Praise for *Nonprofit Fundraising 101*

"Good stuff! A great, incredibly helpful tool for any cause looking to raise money, online or off."

—*Steve Wozniak, co-fou*

"It's not often you find such a distin‌‌‌‌‌‌‌‌‌‌‌‌‌‌ ing. Professionals—and lead volunteers— al, source of reference."

—*Andrew Watt, CEO, Association of Fundraising Professionals (AFP)*

"This must-have book provides a comprehensive breakdown of the strategies and tactics necessary to raise the financial resources essential to bring about the changes we seek."

—*Jody Williams, Nobel Peace Prize Laureate (1997); chair, Nobel Women's Initiative*

"Nonprofits and charities around the world struggle to secure the support needed to maximize impact, but that just got a bit easier thanks to the very practical lessons in *Nonprofit Fundraising 101*."

—*Dan Kammen, professor of energy, University of California, Berkeley; contributing lead author for the Intergovernmental Panel on Climate Change, which shared the 2007 Nobel Peace Prize Laureate*

"Nonprofit fundraising is really, really hard, and almost every nonprofit can use a lot of help with it. This book makes it easier by getting together a lot of useful, effective how-to information."

—*Craig Newmark, founder, craigslist and craigconnects*

"This book is a gift to nonprofit leaders and fundraisers around the world!"

—*Carolyn Miles, President and CEO, Save the Children USA*

"Billions of dollars of support flow to nonprofits around the world every year, and this book will help ensure your cause secures the resources it needs to thrive."

—*Bill Strathmann, CEO, Network for Good*

"Nonprofits are fueled by two things: passion and money. *Nonprofit Fundraising 101* helps show how the two come together and offers a quick intro for the beginner, or a deep dive for the experienced fundraiser."

—*Jacob Harold, president and CEO, GuideStar USA*

"By providing a step-by-step framework for fundraising success across all disciplines, this book makes a much-needed contribution to those dedicating their lives to social change."

— *Charles Best, founder, DonorsChoose.org*

"Whether you are a volunteer, board member, or executive director, *Nonprofit Fundraising 101* is a complete guide to the do's and don'ts of effective fundraising. I don't just recommend it—I'm using it."

— *Greg Baldwin, president, VolunteerMatch.org*

"This is an impressive collection of experts and practitioners, all with ideas and strategies proven by real experience. I'm thrilled to see this compendium of resources available to the nonprofit sector and know every fundraiser and executive director will soon have it on his or her desk!"

— *Amy Sample Ward, CEO, NTEN*

"When nonprofits consider launching social enterprises to supplement charitable income with earned revenue, *Nonprofit Fundraising 101* provides an expert overview of the key factors for leaders and boards to think through at the outset."

— *Jim Schorr, CEO, Social Enterprise Alliance*

"*Nonprofit Fundraising 101* is a wonderful new tool as to ignite your Changemaker™ skills into action!"

— *Nancy Welsh, executive director and CEO, Ashoka's Youth Venture*

"Social entrepreneurs at all levels of experience can benefit from this thorough text, which unlocks the secrets to earning more income and raising more capital for your cause."

— *Cheryl Dorsey, president, Echoing Green*

"If you want to be a force for good in the world, fundraising is essential to furthering your cause. *Nonprofit Fundraising 101* is an extraordinary resource, full of practical advice and wisdom gleaned from numerous sector experts. It has everything you need to succeed, all in one place."

— *Heather McLeod Grant, co-author,* Forces for Good

"Beyond covering the traditional fundraising basics, *Nonprofit Fundraising 101* does a great job clearly breaking down the secrets to success for groups interested moving into the digital age."

NONPROFIT FUNDRAISING 101

NONPROFIT FUNDRAISING 101

A PRACTICAL GUIDE WITH EASY TO IMPLEMENT IDEAS & TIPS FROM INDUSTRY EXPERTS

DARIAN RODRIGUEZ HEYMAN
WITH LAILA BRENNER

WILEY

Published by John Wiley & Sons, Inc., Hoboken, New Jersey
Published simultaneously in Canada

Library of Congress Cataloging-in-Publication Data:
Heyman, Darian Rodriguez
    Nonprofit Fundraising 101 / Darian Rodriguez Heyman.
        pages cm
    Includes bibliographical references and index.
    ISBN 978-1-119-10046-1 (paperback); ISBN
    978-1-119-10050-8 (pdf); ISBN 978-1-119-10056-0 (epub)
        1. Nonprofit organizations.   2. Fund raising.   I. Title.   II. Title: Nonprofit fundraising one
hundred one.   III. Title: Nonprofit fundraising one hundred and one.
    HD2769.15.H49 2016
    658.15'224—dc23

978-1-119-10050-8 (ePDF)   978-1-119-10056-0 (ePub)

                                                                                    2015036883

ISBN: 978-1-119-10046-1 (pbk)

Printed in the United States of America

10 9 8 7 6 5 4 3 2 1

Darian's Dedication

I dedicate this book to my beloved
grandmother, Martha Heyman.
I love you, and I thank you for a
lifetime of service to our family and
to the community. You taught us
all the value of family, the love of
travel, and the joy of serving others.

Laila's Dedication

To my mother, Lori Steele, for teaching me to believe in myself, and that I
could do anything I put my mind to. I love you.

Contents

PART 2: Building Your Toolkit and Tracking Progress   45

Chapter 5

Prospecting and Donor Research   47

Interviewee: Helen Brown, co-author of *Prospect Research for Fundraisers: The Essential Handbook* and president of the Helen Brown Group

Chapter 6

Donor Databases and CRM   57

Interviewees: Suzanne DiBianca, president and co-founder of Salesforce.com Foundation, and Peggy Duvette, director of social impact at NetSuite

Chapter 7

Measuring Impact: Data, Stories, and Organizational Dashboards   65

Interviewee: Stever MacLaughlin, director of analytics at Blackbaud
Inset: Outputs Versus Outcomes
Case Study: charity: water with Kaitlyn Jankowski, supporter experience manager at charity: water

PART 3: Individual Donors   77

Chapter 8

Grassroots Fundraising: Building Your Donor Pyramid   79

Interviewee: Kim Klein, author of *Fundraising for Social Change* and principal of Klein & Roth Consulting
Inset: Don't Be Afraid to Dream Big

Chapter 9

Major Donors: Building Relationships, Making the Ask, and Stewardship   87

Interviewee: Kay Sprinkel Grace, author of *Beyond Fundraising* and fundraising consultant
Inset: Tracking Major Donors in Databases

PART 5: Foundations   205

Chapter 19

Research, Getting in the Door, and Securing an Invitation to Apply   207

Interviewees: Tori O'Neal McElrath, author of *Winning Grants Step by Step* and founder of O'Neal Consulting Services, and Leeanne G-Bowley, manager of capacity and leadership development at Foundation Center and artistic and executive director at In-Sight Dance Company
Insets: The Different Kinds of Foundations; Types of Grants

Chapter 20

Government Grants   221

Interviewee: Joshua Sheridan Fouts, executive director at Bioneers
Inset: Where to Find Government Grants

Chapter 21

Writing a Winning LOI and Proposal   227

Interviewees: Susan Fox, co-author of *Grant Proposal Makeover: Transform Your Request From No to Yes* and fundraising consultant, and Jane C. Geever, author of *The Foundation Center's Guide to Proposal Writing* and founder of J.C. Geever

Chapter 22

Tracking Progress and Reporting Back   235

Interviewee: Beverly Browning, author of *Grant Writing for Dummies* and vice president of grant writing services at eCivis
Inset: Logic Models

PART 6: Corporate Support   243

Chapter 23

Sponsorships   245

Interviewee: Maureen Carlson, president of GoodScout
Inset: Sponsorship Proposal Template

About the Book

"You don't have to know all the answers, you just need to know where to find them."

—Albert Einstein

There's a story I like to tell whenever I address an audience of nonprofit fundraisers. It speaks to what I think of as the single greatest obstacle standing in our way as a community, and especially as a sector—the mistaken notion that when we raise money for an important cause, somehow we're begging for alms, holding out our tin cup.

The story is about a young college student in a philosophy class. One day, the professor greeted his audience of 100 master's and doctoral students with a question. "Is this glass half full, or half empty?" he asked.

The students spent the entire 90-minute class debating and discussing, but as you might imagine, they never solved the age-old riddle. This especially frustrated one of the students, whose family had made great sacrifices to put him through school, even after he finished his undergraduate studies.

He huffed and puffed on his way home, where his grandmother, Gertrude, was there waiting for him.

"How was class today?" she asked as soon as he walked in the door, but the student was upset and didn't want to talk about it. She pressed him, as grandmas are prone to do, and finally he told her about his experience.

"Well, if you really want to know, it was incredibly frustrating. We had a hundred master's and doctoral students sitting around for an hour and a half, and all we did is debate if the glass were half full, or half empty."

His grandmother, with only a second-grade education, didn't miss a beat.

"Well son, *it depends on whether you're pouring or drinking.*"

Pouring . . . or drinking. Brilliant. And the reason I share this story with fundraisers every chance I get is that I believe *the tin cup approach to fundraising is based on a failure of perception.* We mistakenly think of ourselves as the drinkers, relying on the charitable contributions of others to conduct our work. And although it may feel like that at times, nothing is further from the truth.

We are the pourers. *What we do as a sector, as a Movement with a capital "M," is connect people with resources to the change they want to see in the world.* Fundraising is holy work in my mind, and we're privileged and honored to do it for causes we believe in. The world needs us—we are a conduit, a channel. And through us, the world finds the resources and support it needs to thrive, or at least to improve in some small way, one dollar, peso, or pound at a time.

Book Overview and Purpose

Our goal when writing this book was to offer a useful, unique resource to you, the reader. Laila and I may not know you, but we've been where you are. You're passionate, creative, and committed to your cause. Maybe you have resources, expertise, and contacts at your disposal, as we have these past years, or maybe you're like us years ago, starting nonprofits with no budget, no plan, and no experience. Either way, this book will serve you. After more than a decade in the sector, we've seen lots of fundraising books, but there's nothing like what we've pulled together in these pages. *This book is the first comprehensive, practical guide to all aspects of nonprofit fundraising around the globe.*

Ultimately, this is a reference manual, and not every fundraiser needs to know about every tactic or strategy. It's unlikely that you'll read this book straight through, and that's OK; *Nonprofit Fundraising 101* is intended to be your yellow pages for social change. Apply it as needed. Keep it on your desk and when you decide to pursue your first government grant, or your executive director charges you with creating a fundraising plan for your nonprofit, it'll be there. Break it out when you get ready to launch a new crowdfunding campaign or finally commit to taking your cause mobile. Or simply *refer to the various Resource Reviews and the Book Partners if you've already mastered the basics and are looking for resources to advance your professional development.*

Use the book as you see fit and, please, share it with colleagues and peers. All of us can learn a lesson from Chapter 9 interviewee, Kay Sprinkel Grace, who once quipped, "We need to tilt our silos on their sides, and turn them into pipelines."

Book Structure and Style

To make the book as readable as possible, *we've crafted a consistent framework for all of the chapters*, which is in line with the one used in *Nonprofit Management 101*:

- **Introduction**: Each entry starts with a short overview of why a busy nonprofit leader like you should take 20 to 30 minutes out of his or her schedule to learn more about this topic. Which kinds of nonprofits can benefit from this strategy, and what does this approach have to offer your cause?
- **Critical Skills and Competencies**: This portion typically contains 70 to 80 percent of the content for each chapter, and is where you'll find the step-by-step framework for success in each respective arena. We've done our best to distill each interviewee's comments and insights into a how-to formula for success, presented in a logical progression with several main headlines, each of which is followed by a few paragraphs to fill in the specifics.
- **Conclusion**: A paragraph at the end of each chapter helps to underscore key points and takeaways, reminding you of some of the highlights and crucial components of the formula for success.
- **Do's and Don'ts**: These are bullet point lists of concrete, actionable tips from within the chapter and beyond, each of which is distilled down to a sentence or two to make it as easy as possible to digest.
- **About the Experts**: Brief bios for each chapter's interviewees are included at the end of their respective chapters.
- **Resource Review**: The final component of each chapter is where you'll find additional resources to learn more about that particular discipline. Many of these also offer helpful templates, resources, and reports to keep you updated as trends and technologies evolve. These resources are a treasure trove, so be sure to subscribe to the newsletters and blogs, read the annual reports and books, and rely

on the links outlined here to keep abreast of industry trends and
developments.

- **Case Studies and Insets**: Sprinkled throughout the chapters are a
  variety of case studies that showcase specific nonprofits' experiences,
  with a focus on best practices and pitfalls to avoid. In addition,
  you'll also find a range of insets that dive a bit deeper into a specific
  component mentioned in the chapter, or that provide templates,
  checklists, and more.

All the chapters are short and incredibly practical, and ***our goal with this
book is not simply to leave you inspired, but inspired to <u>action</u>***. Short
and to the point, we share concrete, real-world insights, tips, and tools from
globally recognized experts, and leave you with clear takeaways that you can
put to work *immediately*, making you both more effective and efficient at
serving your cause. As recovering executive directors and current fundraisers,
we know you're busy, and the last thing you need are pie-in-the-sky ideas
and concepts that may make you think, but that fail to immediately help,
and even transform, the way you go about your everyday work.

From a style standpoint, we strived to make the book easy to read and
digest. Paragraphs are kept short to facilitate ideas sinking in, and we've
used a conversational tone, since ultimately, we are talking directly to *you*.
We've also formatted things in a way that aims to help you retain the most
important ideas without you feeling like you have to bend every other page
or break out that old, faded highlighter. To this end, important points and
comments are *italicized*, while ***concrete takeaways and best practices are
bolded and italicized throughout the book***. You'll see a wealth of the latter
in each and every chapter, because for us, that's what this publication is all
about.

Admittedly, many of the interviewees and statistics are from the United
States, but ***this book is intended for a global audience of experienced
practitioners and emerging leaders, including university students and
volunteers***. To this end, we've done our best to ensure *Nonprofit Fundraising
101* speaks to nonprofits, charities, and causes all around the world. So
don't worry if you're just getting started, or if you've been in the sector for a
decade. Similarly, there's great content in here for organizations of all sizes.
***The tips and tools shared herein are relevant to organizations ranging
from small, grassroots efforts with no paid staff, to well-established
nonprofits with big budgets and a large team of paid professionals***.

Common Themes

This book covers a wide range of fundraising topics; in fact, our goal was to address a truly comprehensive range of disciplines, offering readers one single book that provides at least a basic sense of everything you need to know. As such, there are a huge diversity of perspectives and topics represented in these pages, but three important common themes and ideas appear throughout:

Plan for Success: Many of the frameworks and formulas for success shared in the chapters start with—or even revolve entirely around—creating a solid plan. *Planning is the lynchpin of any nonprofit's success*, and in fact you'll often hear us share one of the questions we find most helpful when driving this process, "*What does success look like?*" Ask this question at every meeting, every strategy session, and reverse engineer how to achieve your ideal outcome. *Take a moment to step back and envision your path before you dive into any activity or project to ensure you're as impactful as possible*. As Peter Drucker once noted: "Efficiency is about doing things right; effectiveness is about doing the right things." Good planning helps you be both efficient, and effective.

Meet People Where They're at: Several chapters speak to the notion that *you cannot expect donors to come to you; you need to court and steward them where—and how—they're most comfortable*. Whether we're talking about the importance of ensuring your website is mobile-compatible, talking about Facebook and Twitter, or underscoring the huge, continued role of more proven approaches like direct mail, the point is that, to be successful, you must take a dispassionate look at which channels and media are most appropriate for achieving your goals. Along those lines, this book contains some surprises. For example, did you know that 2013 was the first year in U.S. history that Baby Boomers were just as likely to give online versus by direct mail? Or did you realize that odds are, at least 40 percent of your nonprofit's website traffic *today* comes from people on mobile devices? Keep an open mind and be willing to experiment with some of the ideas and tactics shared in this book, always with an eye toward the old mantra, "fail fast, fail forward."

It's Not About You: As we shared in the story at the beginning of this section, nonprofits are a channel, a conduit, between donors and impact. *The most successful nonprofits and fundraisers communicate __not__ about their work, needs, or impact, but rather about the impact the donor or prospect makes* *possible.* Talk with people about what drives *them* to act and contribute—about what their past support has enabled or their future contribution will make possible—and revenue will follow. Several chapters build on this idea by speaking to the power of peer testimonials and creating a movement instead of a campaign. And remember, *people want to be part of a winning team, so framing your work as powerfully as possible is critical.* Always the inspiring and inspired communicator, Kay Sprinkel Grace shares two great sound bites that bring both of these key points home in Chapter 9 when talking about major donors:

> *"People don't give to you; they give <u>through</u> you."*

and

> *"People don't give to you because you have needs. They give to you because you <u>meet</u> needs."*

Flow of the Book

Nonprofit Fundraising 101 is broken into seven parts. After a Foreword from fundraising guru Lynne Twist, we kick things off with Part 1, where you'll learn about a few crucial aspects of planning and maximizing human resources. How can you create a killer fundraising plan without killing yourself? How can you hire and train fundraising personnel and engage your board and key volunteers in fund development?

From there, Part 2 will help round out your infrastructure with a range of tools to track donors and gauge progress. You'll learn how to use tools and technology to identify donor prospects and research their interests, hear about how a constituent relationship management platform can serve as a powerful donor database and coordinate all your communication and contacts, and finally how to collect the right data and personal stories to be able to gauge your efforts and convey impact to donors. All of this rolls up into a powerful organizational dashboard that your staff and board can use to quickly tell whether your nonprofit or program is on track, or if there are red flags that need to be addressed.

Then you'll dive into the meat of the book: actual fundraising strategies. Part 3 focuses on all aspects of individual donors, which represent the lion's share of nonprofit support, at least in the United States. We interviewed some of the sector's best and brightest to ensure this book shares concrete tips and tools for a wide range of disciplines related to cultivating, soliciting, and stewarding supporters at all levels of your donor pyramid, ranging from grassroots supporters to major donors. Part 3 is also where you'll find the specific channels for doing that, including direct mail, annual appeals, membership campaigns, and events, as well as learn about how to raise money from people both young and old.

Part 4 explores the exciting world of online giving, starting with tips for optimizing your website and email, which is where the majority of technology-based fundraising currently occurs, and then looking at social media and crowdfunding's ability to turn your donors into fundraisers, and finally, what can be argued is the future of giving: mobile. Here our experts will share tips for doubling your online giving in just thirty days. And if you're hoping to create the next ALS Ice Bucket Challenge, this is the section where you'll hear from the folks who orchestrated that campaign via a detailed case study, as well as learning from a wide range of experts with decades of experience under their belts—and literally more than a billion dollars raised online between them. With their help, you can take your nonprofit into the future, today.

Parts 5 and 6 share a range of tips and tools for institutional giving. Learn how to identify the most likely prospects, secure the all-too-elusive call or meeting, and not only be invited to apply for foundation, corporate, or government support, but how to secure crucial pieces of information that will catapult your odds of success from 5 percent to 50 percent. The interviewees follow that with tips for writing a great proposal and how to monitor your progress and report back in a language that funders appreciate and expect. And beyond straight cash support, we've devoted a chapter to in-kind and media sponsors, as we've witnessed firsthand the transformative impact those partnerships can have on both a fledgling nonprofit and a well-established organization, even though they're infinitely easier to secure.

Finally, the book ends with Part 7, where guest contributor Rick Aubry shares and explores the ins and outs of earned income for nonprofits. If you're considering launching a social enterprise in an effort to diversity your revenue base, don't miss this chapter. And as long as we're in the world of social enterprise, what better way to wrap things up than with an inspiring Afterword by Kiva.org founder Premal Shah.

Again, **this book is a reference guide, so feel free to skip around**. Pick the chapters that you find most compelling and useful today, and don't be surprised when other topics pop up on your radar as times goes by. After all, change is the very essence of life, and it's ultimately the goal of all nonprofits, isn't it?

Fundraising Ethics

We'd be remiss if we neglected to introduce this book without a quick note on fundraising ethics and, most notably, commission-based fundraising. As you implement the best practices shared in the coming pages, always remember that *the public expects you to be honest, accountable, and transparent.* The Association of Fundraising Professionals (AFP) Code of Ethical Standards (www.afpnet.org/files/ContentDocuments/CodeofEthics. pdf) provides a comprehensive overview of ethical aspirations and boundaries for fundraisers. An ethical fundraiser applies the Code of Ethics and all relevant laws and regulation to their work.

In particular, unlike the corporate world, in the nonprofit sector, donors and funders can mandate exactly how their gifts are to be used. *You are ethically and legally bound to use funds as directed by the donor.* If someone states he wants his donation or grant to be used exclusively for a specific program, or even a particular line item in your budget, then you need to take all proper measures—especially bookkeeping, accounting, and measuring program expenditures—to ensure those funds are used as directed.

Whether you're a consultant or a paid staff member, remember that *in the nonprofit sector, commission-based fundraising is considered unethical.* Standard 21 in the AFP Code of Ethical Standards addresses this principle. Deviating from this simple guideline can have devastating implications for your nonprofit and on donor relationships. Supporters want to know their gifts go to the mission-based work of your organization, not to a glorified salesperson. This, too, is very different from the corporate world, where performance-based compensation is common. In short, in the nonprofit or social sector, every fundraiser is expected to do his or her best to represent the organization or client, and to be paid fairly for work out of the organization's budget.

As you begin, or continue, your journey doing your best to represent a cause you care deeply about, may this book serve as a useful guide—to you, to your cause, to the people whose lives you make better every day you go about your work, and ultimately to the public trust we serve as fundraisers.

Acknowledgments

First and foremost, I offer thanks and congratulations to Laila Brenner, without whose contribution this book never would have been possible. Laila, you are a joy to work with, and I admire your great writing and unwavering commitment, even while expecting your second child. I look forward to working with you again.

Thanks also to John Wiley & Sons for graciously offering to publish my second book and for being an understanding and flexible partner. I offer a deep bow of humble appreciation to the 121 interviewees and partners who shared their time, insights, and resources, ensuring this book offered truly useful tips and tools for nonprofits and fundraisers, and providing invaluable marketing support around its release. Thanks to my colleagues at Sparrow for their support of this project and for their work helping nonprofits employ the power of mobile technology to better serve the poor. I also want to thank the two other sponsors of this book, Eventbrite and CommitChange, for their invaluable support as well as the Association of Fundraising Professionals for their incredible endorsement, and Social Media for Nonprofits' Ritu Sharma, for being the catalyst for this project.

I thank my family in Argentina for showing me firsthand how challenging yet rewarding philanthropy can be on a personal level. To the Heyman family, my *mishpocheh*, thanks for providing me with the support and love I needed to experiment and discover my path. In particular, I'd like to thank my brother for being the best thought partner I could ever ask for and for always being in my corner, even when things get hard. Paulo, you can never lose me. And most of all, I offer gratitude to my mother, Annette. Mom, you taught me how to love and helped me see that, no matter how much I work to change the world, ultimately what really matters is helping one person at a time.

Foreword

Discovering What It
Means to Be a Fundraiser

Lynne Twist

"You will find as you look back upon your life, that the moments
you have really lived are the moments when you have done
things in the spirit of love."

—Henry Drummond

I discovered my passion for fundraising when I was in kindergarten in
Evanston, Illinois. My oldest sister had just gotten the lead role in the school
play, but there wasn't enough money to buy costumes or sets because of a
budget crisis. I saw how heartbroken she was, so I went to my teacher and
asked if there was anything our class could do to help. Turns out I wasn't
alone in wanting to support the cause, and I've often found since then that
*when you take a stand for something you believe in, it inspires others to
follow your lead*.

As Goethe once said, "Be bold, and mighty forces will come to your aid."
The entire kindergarten class ended up selling chocolate chip cookies and
lemonade outside our school every afternoon, and on weekends, until we'd
raised enough money to support the play. Our actions inspired the rest
of the school, including the PTA and Board of Education, to step up and
look at how they could solve the budget crisis. At just five years old, this
was a life-altering experience for me; it ignited my passion and helped me
realize that *fundraising is an act of love*. We were a bunch of children
who couldn't read or write, add or subtract, but we could fundraise with
homemade cookies and lemonade! I remember thinking how amazing it was
that, out of an act of love for my sister, we were able to solve a problem and
help turn the tide for the whole school.

This first experience with fundraising taught me that it took commitment and courage to raise money. Ever since, I've seen it as an act of love and affirmation. We all know that giving is an act of generosity, and often love, commitment, and vision; but I think that asking also taps into a very powerful part of the human heart. To me, fundraising is sacred—it's holy work, and I'm privileged and honored to do it. Fundraising enables people to move their resources toward what they really believe in. It's how we shift people's relationships with money, showing them it can be used to empower and inspire us to be the best people we can be, while nourishing others around us.

At this time in history—the first decades of the 21st century—one of the greatest things we need to come to terms with as a species is our use of resources: the earth's resources; human resources; and, of course, financial resources. We need to recognize that we're at a critical juncture, where *until we learn to live within our ecological means, we won't learn to live within our economic means.* We need to look at how to move away from overconsumption, destructive causes, and depletion of the natural world, and reallocate resources toward our highest commitments, allowing them to nourish our lives, and the health and well being of all humanity. Fundraising is how we can, and are, doing this. ***Every time you raise money for a cause you care about; every time you cultivate or steward a donor; and every time you make an ask, you're taking a stand for the just, equitable, and sustainable world we all dream of.***

As fundraisers, when we ask someone for money, whether it's online, in person, or through a letter or phone call, what we're actually doing is saying to that person: "I see you. I see your heart and your generosity. I see that you have a vision, and that you care about the world. That is why I am asking you to help." You aren't trying to manipulate people—you are *affirming* them. You're inviting them to leave our planet in a better state than we found it. ***As fundraisers, our job is to listen to who people really are and then to reconnect them to their courage, and to their heart.*** Is your cause a match for what they *really* care about? It's been my experience that if an ask is done with respect and love, regardless of that person's capacity to give, the encounter ennobles both parties and inspires us to step into our best selves.

In my workshops, I talk about the three rules of fundraising. The first rule is *ask for the money.* You can't be afraid to ask. It's critical that you are willing, eager, and completely comfortable asking people for money. You need to ask clearly and unapologetically. Be proud to invite support for a cause both you and they care about.

Rule number two is *ask people who are committed and want to make a difference*. Find people who want to leave this planet better than they found it. In fact, they're all around you, every day you go about your good work. People care, and they want to be part of the solution. Your cause or organization can represent that solution.

That leads us to rule number three, which is *ask everyone*, because everyone is committed at some level and wants to make a difference with their lives. **Your role as a fundraiser is to help people see their commitment, and then to show them a way to make a difference.**

One of the most important lessons to learn as a fundraiser, is that *it's OK to ask people and have them say no*. If done with respect and love, and acknowledgment and the affirmation that people want to make a difference with their lives, every fundraising ask can open the heart and is a win for humanity. Fundraising encounters will not always create money for your cause, but regardless they can unlock something in people and help their generosity to flow in the direction that's right for them. Often when people say no, you've helped them realize that they actually want to give to something else that they care more about. We're all in this together, so it's important you still see this as a win.

One of the other most important fundraising lessons I've learned is that coming from a place of need is not sustainable. In Chapter 9, Kay Sprinkel Grace shares that **people don't give to you because you <u>have</u> needs; they give to you because you <u>meet</u> needs**. Crisis fundraising—especially in the aftermath of things like natural disasters—has its place, but it's not a strategy that can lead to long-term success. Effective asks don't come from a place of crisis or scarcity. **To be successful, fundraising must be expressed as an opportunity to partner with a nonprofit to make a difference**. Rather than "we can't do this without you" or "our work depends on your support," aim instead for the sentiment: "Who's with us?" This way, there is dignity and respect in the relationship, and you create a partnership where everyone is pulling together to make a difference, whether it's saving the rainforest or ending world hunger.

Another lesson I like to pass on to fundraisers is what I call *the truth of sufficiency*. We live in a very intense global consumer culture that constantly tells us that we don't have enough; that we need more. Fundraising interrupts this toxic notion, allowing us to rest in the "enough-ness" of bounty and bear witness to the blessing of our lives. Fundraising helps people realize that they are sufficient, whole, and have what they need to live fulfilling lives. After all, *generosity is a demonstration of abundance*, both to the recipient and the donor.

Even those of us struggling to pay rent or get out of debt can have these realizations when we stop comparing ourselves to others who have more. By realizing the fullness of our lives, we can truly experience gratefulness—of the friends we have, the rich tapestry of love in which we dwell, the people who care about us, our families, the work we get to do, the health we enjoy, and more. And once we dwell in this realization, the fullness of our lives grows. I like to say, "*What we appreciate, appreciates.*" For me, fundraising is the opportunity to help people appreciate the bounty that they live in and share that with others. Of course, this saying also relates to stewarding relationships after the gift, since ***expressing gratitude and demonstrating the impact someone's generosity enables is the surest way to secure additional support***.

Notwithstanding the name of this book, thinking of yourself as a "nonprofit" fundraiser is actually a bit of a misnomer. The social sector actually generates an enormous profit—a long-term social profit for humanity, the environment, and all future life. Think about the great leaders of history: Mahatma Gandhi, Mother Teresa, Martin Luther King, Jr., Elizabeth Cady Stanton, Nelson Mandela, and Susan B. Anthony, to name a few. The work they did is still yielding a profit today and will continue to do so for many future generations. And *they were all fundraisers*. Had they not been successful in raising the financial resources that were required to do their work, we would not know their names nor benefit from their movements. These leaders are your colleagues. You are following their example and working to change history. You are creating a *permanent* profit for society, not the kind of profit that can be spent, or wasted. This is the work you are here to do, and the world needs it.

As a fundraiser, you are not only creating profits, P-R-O-F-I-T-S, but in fact you are a social prophet, P-R-O-P-H-E-T. In other words, whatever your cause, your work aims to achieve a beautiful prophesy of the future, where things are better than they are today. This takes courage, grace, and heart. That is who *you* are as a fundraiser. You have the guts to garner the resources needed to shift the direction of history. And so I bow to you—and to all fundraisers—for using your courage and heart to make our world a better place in which to live. Thank you.

About Lynne Twist

For more than 40 years, **Lynne Twist** has been a recognized global visionary committed to alleviating poverty and hunger, supporting social justice, and promoting environmental sustainability. From working with Mother Teresa in Calcutta, to serving in the refugee camps in Ethiopia, and helping save the threatened rainforests of the Amazon, Twist's on-the-ground work has brought her a deep understanding of the social tapestry of the world and the historical landscape of the times we live in. Her best-selling book, *The Soul of Money: Reclaiming the Wealth of Our Inner Resources* (W.W. Norton & Co.), shows us that examining our attitudes toward money—earning it, spending it, and giving it away—can offer surprising insight into our lives, our values, and the essence of prosperity.

Part

Planning for Success and Preparing Your Team

1

Creating a
Fundraising Plan

"A goal without a plan is just a wish."

—Antoine de Saint-Exupery

Introduction

Your organization has a mission, and to accomplish it you need to raise money. But where do you start? That's simple: with a plan. You need a clear set of objectives, and a map of how you aim to get there. Your fundraising plan will be unique to your nonprofit. Every organization has different needs, goals, strengths, and priorities, and your fundraising plan will address and incorporate these in a written document.

Being strategic about fundraising in this way generates better results, creates efficiency, and ensures everyone involved is on the same page and accountable. It will also allow you to evaluate progress and assess the effectiveness of different fundraising channels, facilitating strategic shifts when necessary.

The rest of this book will help you understand each of the various fundraising channels and tactics, enabling you to make informed decisions when creating your fundraising plan. But before you dive in, remember to take stock of what you have going for you and your cause, and to look at what you're already doing successfully if you've already launched the organization. Your plan is a living document wherein you'll spell out your proposed recipe for success, and its goal is helping you focus on your strengths, while challenging you to identify new opportunities. Be mindful of the resources you have and don't stretch them too thin, but also bring an open mind to considering assets you've underutilized or ignored and look at how you can put them to work.

To learn more about the basics of creating a nonprofit fundraising plan, I sat down with Andrea McManus, president of the nonprofit consultancy The Development Group, and she outlined the six things you need to know to succeed when creating an effective fundraising plan.

Critical Skills and Competencies

1. Understand the Big Picture

Creating a fundraising plan means answering two basic questions: How much money do you need to raise? and Who do you plan on raising it from? In your plan, you'll create realistic program goals based on the expenses of running your programs and organization today—assuming you have some past experience with the work—as well as aspirational goals that inspire your team by clarifying exactly what kind of additional impact is possible if you secure even more resources and support.

Your plan will also be a vehicle for detailing your sources of revenue and how much income you expect from each, whether it's individual donors, corporations, foundations, the government, or earned income. *It is critical to have multiple, diverse sources of revenue, so that if you unexpectedly lose one, you still have others to rely on*.

Once you've identified your revenue sources, perhaps benefiting from the rest of the book to determine which channels are most appropriate for you, you'll articulate your strategies and tactics for each source. If you plan to raise money from individuals, will you be cultivating and asking major donors, running an annual fund, doing direct mail, online fundraising, or utilizing other approaches? Will you be soliciting businesses and corporations for gifts of cash or in-kind donations? While many of the remaining chapters of this book, especially those related to marketing and donor communication, propose a "less is more" style, when planning for success, the more detailed your vision, the more likely you are to succeed.

2. Know Your Finances

Now that you have a sense of everything your fundraising plan is meant to accomplish, and some of the various sections it will include, let's get into it. Knowing how much money you need to raise starts with good financial planning. *You can't create a fundraising plan without a budget.* How much does the work you do cost? What are your programmatic, fundraising, and overhead expenses? Once you know your expenses, you need to figure out how you will pay for them; in other words, how will you raise the money to pay for them? And don't forget that fundraising itself costs money. You can't raise money without spending money.

Dispelling the Overhead Myth

At least in the United States, the IRS dictates that all nonprofit expenses be classified as either program, fundraising, or administrative. This adds not only an extra layer of bookkeeping, but also creates some difficulties with fundraising, since some donors and funders will ask for their contributions to be allocated only for programs. Others still will want to know whether more than 80 percent of the funds you raise go toward programs, a common industry benchmark.

Part of your job as a fundraiser will be using the tactics outlined in this book to convey the importance of not just some of your work, but all of it. Just as you cannot provide medical attention only to the lungs and expect someone to stay healthy, you'll need to refine your ability to make the case for "general operating support" or "unrestricted gifts," both of which are discussed in detail in the sections on individual donors and foundations.

For now, we'll focus on dispelling the notion that staff payroll, rent, and utilities should all be categorized as overhead. Not true: *the staff time spent implementing programs is a program-related—not an overhead—expense.* The way to calculate overall payroll allocations, which are also used for rent and utilities, is as follows:

- Have staff members break down how they spend a typical week in a spreadsheet. No need to get too specific; simply create 8 to 12 "buckets" for their time, for example, client meetings, fundraising calls, answering email, etc.

(continued)

(*continued*)

- Assign a time estimate for how many hours of each week is spent on each bucket; an average over time is sufficient.

- Allocate each bucket: What percentage of that activity relates to programs, versus fundraising, versus purely administrative details?

- Based on this, you can use a fairly simple spreadsheet formula to figure that employee's overall allocation, that is, what percentage of his or her time is spent on programs versus fundraising versus administrative duties.

- After doing this for each paid staff member, you can factor in each person's compensation to weight his or her personal allocation, and then combine everyone into an overall staff allocation.

- Use this same allocation for staff-related expenses, such as benefits, rent, utilities, and so forth.

3. Create a Process

Developing an effective fundraising plan cannot be done in a silo by the fundraiser alone. Involve your executive director, senior staff, and board members. Assemble your team and outline the process you'll go through to create the plan, so everyone knows what to expect. Here are the steps McManus suggests:

1. **Assess your environment**, both internally and externally. Internally, look at things like organizational priorities, programs, and resources, including staff, technology, and capabilities. Capabilities should include expertise in fundraising, marketing, and other key areas. Externally, discuss things like fundraising trends, best practices, industry benchmarks, and how peer organizations (those doing similar work with similar budgets) are succeeding at fundraising.

2. **Assess your donors**, both current and aspirational. What kind of support can you conservatively expect from your current donors and prospects? What does your current donor base look like, and what do you *want* it to look like? Gaining a realistic sense of how much money you can raise from your base, combined with other potential strategies, will enable you to determine the feasibility of the financial goals you'll tackle later in the discussion.

3. **Outline your goals.** In order to achieve the impact your organization envisions, what kind of fundraising infrastructure and results are needed? A couple examples are included below to help kick-start your discussion, but don't just think about financial targets from different channels, although those are certainly crucial. Consider also the kinds of capacity that you as an organization need to build to thrive, for example, increasing board participation in fundraising and contributions; launching your first successful crowdfunding campaign, etc.

4. **Identify your objectives.** What are the three or four (or more) things you need to accomplish in order to achieve the big-picture goals and strategies you've outlined? Break down the goal into the elements required to ensure it happens. Again, some examples to get you thinking are below.

5. **Identify your tactics.** This is where you get into the nitty-gritty details, breaking down each objective one more step. In other words, the who, what, when, where, and how. Who will you be raising money from, and *how*? What are the concrete actions that need to occur to achieve your objectives? Be *very* specific and include measurable goals, such as: We will apply for six grants from private foundations by the end of the second quarter.

6. **Identify your budget and resources.** How much will it cost to raise this money, and who will do it? Do you have the necessary tools in place, including a CRM platform, staff, subscriptions to foundation or donor prospecting databases, marketing and communications support, an online fundraising platform, etc.?

Once you've outlined your process, *assign responsibilities and create deadlines*. Keep people accountable by assigning them duties and clarifying who is personally charged with ensuring the fulfillment of each tactic, as well as deadlines for each.

4. Document the Plan

Once you've gone through the steps in this process and answered all the relevant questions, it's time to document your plan. *Without a written plan, you have no plan at all*. This document should be specific, but also as short as possible and easy to read. *Organize the plan by two to five goals and associate each goal with three to six objectives, and then associate each objective with tactics*. Assign a lead person and deadline for each tactic.

Here is an example:

ABC 2016–2018 Fundraising Plan

Goal 1: To build a strong and adequately resourced fundraising infrastructure that includes staff and volunteer resources, technology, policies and procedures, and professional development that provides a foundation for fundraising sustainability and growth as required.

Objective 1: Build fundraising personnel resources.
> **Tactic 1**: Hire a Development Associate. Lead: Development Director. Deadline: 8/10/16.
> **Tactic 2**: Secure at least one skilled volunteer to help with administrative fundraising tasks. Lead: Development Associate. Deadline: 1/12/17.

Objective 2: Build a strong board with reach and influence, as well as fundraising and giving capacity.
> **Tactic 1**: Create and implement a board member agreement detailing board responsibilities, including financial and fundraising commitments. Lead: Development Director. Deadline: 11/10/16.
> **Tactic 2**: Recruit at least three new board members able to contribute major gifts and facilitate introductions to major donors. Lead: Development Committee. Deadline: 6/15/17.

Objective 3: Build a strong annual fund program that will contribute sustainable revenue toward operating expenses.
> **Tactic 1**: Select and implement a CRM platform to serve as our donor database. Lead: Development Director. Deadline: 3/15/17.
> **Tactic 2**: Build prospect list with 15,000 mailing and 25,000 email addresses. Lead: Marketing Director. Deadline: 5/1/17.
> **Tactic 3**: Select and implement an online fundraising platform. Lead: Development Director. Deadline: 6/15/17.
> **Tactic 4**: Create an editorial calendar mapping out all 2018 mail and email solicitations, plus major marketing communications. Lead: Development Director. Deadline: 9/15/17.

Goal 2: To increase fundraising revenues by 25% and raise $1,000,000 in FY 2017/18.

Objective 1: Increase revenues from foundations by 30%.
> **Tactic 1**: Research, qualify, and prioritize 10 new foundation sources each year. Lead: Development Associate. Deadline: 6/30/16-18.

> **Tactic 2**: Prepare Letters of Intent and/or grant proposals according to foundation deadlines. Lead: Development Associate. Deadline: FY according to required deadlines.
> **Tactic 3**: Maintain schedule for research, qualification, prioritization, grant preparation, and follow-up. Lead: Development Associate. Deadline: Ongoing.
>
> **Objective 2**: Build a strong and compelling Case for Support for fundraising purposes.
> **Tactic 1**: Consult with staff, volunteers, donors, and clients regarding why they give and key messages. Lead: Development Director. Deadline: 3/30/16.
> **Tactic 2**: Draft key messages and circulate in small but representative group for feedback. Prepare final Case for Board Approval. Lead: Development Director. Deadline 6/30/16.
> **Tactic 3**: Develop mini Cases of Support for each program. Lead: Development Director. Deadline: 9/30/16.
> **Tactic 4**: Communicate Case messages through various formats, including print, proposals, social media, website, marketing, etc. Lead: Development Director. Deadline: 9/30/16.

5. Gather Your Prospects

Donor prospecting is absolutely crucial to fundraising. So much so that we've dedicated all of Chapter 5 to it. *Your prospect list will be critical to the development and implementation of your fundraising plan.* You will need it to assess your current donors and determine where to focus your efforts, as well as to identify new opportunities. Ideally, this information should be stored in your CRM or database (see Chapter 6), but you should export it into a spreadsheet to visualize the full list and better prioritize and discuss it with your team.

Assign a lead fundraiser to each prospect, so you know who is accountable and can provide updates during regular reviews. Create separate tabs for each type of prospect, especially foundations, companies, and individual donors. Add to the list regularly and review it frequently with your team to measure progress and identify fundraising opportunities. As detailed in Chapter 5, it's helpful to implement a ranking system, even a simple one, to help you prioritize prospects and determine where to focus your efforts. How connected to your cause and organization are they, and what's their giving capacity? Focus first on people in your inner circle, such as your board and close connections. Then think beyond the usual suspects, like the wealthy donors in your town known for their philanthropy. Try to identify people off of the radar who are connected to your cause, and devise a strategy for your most important prospects.

6. Keep It Alive

Once you've spent precious time and resources creating a solid fundraising plan that secures board approval, the worst that can happen is for it to sit on a shelf. *Your plan must be a living document that guides your activities, and it must be updated or at least reviewed annually*. At each review, involve the board, key staff, and volunteers and evaluate whether you are on point or falling behind. This will allow you to hold people accountable, make strategic decisions, and shift tactics as needed. It will also enable you to recognize and celebrate your successes, something too few of us fundraisers take the time to do! Use your objectives to create key performance indicators and include them in your organizational dashboard, as outlined in Chapter 7, so that evaluation of your fundraising efforts is integrated into the evaluation of your overall organizational health.

Conclusion

Muhammad Ali once said, "The fight is won or lost before I even get in the ring." To succeed in fundraising you need to know where you're going and how you'll get there. How much money are you trying to raise? and Who are you going to raise it from? You need to be strategic and think long-term, but also clarify the interim steps required for you to succeed. Prosperity for your cause typically doesn't come quickly; it comes from hard work, a well-conceived strategy, diligent execution, and the investment of time and resources. You need to identify your revenue sources, your resources, and your prospects before you get started to ensure a more mindful approach. Be crystal clear on both your strategies and tactics, and hold yourself and your team accountable to concrete deadlines. Engage key leadership, like your board, and volunteers in your efforts, and revisit your strategy and progress regularly with everyone involved. Create the systems to measure progress, learn from shortcomings, and celebrate successes. When done right, a fundraising plan will do all of this for you; it's simply a matter of creating it thoughtfully, keeping it alive, and holding yourself to it.

Do's and Don'ts

Do. . .

> . . . include as many key staff, board members, and volunteers as possible in your fundraising planning process.

> . . . review your prospect list in advance to ensure your goals are realistic and achievable.

> . . . build a diversified fundraising plan that includes goals and objectives, plus tactics that are assigned to an owner with a deadline for each.

> . . . review your tactics in the fundraising plan monthly.

Don't. . .

> . . . create a fundraising plan without the input of your communications and marketing team, or one that lacks a budget to ensure implementation.

> . . . assume that all staff payroll, benefits, rent, and utilities are overhead or administrative expenses.

> . . . believe you have a fundraising plan in place if you fail to take the time to document it in writing.

> . . . create a fundraising plan without integrating your strategic plan into it.

About the Expert

Andrea McManus is president of The Development Group and a recognized leader in the nonprofit sector. With more than 29 years of experience in fund development, communications, media, public relations, and marketing, McManus has particular expertise in environments where major changes, restructuring, or transition require innovation, leadership, creativity, and an entrepreneurial attitude.

Resource Review

The Association of Fundraising Professionals (AFP) (www.afpnet.org)
    AFP is a great resource for fundraisers. They have regional chapters all over the world that produce quality events, as well as a large international

conference, and a storytelling conference. You can also find helpful resources on their website.

Future Fundraising Now (futurefundaisingnow.typepad.com)
Jeff Brooks is a regular contributor to *Fundraising Success Magazine*, and his blog is full of great posts and resources. Check out his podcast, "Fundraising Is Beautiful."

Ahern Donor Communications (www.aherncomm.com)
Tom Ahern's blog is a great source for case studies, sample critiques of fundraising materials, and links to useful resources.

The Fundraising Authority (www.thefundraisingauthority.com)
Find helpful resources including articles, webinars, books, and podcasts. Check out their "Beginner's Guide to Fundraising" and the article, "How to Write a Successful Fundraising Plan."

Joyaux, Simone P. *Strategic Fund Development: Building Profitable Relationships That Last* (3rd ed.). John Wiley & Sons, 2011.
This book focuses on long-term strategic fundraising, rather than the typical transactional approach that fails to nurture your most important donor relationships.

Network for Good's Fundraising 123 blog (www.fundraising123.org)
Find a variety of posts and resources on all things fundraising, including the "Fundraising Planning Worksheet: A Tool for Creating Your Annual Fundraising Plan" by Mimi Ho and Priscilla Hung.

Nonprofit Quarterly (https://nonprofitquarterly.org)
A print and online publication that provides articles on a variety of nonprofit topics. Check out their webinars, and sign up for their daily digest.

M+R Lab (www.mrss.com/lab)
A free collection of articles and advice from a group of experienced nonprofit consultants; includes case studies and covers a wide variety of topics, including reports on industry benchmarks.

The Agitator (www.theagitator.net)
A great online blog from industry experts Tom Belford and Roger Craver that provides information and advice on nonprofit fundraising and marketing strategies.

Idealist (www.Idealist.org)
A very robust website that offers tons of links to useful resources and articles, plus it gives you access to a global community of volunteers and nonprofit peers.

Hiring and Training Development Staff

"Good plans shape good decisions. That's why good planning helps to make elusive dreams come true."

—Lester R. Bittel

Introduction

I've gone to great lengths to document and articulate all the tips, tools, and tactics you need to succeed at fundraising in this book. But without the right team in place, none of them matter. ***The staff, board members, and volunteers charged with spearheading your development efforts are the single most important factor in your success.*** From interns to senior management, event volunteers to engaged board members, each and every person driving your fundraising machine is a critical part of building a successful, high-functioning development infrastructure. Surrounding yourself with the right people, properly training them, and fostering their professional growth will result *directly* in you raising more money. It will also keep employee morale high and provide stability for your organization and its donors. Fundraising is about building relationships, and each person on your team plays an important role in your interaction with supporters. From entering gifts into your database, to sending acknowledgment letters, to answering the phone, and making an ask, each team member represents a link in the chain and influences how contributors feel about your organization.

Building your fundraising dream team is only possible if you learn and follow best practices around hiring and training. Investing resources in the hiring process will help ensure you bring the right people on board and keep employee retention high, saving valuable time and resources in the future. And by dedicating resources to training and professional growth opportunities for employees, you can grow your team from within, expanding their expertise and capabilities, and helping you promote from within. Ultimately, *a stable development staff leads to more knowledgeable and passionate fundraisers who can develop deeper relationships with donors*.

To learn more about how to hire the right staff, efficiently and effectively bring them into the organization through training, and foster their growth, I sat down with Missy Sherburne, chief partnerships officer at DonorsChoose.org, who outlined the following seven tips.

Critical Skills and Competencies

1. Know Yourself and Your Needs

You can't surround yourself with the right team unless you know who you are and who you need. Ask yourself: What is important to my organization, in terms of alignment with the mission, vision, and values standpoint? What skills and experiences are most important in your new hire as your organization grows? Do you need a relationship builder that can secure major gifts, or a more detail-oriented person who can build the infrastructure and systems you need to succeed? By looking at the opportunities and challenges facing your organization, you will often identify needed positions. Whether you're a staff of one or 100, being crystal clear about what you're looking for will help you recruit and retain the right people.

If you are hiring your first fundraising staff, and your executive director (E.D.) or founder is an effective fundraiser, hire a development associate or a development manager to provide support and help with administrative tasks. In this scenario, odds are your E.D. will continue to be your best fundraiser, so "backfill" him or her to free up additional capacity, instead of hiring a more senior person that you hope will take over this role. If your leader is not a natural fundraiser or you have huge fundraising goals, then you do want someone with experience and contacts, so you'll likely want to hire a development director. Also, use fundraising consultants wisely. Do not hire them if you really need an employee. Bear in mind that *consultants can help with strategy, but they rarely drive actual fundraising. Your organization typically needs to conduct its own fundraising efforts*. As such, consultants are typically best utilized for specific campaigns, initiatives, and for strategic or development planning. In fact, DonorsChoose.org doesn't use consultants at all, instead opting to hire yearlong fellows prior to making a full-time hire if they're unsure of their needs.

2. Create a Job Description

Now that you know what you're looking for in a new hire, *write it down*. See the Resource Review at the end of this chapter for some websites that provide great templates for, and examples of, nonprofit job descriptions. Sherburne also recommends looking to similar, respected organizations for ideas on building job descriptions that reflect the role and your organization's style, values, and needs. Crafting a compelling, authentic job description is key to bringing the best candidates in the door. It should *convey not only what you want this person to accomplish and the required skill set and experience base, but also the culture of your organization*. If you have a fun and quirky office, make sure the job description relays that personality. Remember to frame your work in the most powerful way possible. Just like donors, potential employees want to be part of a winning team, so share your organization's accolades and accomplishments. Describe the role as it relates to the rest of the organization, as well as the benefits of working there.

It's common to list compensation as "based on experience," but *if you are a very small organization that needs to offer significantly less than the industry standard, be honest and explicit about your budget*. It will save you a lot of time interviewing candidates who are unwilling to work at that compensation level. When laying out the qualifications for the role, write in the second person, for example: "You enjoy diligently following up with people to get them to yes." Also, *include specific information on what materials applicants should submit in order to apply*, and where and how. Do you want a writing sample or references in addition to a résumé and cover letter? Should they email it to a specific person? Candidates' attention to detail when submitting their materials is one of the first things you should assess.

3. Select the Right Candidates

Often, the best candidates come from within your organization, or from the personal and social networks of your employees, board members, and volunteers. Look within your own team first, and if you still need to look externally, ask your network to reach out to relevant candidates and spread the word more broadly through email and social media. Consider providing a referral bonus to team members who refer candidates whom you hire for a full-time position. Provide email templates and sample social media posts to make it easy for people to help you source candidates. If possible, give this process a week or two before posting the opportunity to more public outlets, including those outlined in the Resource Review.

If you anticipate being inundated with applicants or are making an entry-level hire, consider asking candidates to complete a simple assignment (e.g., crafting an email), along with submitting a résumé and cover letter. Only committed applicants will take the time to do a brief assignment, plus this will give you a good sense of their work ethic, follow through, and communication style. Once you review résumés and cover letters, your next step will be narrowing it down to the candidates you'd like to do phone interviews with. Create a rubric by which to evaluate applications based on what's most important for the position, such as communication skills, experience, or strategic thinking. Typically you'll only want to call 5 to 20 people, but be sure to honor the time each person put into applying by responding to <u>every</u> applicant with at least a brief and courteous email.

4. Conduct Interviews

Sherburne recommends a three-step interview process, which is directly in line with what I've found to be most effective for identifying and hiring the best candidates:

Phone Interviews

Before your phone interviews, prepare four or five basic questions for each of these 30-minute conversations, and communicate that time limit to applicants beforehand. Consider asking foundational questions, like why they're interested in the role and what excites them about working for your organization. *To unearth how they align with the personality traits and attributes you most desire, ask open-ended behavior-based questions*. For example, if you want someone who's not afraid to experiment, but who needs to learn quickly and fail forward, ask something like, "Tell me about a time you failed at something, and what you learned from it." You'll likely also want to ask candidates to walk you through their most recent fundraising positions, and share what they learned from each. Leave room for candidates to ask their own questions, as these can also give you insight into how they think and how they prepare for an important meeting. Based on their responses and your overall impressions of the phone interviews, narrow down the candidate pool to the three to five individuals you'll interview in person.

First Interviews

During the first in-person interview, your mission is to learn as much as possible about each candidate and determine who will be the best fit. Keep the needs and qualifications detailed in your job description at the front of your mind, and ask behavior-based questions that help you ascertain how their interests and skills align with your needs. Before the interviews, **create a question bank to guide you, and ask likeminded or allied organizations for suggestions**.

A question bank organizes questions by skill set, so the interviewer can thoughtfully tailor the interview for each candidate. For example, if the phone interview left you with concerns that a candidate isn't goal-driven or detail-oriented, the question bank will provide questions that help you get at these areas of concern. Examples of great questions and prompts include, "What's the most useful piece constructive feedback you ever received, and how did you use it?" "How do you manage your time?" and "Tell me about the last time you were asked to do something you had no experience in." You're looking to see how they think on their feet, and how they'd handle some of the tasks and needs of the position.

Consider giving applicants a small, clearly defined assignment so that they can demonstrate their interest and excitement. Sherburne has asked candidates to draft an email to the CEO of a specific company overviewing their organization and asking for a meeting, which offers her insights into not only their writing skills and research acumen, but also how they think about the work of DonorsChoose.org. See http://www.managementcenter.org/article/how-to-ask-job-candidates-for-work-samples-exercises-or-simulations/ for tips on how to conceive and request reasonable assignments, and work samples.

Final Interviews

After the first round of in-person interviews, narrow it down to 2-3 final candidates. Have these finalists meet and interview with a variety of other people within the organization. Make it clear that this is a top priority, which merits taking time out of busy schedules. Invite other staff members, leadership, and key board members to meet with the candidate and give you feedback. Which of the candidates do they think is the best fit for the role and the organization? Be sure to **check all the references of your final candidates, even though most large employers won't say anything critical** for legal and liability reasons. Even still, share a bit about the role that you're hiring for and ask them if this person would be a good fit. If you're not sure what questions to ask when you check references, check out The Management Center's suggestions at http://www.managementcenter.org/resources/suggested-reference-check-questions.

5. Make an Offer

Once you've interviewed all the candidates, narrowed it down to finalists, received feedback from your team, checked references, and made a decision regarding whom you want to hire, you are prepared to make an offer. Call the candidate with the good news and share your excitement about him or her joining your team. Do not press for a commitment on the phone; rather, let the applicant know that you will send an offer letter so he or she can formally accept. *Your offer letter should include the proposed start date and all compensation and benefit information*, including paid time off, healthcare, retirement, and other details. Both the organization and the candidate need to sign the letter, but send it to the candidate with your signature already in the document. If and when you receive the countersigned letter back, share the good news with your team, especially those who helped with interviews. Follow up with your new hire by emailing your employee policy handbook if you have one.

6. Onboard Over Time

Don't throw your new employee in the deep end on his or her first day; *space training and orientation out over one or two weeks to ensure everything has a chance to sink in*. Give the new hire time to get to know your organization, the team, and the tools and resources on hand. *Start with a presentation on the organization, its history, and its current work and goals, ideally led by your executive director*. Set up meetings or lunches between the new team member and key colleagues. Provide time and orientation so he or she can get up to speed on your fundraising efforts, systems, and donors. *Share all key fundraising and marketing materials, including everything you share with the public and your donors*, to provide a sense of your communication points and style. Wait a few weeks before having new hires do larger tasks, like creating an individual fundraising plan or going on donor meetings.

7. Develop Your Team

Hiring is only the beginning of your effort to develop a successful fundraising team. Training and professional development are ongoing processes worthy of your time and resources. *Create a professional development budget for your employees*, even if it's only $500 a year, and encourage them to bring you classes, trainings, and conferences they'd like to attend. Buy subscriptions to fundraising publications like *The Chronicle of Philanthropy*, *The Nonprofit Times*, *Fundraising Success Magazine*, and others, including industry-specific publications that match your focus. Offer regular opportunities and suggestions for ongoing educational opportunities that will improve capabilities and skills. Consider suggestions in excess of your professional development budget if it's in the organization's best interest. These investments will show your team that you care about their personal and professional growth and success, and that you're willing to support them as they work to make your nonprofit successful. This will keep employee morale and retention high, and most importantly, will lead to more successful fundraising efforts.

Get Your Executive Director to Love Fundraising

This chapter focused on hiring and training development staff, but what does it look like for these leaders to "manage up" and train your executive director or board chair? After starting his new role as director of major gifts at Worldreader, a nonprofit focused on bringing e-books to every child and family, Brian Gougherty was surprised when his E.D. told him that he didn't like fundraising. The group had already raised millions, so Gougherty knew he had a lot to work with, and assumed that if he could change his manager's perspective, the group could raise even more funds and educate more children. It worked, and here's how he did it and what you can learn from his experience:

Focus on the cause. Fundraising is not about the money; it's more about the cause and your personal connection to its impact. Constantly remind your E.D. of this, and *invite him to share why he chose to devote a career and time to the organization when meeting with prospects*. If your E.D. can let the passion flow, the dollars will follow. Gougherty did this and subsequently, his E.D. found conversations with donors to be surprisingly engaging. He now views questions they ask as a challenge that drive new ideas at the organization, some of which have even led to new programs. He's grown to really love having donor meetings, not just because they bring in money, but because they bring forward new thoughts and ideas.

(continued)

(continued)

Establish credibility. Take the time to educate your E.D. on your donor cultivation and stewardship process. Make sure he or she knows *exactly* how you plan to follow up with donors, and what you're doing to build and strengthen relationships with them. This will make your E.D. more comfortable and confident in engaging and soliciting major donors, as well as bringing their own personal prospects to the table.

Engage wisely. Value your E.D.'s time and utilize it in the best way possible. Don't ask her or him to do cold calls, instead of cultivating major leads and closing big gift opportunities. You can write acknowledgment letters and proposals, but *your E.D. should focus on making personal thank you calls to major donors, attending key donor events, and the other things that really benefit from your leader's personal touch*. Along these lines, draft sample correspondence, such as follow-up emails and thank you letters to facilitate fundraising. Think "low touch, high value," as this process is very much akin to what's detailed in chapter 3 for board engagement.

Point to success. When your E.D. secures a major gift that inspires other major donors to contribute, make sure he or she knows about this ripple effect. When you receive an unexpected gift from a key donor after your E.D. sent a note, made a phone call, or took a lunch meeting, share the good new! Success breeds success, and the more your E.D. sees the fruit of his or her labor, the more engaged he or she will be.

Conclusion

Raising money for your cause depends directly upon the strength of your team. Hiring the right people, training them properly, and fostering their professional growth are critical to building a, efficient, cohesive, and successful fundraising team. Doing this requires an investment of time and resources that, too often, nonprofits aren't willing to commit to. However, the investment is far outweighed by the tremendous benefits, most notably increased revenue, higher employee morale and retention, and deeper relationships with donors. Simply put, you will raise more money with the right people at your side. So invest what's needed to find, keep, and empower them!

Do's and Don'ts

Do...

> . . . send a very brief email to applicants you won't interview to thank them for their interest but let them know they're not a fit.

> . . . create a bank of interview questions for each phase of the interview process.

> . . . have key staff and board meet a final candidate before hiring.

> . . . ask your network whether they know any viable candidates before utilizing public job posting resources.

Don't...

> . . . let the hiring process take longer than a few weeks.

> . . . hire a consultant to act as your development director.

> . . . forget to include a professional development budget for every staff member in your organization, however small.

About the Expert

Missy Sherburne is the chief partnerships officer at DonorsChoose.org, a nonprofit that connects individuals, companies, and foundations with the needs of public schools. Previously, she served as the founding executive director of DonorsChoose.org North Carolina and South Carolina, and North Carolina Executive Director with Teach For America.

Resource Review

The BridgeSpan Group (http://www.bridgespan.org/Home.aspx)
  This group provides a great nonprofit job board, and their website is a great starting point to look for job description templates, plus it offers a wide range of reports and resources.

Both Sides of the Table (www.bothsidesofthetable.com)
  Mark Suster's blog is a helpful resource for organizations looking to grow, and has a lot of tips for hiring the right people.

Young Nonprofit Professionals Network/YNPN (www.ynpn.org)
   This is a great place to connect with younger nonprofit leaders, and you
   can post jobs for free on their regional listservs.

Great places to post (and find) fundraising jobs:

- Association of Fundraising Professionals (www.afpnet.org)
- Foundation Center (www.foundationcenter.org)
- Idealist (www.idealist.org)
- The BridgeSpan Group (http://www.bridgespan.org/Home.aspx)
- Glassdoor (www.glassdoor.com)
- OpportunityKnocks (www.opportunityknocks.org)
- *Chronicle of Philanthropy* (www.philanthropy.com/jobs)
- Indeed (www.indeed.com)
- craigslist (www.craigslist.org)

Blue Avocado (www.blueavocado.org)
   This online magazine writes about a variety of nonprofit management
   issues, including hiring and training staff.

GuideStar USA Nonprofit Compensation Report (www.guidestar.com).
   Every year, GuideStar conducts the most comprehensive analysis available
   on nonprofit executive compensation practices, the only large-scale
   examination based entirely on IRS data. Available for a fee, the report
   is based on observations from over 100,000 Forms 990 filed by 501(c)
   organizations with the IRS for the prior fiscal year.

Collins, James C. *Good to Great: Why Some Companies Make the Leap—and
Others Don't.* HarperBusiness, 2001.
   Collins and his team outline the key determinants of greatness for
   companies—which are equally relevant to nonprofits—and speak to
   why hiring the right people and setting them up for success is critical to
   building a thriving organization.

The Management Center, DC (www.managementcenter.org)
   Find great resources on hiring and training on their website, plus a
   helpful monthly newsletter with a hiring section that shares useful tools,
   like sample interview questions and exercises.

Association of Fundraising Professionals/AFP (www.afpnet.org)
   This is a great place to connect with fundraising professionals. Check out
   their job board and annual conference.

Foundation Center (www.foundationcenter.org)
Find resources on their website, free events at local chapters, and check out their job board.

Cause Marketing Forum (www.causemarketingforum.com)
This is a great place to find a nonprofit community that will provide referrals and sounding boards, as well as access to tips and resources.

Engaging Your Board

"Change is inevitable, but progress is optional, and leadership makes all the difference."

—Andy Stern

Introduction

Board members are part of the core leadership team of your organization, and they're in one of the best positions to serve as passionate advocates for your cause. When effectively engaged and utilized, boards will step up, and step *in* to fundraising. Board members have unique connections and relationships in the community that are valuable and even transformative when properly leveraged. The right board, successfully employed, can catapult both your impact and fundraising efforts to the next level. Board members should also be among your most dependable and generous donors. For most nonprofits, the sum of these contributions makes a big difference on their budget.

Unfortunately, this rosy picture isn't as common as it should be. Many small nonprofits launch with a friends and family board that simply lends their names to the NGO application, and still others are grassroots organizations that leverage a "working board" to augment their staff, assuming they even have a payroll. Either way, transitioning your organization to one that effectively recruits and engages a powerful board that contributes on all levels to your fundraising efforts—donating, asking, prospecting, and more—is one of the most vexing challenges facing many nonprofits. But there's hope: it doesn't have to be that way.

In an effort to identify tips and tools that can help nonprofits successfully partner with their boards to drive fundraising results, I sat down with nonprofit executive coach and fundraising and board development consultant Lisa Hoffman. We discussed six tips to foster your board's passion in your mission and increase their participation in your fundraising efforts.

Critical Skills and Competencies

1. Know What You're Looking For

Building the right board is the first critical step in achieving fundraising success, but of course, transitioning to your ideal board is difficult. The key is gaining consensus on what you're after. It's a lot easier to recruit from your network when you know that you're hoping to find a Latina lawyer with solid corporate connections who's committed to our cause of combating homelessness, versus just telling folks you want more members. Your goal should be identify the top three things you're looking for in new candidates, and share that with the world. *A board matrix is a powerful yet simple tool that clarifies exactly what kind of characteristics, assets, and skillsets you want on your board:* someone with business or foundation connections in a certain location; an issue area expert well-versed in your cause; a person who contributes geographic, racial, or gender diversity; someone who can make a large annual gift; an accounting, fundraising, or marketing maven, etc.

A simple spreadsheet does the trick nicely—use the rows to write down all the characteristics of your ideal board, including assets you may already have in place. Typically, it's helpful to organize these into "buckets," including leadership, expertise and connection to the mission, financial capability and connections, demographics, and so forth. The columns are for the names of your current and potential board members, as well as other prospects identified over time. Here's a simple example:

Nonprofit Board Matrix Template

Categories	Current Member 1	Current Member 2	Current Member 3	Prospect	Prospect
Leadership and Expertise					
Visionary	X	X	X		
Spiritual					
Legal				X	
Accounting					
Entrepreneur	X	X	X	X	
Nonprofit Management				X	
Our Issue: Peace					
Scientist					
Recognized Leader	X	X	X		X
Community Contacts	X	X	X		X
Entertainment/Media					
Media Contacts	X		X		X
Music Contacts	X	X	X		X
Arts Education			X		X
Financial Support					
Major Donor		X	X	X	
Donor Contacts	X	X	X	X	
Foundation Contacts			X		X
Corporate Contacts	X	X	X		
Time/Availability		X	X		X
Geography					
International Relations	X		X		X
Brazil					X
South Africa				X	
Austin					
India			X	X	
Demographics					
Youth					
Latino					X
African American				X	
Female			X		X

Although undoubtedly a powerful tool, ***the board matrix must be
presented with finesse.*** Start by getting your board chair sold on the idea,
even before you take a stab at a first draft, which you can create together.
Ideally, the board chair then convinces the other members to create a

blueprint to guide recruitment as the organization matures. Once they're sold on the idea, there's usually a discussion about what's called for, using your draft matrix as a starting point. When this is in place, you're ready for the real exercise. Everyone simply puts an "X" under his or her name for the characteristics he or she possesses. Finally, quickly tally the results and discuss what's missing, and what you need more of.

Then it's time to share this profile with your colleagues and contacts. Work your network, reaching out to the most connected, established people you know, and have staff and board members do the same. *Consider creating a board development committee to drive recruitment and onboarding*. Don't compromise: you need people who are passionate about your mission, have the time to serve, and who will prioritize your organization. When a potential board member is identified, someone needs to meet or talk with the candidate to share your story and feel him or her out. If there's a good fit, your ambassador should then clarify what's involved, which leads us to our next tip.

2. Set Expectations

A board member agreement is one of the most powerful tools for engaging your board in fundraising, and beyond. This is a one- or two-page document, written plainly, that details the responsibilities of all board members. Simply put, it's a checklist of expectations, written in clear terms that aren't subject to interpretation. So instead of "I'll make a good faith effort to attend all board meetings," it should say something more like, "I will attend 75 percent of all quarterly board meetings." This document serves as a perfect basis for onboarding new members, avoiding most surprises and miscommunication.

Of course, you can't expect the new guy or gal to sign up something that the old guard isn't subject to. Follow a process exactly like the one for the board matrix to ensure the current board buys in and agrees on the requirements, and then *have every current board member sign an agreement*, all co-signed by the board chair. This creates a helpful dose of accountability for both new and seasoned members, and your chair should *use the board member agreement as the basis for annual board reviews*. Simply go through the agreement point-by-point, ensuring each item was completed, and exploring any shortfalls by asking whether the trustee needs more training or support or, if it's simply not possible for the person to deliver, invite him or her to consider transitioning to an advisory role. This approach can help make move inactive board members out much more gracefully than a subjective "I don't think you're doing a good job" chat, thereby increasing the chance of the person continuing to provide financial support.

Now let's talk a bit more about the terms of the board member agreement. First, it must include an outline of required activities and their frequency: board meetings, committee participation, special events, fundraising and marketing campaigns, board recruitment drives, site visits, and so forth. Be honest about the time and level of commitment you expect, but remember *the best way to engage your board is with a "low touch, high value" approach, where you focus their contribution on the things that only they can do.* Leave the heavy lifting and the mundane tasks to staff and volunteers.

The agreement must also *outline all fundraising responsibilities of board participation*, starting first and foremost with a personal financial contribution. Rather than arbitrarily setting a minimum requirement, which is especially tough if you have a diverse board, **require an annual capacity gift of every board member**. A capacity gift is defined as the largest gift someone can comfortably make and one of his or her top three philanthropic investments of the year. It may be $20 for the student on your board, or $1,000 for the accountant who also gets her company to kick in $10,000 for your annual event, but having even one board member fail to contribute *personal* funds undermines your chances of securing other donations and grants from foundations requiring 100 percent board giving participation.

In addition to making a personal contribution, *all board members must also be engaged in the fundraising process.* As Kay Sprinkel Grace suggests in Chapter 9, it's unlikely that every member of your board can be an asker, but every member should be identifying prospects, utilizing connections, and setting up meetings and calls, spreading awareness about your organization, and supporting fundraising campaigns via social media and email. Some organizations have a "give/get" requirement to encourage the board to donate and fundraise in meaningful ways, but again this can be problematic if your board is diverse. If one lowest common denominator "get" number is inappropriate for your organization, which is, in fact, the norm, there are two things you can and should do to still engage your board in fundraising. First, rather than setting a dollar limit in the board member agreement, **require a minimum number of donor, funder, and sponsor prospect introductions annually**, perhaps three or five so you don't scare prospects away. Second, set an individual fundraising goal with each board member, as discussed more in Tip 4, below.

3. Provide Training and Support

Most board members will come into your organization without any fundraising experience or training. *It is your responsibility to transform their passion for your mission into successful fundraising activity.* It is critical to give board members tools like talking points, personal stories and case statements, and fact sheets about the organization.

Don't assume your board members know how to talk about your work, nor that they're comfortable advocating on your behalf. ***Hold a board training session every year or two***, conducted by your executive or development director or a professional consultant. Leverage these regular trainings to teach your board how to articulate your organization's mission compellingly and passionately. They should learn how to incorporate their own personal stories of how they're connected to the cause and why they care. Role playing is a great, fun way to practice this.

Finally, be sure to use the training to address any fears or discomfort your board has around fundraising. You need to *make them feel proud to fundraise* and help them see that an ask is simply presenting people with an opportunity to affect the change they want to see. Have them read the foreword of this book and Chapter 9, or at least the part where Kay shares her thoughts on transformative versus transactional giving. Whatever it takes, your board must be willing, and proud, to reach out to their networks and contribute to building your base of support. Some board members will be naturals at asking, and others will prefer to make introductions and let you or fellow trustees do the asking. In the latter case, ***always try to involve a board member in calls or meetings with prospects they've identified***. This provides ongoing training, enabling those who are less comfortable to witness respectful and effective asks firsthand, and hopefully leading to them becoming askers over time.

4. Engage Each Board Member Individually

It's important to foster relationships with each board member and meet with them individually on a regular basis. At the very least, ***meet with each board member annually to identify what support is needed in achieving their annual fundraising goal***, which they set with you or, ideally, the board chair. If at all possible, connect more frequently to check in on their progress, but let each board member dictate how often he or she wants to talk or meet. Ensure that not only are they engaged and active in their role, but more importantly, that all members also feel satisfied and fulfilled with their participation. Remember, it's actually the board chair's job to manage the board, and you should only be focusing on getting them what they need to be fully engaged and equipped to participate—of course, that's certainly not always the case. Either way, these meetings are a perfect forum to figure out whether you're getting what you need out of them, and whether they're getting what they want out of you. If they haven't been attending meetings regularly or following through on their commitments, this is a good time to see whether there's anything *you* can do about that. Is there any help, materials, stories, or training that'd be useful as they pursue their leads? These one-on-one check-ins also help to establish a personal connection between you and your board, helping each member feel comfortable reaching out with questions and concerns over time.

5. Let Your Board Lead

Generally speaking, *your board chair needs to take charge of getting other board members involved in fundraising*. For larger boards and well-established organizations, your development or governance committee chair can also take on this responsibility. Either way, just as with all fundraising, *the most powerful form of ask is a peer ask*, as in "I just gave to Save the Children—won't you join me in supporting their good work?" The same holds true for board engagement, and it's always better when a peer— the board chair—asks members to step up and actively contribute.

Your chair should regularly communicate that fundraising is a core responsibility and must hold each member accountable for his or her fundraising commitments and annual donations. Your executive or development director should be regularly meeting with the board chair about the board's fundraising progress and needs, so that that he or she can properly support the board and unlock their full, active participation. Of course, this entails the board chair having a clear understanding of the organization's fundraising goals and its strategic plan, as well as progress made to date. You can also *create a development committee within the board to focus on fundraising*, as long as the rest of the board understands that this doesn't let them off the hook for fundraising. This can be a great platform to further engage people who want to contribute more to your fundraising efforts, as well as create an opportunity for potential board members to start helping out. A development committee is a tool to foster board and community involvement in fundraising and provides support and coordination for fundraising activities. In order to avoid confusion between the committee's role and that of the chair and staff, *the first order of business for any committee should be drafting a charter outlining its function and role.*

One of your board chair's most important responsibilities is making personal asks of each board member annually. Again, the exception to this is large organizations that task the development or governance committee chair with this responsibility, but either way, it's crucial that it's board-led. You can provide support and training to ensure these asks are made respectfully, and effectively, but again, peer asks simply work better. Your role is to support the chair in these asks, as it is with all the members. Providing your chair with information on each member's giving capacity and any other major gifts they've made to other organizations is always helpful. You'll also want to share their giving history to your organization, as well as the programs and impact they're most connected to. This will help your chair customize each ask and maximize dollars raised.

6. Maximize Board Meetings

There should be time allocated at every board meeting to quickly look at fundraising results to date, and compare them to your overall plan and goals. The board should be familiar with your strategic fundraising plan and be able to ask focused questions about progress and results. You should also use board meetings to continue to inspire members to participate in fundraising efforts. *Have one or two members share success stories about progress they've made with leads, or donations they've secured.* It's also helpful to have board members share how they've handled any "no's" they received, hopefully showing the others that you don't need to take a "no" personally. You can also share what Kay Sprinkel Grace calls "mission moments" by having a client or stakeholder come in and share how the organization has helped improve his or her life. These moments powerfully connect board members to your organization and its impact on those you serve.

Finally, one way to ensure board engagement at meetings—in fundraising and in general—is to ensure that there's more dialogue than monologue. *Board meetings should be a place for discussion, and reports and updates should be kept brief and focused.* As covered in Chapter 7, organizational dashboards help streamline meetings by providing a quick, bird's eye view of the health of the organization and progress toward goals. Another great tool is a docket agenda, also known as a consent calendar. *Docket agendas are short documents that include minutes from your last board meeting, plus top-line updates* of no more than two or three paragraphs each. Keeping your board up-to-date is important, but almost all reports and updates can be condensed down to a couple of paragraphs. Distribute the document in advance, but even still, ***start each board meeting with five or ten minutes of silence as everyone reviews the docket agenda***, after which it's voted on and approved. If there are items from the agenda that warrant further discussion, they can be removed and added to a proper meeting agenda.

Conclusion

Your success in fundraising depends largely on having an engaged and active board. The first step is recruiting effectively and making sure you build a board that has the traits and skill sets your organization needs. As Jim Collins says in *Good to Great*, it's about getting the "right people on the bus." But what's enormous potential if it's not tapped? Board members also need to be trained so that they can speak passionately and articulately about your mission and feel proud to invite others to support your cause. Not every board member will feel comfortable making direct asks, but everyone needs to help identify prospects, foster connections, and spread awareness. Cultivating leadership on your board and having a strong, engaged chair is key to securing personal board contributions and fundraising participation throughout. When effectively leveraged, your board can be your strongest asset, and each member deserves personal attention and regular updates on the impact his or her contribution has on your overall work. Follow this recipe and your board will catapult your fundraising efforts, enabling your organization to thrive.

Do's and Don'ts

Do. . .

> . . . be clear about fundraising and all other expectations when recruiting board members.

> . . . provide fundraising training and materials to all board members annually.

> . . . ensure each board member has an individual fundraising goal and plan for the year.

> . . . have each member sign a board agreement when first recruited.

Don't. . .

　　. . . spend the majority of board meetings giving updates, instead of engaging in dialogue.

　　. . . recruit board members without first creating a board matrix.

　　. . . fail to communicate with board members who are not meeting expectations.

About the Expert

Lisa Hoffman is a nonprofit coach, consultant, and facilitator with more than 25 years of experience in helping nonprofits thrive by moving boards from good to great. Hoffman is also an ordained Zen priest, bringing the Buddhist practices of compassion, active engagement, and leaving the ego at the door to her nonprofit coaching and consulting.

Resource Review

Grace, Kay Sprinkel. *The Ultimate Board Member's Book: A 1-hour Guide to Understanding Your Role and Responsibilities.* Emerson & Church, 2004. This quick and easy to read book explains what board members must do to help their organization succeed.

Grace, Kay Sprinkel. *Beyond Fundraising: New Strategies for Nonprofit Innovation and Investment* (2nd ed.). John Wiley & Sons, 2005. Fundraising expert Kay Sprinkel Grace presents her internationally field-tested core beliefs, principles, and strategies for developing long-term relationships with donor-investors and volunteers.

BoardSource (www.boardsource.org) This is the go-to source for board development resources. They do live and online trainings, have membership programs, and also provide a wealth of articles and publications on their website.

Blue Avocado (www.blueavocado.org) This is a great online magazine focused on all aspects of nonprofit management. Search for board fundraising and find a wealth of content.

Masaoka, Jan. *The Best of the Board Café: Hands-On Solutions for Nonprofit Boards*. Amherst H. Wilder Foundation, 2003.
This book gives nonprofit board members just-in-time guidance to the issues at hand. Because board members' time is scarce, articles are "short enough to read over a cup of coffee."

CompassPoint Nonprofit Services (www.compasspoint.org)
This is a great resource for in-person workshops in the San Francisco Bay Area and online trainings for nonprofits nationwide. You can also find publications and articles on their website.

Klein, Kim. *Fundraising for Social Change* (5th ed.). Jossey-Bass, 2007.
This book provides a soup to nuts description of how to build, maintain, and expand an individual donor program, and is often called "the Bible of grassroots fundraising."

Grassroots Fundraising Journal (www.grassrootsfundraising.org)
Search for board fundraising to find a lot of great content and resources.

Andy Robinson's blog (http://andyrobinsononline.com)
Find links to articles, resources, and videos about fundraising.

Rosso, Henry A. *Hank Rosso's Achieving Excellence in Fundraising* (2nd ed.). Jossey-Bass, 2003.
This book explains the fundraising profession's major principles, concepts, and techniques, clearly defines each step in the fundraising cycle, and demonstrates why fundraising is a strategic management discipline.

Robinson, Maureen K. *Nonprofit Boards That Work: The End of One-Size-Fits-All Governance*. John Wiley & Sons, 2001.
This book offers practical yet flexible strategies that can be tried by any nonprofit board, whatever its current effectiveness toward accomplishing the goals they seek.

Zimmerman, Robert M., and Ann W. Lehman. *Boards That Love Fundraising: A How-to Guide for Your Board*. Jossey-Bass, 2004.
This workbook explains fundraising responsibility as a board member while providing information on board structure, its impact on raising money, and outlining the concepts that will empower a board to ask for money effectively and fearlessly.

Chapter 4

Volunteer Fundraising

"Until you ask, the answer is always 'no'."

—Nora Roberts

Introduction

If you don't realize that your volunteer strategy and your fundraising efforts are linked at the hip, you're missing the boat. In fact, according to Fidelity's *Charitable Gift Fund Volunteerism and Charitable Giving Report*,[1] **two-thirds of volunteers donate to their nonprofits,** and **people who volunteer donate ten times more money**. Volunteers are also a great source of capacity and connections, and they can bolster and expand your existing development efforts, especially if put to use in the right way. They can also serve as passionate advocates for your cause, connecting you to cash and in-kind supporters, strategic partners, and expanding what your staff and organization can achieve.

But how can you tap this immense potential, and what are the best practices for gracefully inviting these key supporters to also open up their wallets and support your organization financially? To answer these key questions, I sat down with volunteer engagement expert Simon Tam, who managed 2,500 volunteers at the American Cancer Society.

In our conversation, Tam outlined eight crucial tips for engaging volunteers.

Critical Skills and Competencies

1. Dedicate Staff

Having a dedicated staff member who can manage your volunteers, provide guidance and training, answer questions, and serve as a main point of contact is critical. It doesn't necessarily need to be a full-time position, but *someone needs to manage these important relationships and potential donors.* Volunteers need a person to turn to for questions and feedback; someone who can help them understand the workflow and politics of the organization, its style and values, and key talking points. This dedicated staffer should be responsible for onboarding new volunteers and thereafter tracking them, from simple contact information, to volunteering history and hours, to donor research—more on the latter in Tip 4, below.

2. Define Clear Roles

Volunteers need to be given clear direction so they know what's expected of them; this is crucial to them feeling their time and work is valuable and maps to impact. This can be as simple as creating a job description or having them sign an agreement before they start—typically, less is more, and even a few simple bullet points can go a long way. The point is that *you need to let volunteers know that, even though they aren't being paid, they're still going to be held accountable for their work*, and it's still crucial to your nonprofit's work in the community. Creating an agreement or contract also helps document hours needed for school credits or résumés, and creates a paper trail that can help later with letters of recommendation and job references. ***Clarity of purpose, goals, and expectations is the key to successful volunteer engagement.***

3. Create a Toolkit

Remember that scene in *The Matrix* where Neo instantly learns martial arts? Well, your nonprofit needs a program like that to quickly and effectively orient new volunteers. This kind of toolkit not only provides your volunteers with basic, yet important, organizational information and talking points, but it also gives them a sense of belonging and pride. It demonstrates that you're investing in them, that they are a crucial part of your team, and that you *want and expect* them to represent you.

A toolkit can include things like basic talking points on the organization and its history, marketing brochures and communication materials like FAQs, simple training materials (e.g., database training manuals), contact information of your staff (especially their dedicated liaison), and perhaps a gift, such as a t-shirt with your logo on it. Over time, you can even consider adding in business cards for key performers, as these really help to develop a sense of commitment. Building volunteer toolkits is a small, smart investment when you consider how many hours volunteers contribute, not to mention potential fundraising revenue.

4. Track Everything

As outlined in Chapter 5, having a database or constituent relationship management (CRM) system is critical to not only tracking your donors, but info on volunteers as well. This lets you track each volunteer, including contact information, staff contacts, and hours donated; plus it allows you to track their fundraising leads. This will help you better manage volunteer relationships, stay in touch, and maximize volunteers' fundraising potential. When appropriate, volunteers should be involved in using your CRM, so that they can track their own progress and see how they're making a difference, not to mention saving your staff time. And when it comes to the donor prospects they share with you, be sure to ***document valuable connections, including contact info, giving interests, and capacity***. This allows you to better manage and cultivate these relationships, particularly when you engage multiple volunteers.

5. Think Small, but Dream Big

Creating small workgroups, such as committees or teams dedicated to a particular task, can expand organizational capacity and enable you to more deeply engage key volunteers. So the next time you're launching a new campaign, producing an event, or contemplating expanding into new geographic areas, create a team or committee to spearhead your efforts, thereby enabling you to stay focused on the big picture and other key areas. The big point here is that *volunteers can do more than just execute on your orders*; they can think for themselves and strategically contribute to the future and success of your nonprofit.

6. Communicate Regularly

Having weekly or monthly check-ins with volunteers allows you to review their work, ask whether they have questions or concerns, and provide guidance. This ensures both sides are satisfied with the relationship, increases accountability, and gives you an opportunity to show your gratitude. (Plus it minimizes the unlikely scenario that a volunteer goes off course and undermines your work.) It can be as short as 10 minutes, and a check-in can be something as simple as taking the volunteer out for coffee or lunch or scheduling a brief meeting or call. Either way, these *regular forums are critical to optimizing the contributions of your pro bono support network*.

7. Never Say Goodbye

Once volunteers are no longer actively working with you, it's important to continue to engage them. They've already invested in your organization, and keeping them apprised of new accomplishments, activities, and even challenges allows them to feel connected and appreciated—a part of your inner circle. But this doesn't have to be a lot of work, and you don't need to reach out to each past volunteer individually with updates; instead, *create a Listserv for alumni volunteers*, and be sure to invite them to key events. All this goes a long way toward cultivating these relationships and can certainly lead to fundraising results—remember, *volunteers are some of your best donor prospects and must be treated accordingly*!

8. Invite Financial Support

Asking volunteers directly for donations is inherently sensitive. Many times, however, volunteers are waiting to be asked. The key is building a relationship with your volunteer first, just as you would with any donor. Just about all volunteers want to make a difference, but they don't always know how, both in terms of their volunteer service and contributing financially.

We covered a lot of tips for effectively engaging their time in this chapter, but beyond that, if you make the ask properly (see Chapter 7) and the volunteer is *not* in a position to donate at the time, he or she should feel honored to have been invited. That's the art of fundraising—inviting people to support work you've clearly established they believe in; and *it's your job to ensure they can reply gracefully no matter what their answer*. Beyond the tips for doing this with all donors, when it comes to volunteers, before making an ask it's especially critical that you make your volunteer feel appreciated and frame the invitation to donate as an additional or incremental opportunity, so that you in no way undermine the contribution of his or her time and energy.

Examples of Volunteer Activities

Depending on the fundraising strategy and needs of your organization, you'll want to engage your volunteers in different ways. At the American Cancer Society (ACS), Tam managed volunteers who *conceived and implemented their own fundraisers*—bake sales, car washes, silent auctions, etc. To facilitate this, ACS volunteers dedicated staff members who provided branding and communication materials, plus best practices for throwing these kinds of self-directed fundraisers. Nonprofits like ACS with enough resources can even provide tools like Convio or StayClassy that allow volunteers to create their own fundraising pages, further strengthening their ability to raise big bucks for you. (See Chapter 15 for effective crowdfunding tips.)

Now that he's at the Oregon Environment Council, a much smaller membership organization, Tam and his staff utilize volunteers to *call lapsed donors and ask them to renew their memberships*, as well as calling current monthly donors to ask them to increase their giving. To do this, they provide volunteers with a call script and guidelines and have them work from the office to ensure that staff is there to provide support. Tam is also a big fan of utilizing volunteers to *help fundraising staff with administrative tasks*, including processing donations, entering new donors into the database, and preparing donor acknowledgement letters. Again, volunteers can help with both the mundane tasks associated with raising money for your cause, but also the big picture, strategic opportunities that can really move your organization forward.

So don't be afraid to get creative and engage your volunteers as thought partners—maybe you invite their input on a letter writing campaign and ask them to contribute ideas and language, or you talk with them about sharing fundraising and marketing materials with their personal networks via email and social media to see who might be interested in becoming a donor or attending an event, and then you solicit ideas for how to make the appeal more viral—the point is *you don't need to have all the answers and can make it a conversation instead of an assignment.*

Case Study: APANO

Tam was impressed and learned something himself when he volunteered for APANO, the Asian Pacific American Network of Oregon. They needed to raise $20,000 for a new community center. They looked through their database and identified their "superstar" volunteers, then narrowed down the list to folks who were also influential community leaders. They invited Tam and the others out to dinner, where they presented their vision, the impact it would have, the fundraising need, and their intended strategy

(continued)

(continued)

for raising the cash. Their focus was on a tight list of key major donor prospects—they already had their contact info and invited the volunteers to share any existing relationships they had with the prospects. Since they stacked the deck with well-connected supporters, almost everybody in the room was tied to somebody and offered a personal intro. They also asked for additional names and encouraged everybody to list two to five names of people who might be interested in this particular project, and made sure to confirm they felt comfortable with approaching them.

By the end of one well-executed night, APANO had a list of more than 100 targeted prospects, each associated with a personal connection, plus they had lots of inroads with the leads they previously identified. From there, they provided packets, email templates and talking points, and a top-level brochure and one-pager. The APANO staff also checked in with their volunteers on a call or email every week or two, asking about updates and challenges and inquiring about possible meetings that staff could support by participating. Throughout the campaign, whenever a volunteer had a fundraising victory, APANO sent an email saying something like "Haley just got a pledge for $1,000," "John Smith just pledged $5,000," "Jane Betty is in for $20 a month," and so on. This kept the momentum going and created an environment of friendly competition. APANO even kept an updated list of total contributions that all the volunteers viewed regularly, ultimately making the campaign a huge success, generating $25,000, with the extra cash going toward the complete remodel of their offices, as well as building a new community center. They also leveraged this momentum to double the funds raised at their annual gala shortly thereafter.

Conclusion

In short, if you ***treat volunteers the way you do staff and potential donors***, you're on the right path. Volunteers are not only freely giving their time to advance your cause, but they are also statistically likely to be your best donors. Take the time to plan their contributions properly and make sure to provide them with the support and resources they need to maximize their engagement, including staff, materials, and most of all, access to your time, attention, and appreciation. *Train and appreciate your volunteers and they will thrive.* Get out of your comfort zone when it comes to actively engaging them as thought partners in your fundraising efforts. Finally, *never underestimate the importance of regularly showing them the positive impact they are having on your organization and cause.* By creating and maintaining a relationship of trust and accountability, you will create a more fulfilling and prosperous relationship for everyone involved.

Do's and Don'ts

Do. . .

> . . . have clear expectations documented in an agreement that's signed by *both* your organization and the volunteer.

> . . . check in with volunteers at least monthly to provide feedback and show gratitude.

> . . . engage volunteer alumni by regularly sending out key updates and invitations after their terms of service end.

> . . . offer business cards to top-performing volunteers to get them more engaged.

Don't. . .

> . . . bring volunteers on without a clear sense of what's required of them, who's going to manage them, and systems to set them up for success.

> . . . be afraid to ask volunteers for their input on ideas in progress, or to contribute financially.

> . . . make assumptions about volunteer experience, skillsets, or commitment; ask them what they want and don't want to do.

> . . . ask volunteers to do something that staff would not be willing to do themselves.

About the Expert

Simon Tam is currently the director of marketing for the Oregon Environmental Council, the author of *How to Get Sponsorships and Endorsements*, and was previously the community relationship manager at the American Cancer Society, where he managed more than 2,500 volunteers.

Note

1. Fidelity Charitable Gift Fund. "Fidelity® Charitable Gift Fund Volunteerism and Charitable Giving in 2009 Executive Summary." www.fidelitycharitable.org/docs/Volunteerism-Charitable-Giving-2009-Executive-Summary.pdf. December 9, 2009.

Resource Review

VolunteerMatch (www.VolunteerMatch.org)
Great resource for finding volunteers, articles, and content on volunteer engagement; useful for recruiting volunteers, board members, and fulfilling skills-based requirements.

Idealist (www.Idealist.org)
A very robust website that offers lots of links to useful resources and articles, plus access to a global community of volunteers and nonprofit peers.

J. Maxwell & S. Covey. *The 21 Irrefutable Laws of Leadership: Follow Them and People Will Follow You* (10th ed.). Thomas Nelson, 2007.
Insightful book that offers great leadership advice, with direct implications for staff and volunteer engagement.

HandsOn Network (www.HandsOnNetwork.org)
A U.S.–wide network of volunteer centers, many of which organize events to share best practices for volunteer recruitment and engagement.

National Council of Nonprofits (NCN) (https://www.councilofnonprofits.org/tools-resources/volunteers)
The NCN is a network of state associations of nonprofits, but their website has a wealth of resources and links to useful data on volunteers, as well as tools and best practices for their engagement and management.

Nonprofit Resource Center (www.nprcenter.org/volunteer-management)
Besides providing training and support to Sacramento-based nonprofits, NPR also publishes a great list of useful volunteer resources.

Foundation Center's GrantSpace (http://grantspace.org/tools)
In the Tools section, you can search for "Recruiting and Managing Volunteers" and there's an extensive list of resources, links, and research on the topic.

Career Resource Centers at Community Colleges
These are great resources for finding volunteers, as they provide access to working adults looking to expand their résumés. Google is a free and easy tool for finding these.

Building Your Toolkit and Tracking Progress

Prospecting and Donor Research

"By failing to prepare, you are preparing to fail."

—Ben Franklin

Introduction

Prospecting and donor research are absolutely critical to a nonprofit's long-term fundraising success. It's about more than just collecting data; it's about creating fundraising intelligence. To raise money, you need to be able to identify fundraising prospects, track your activities, and gather information on donors and prospects that will help you connect and develop relationships. Without intelligence, you will be operating in the dark, and at some point you'll need to turn the lights on but won't be able to. This is where prospecting and research tools will help.

Fundraising research helps you identify and prioritize donor prospects and provides helpful information to frontline fundraisers for their interactions with foundations, corporations, and major donors. Ultimately, it enables you to build a clear picture of your top prospects and craft appropriate strategies to maximize results. Your budget and organizational capacity will determine how deep you go, but *every nonprofit trying to raise money needs to research prospects*, and in particular you should focus on your top 5 to 10 percent, but of course that means you need to be able to identify them.

Having a system in place for donor research will lead to larger pools of funding prospects and increased fundraising revenue. Advances in technology and information storage have been a game-changer for nonprofits and fundraisers in particular. To learn more about this topic and the tools that will help you be successful, I sat down with Helen Brown, co-author of *Prospect Research for Fundraisers: The Essential Handbook*, and president of the Helen Brown Group. In her words, she says this topic is crucial since, "Research is the foundation that all great fundraising is built on."

Critical Skills and Competencies

1. Assign the Right Staff

Someone will need to take point on your fundraising research efforts, but who? The staff member you charge with gathering fundraising intelligence will need to possess or acquire specific skills and characteristics. Try to pick someone who has a natural curiosity, combined with the ability to find, synthesize, and communicate information skillfully. Of course, he or she should also possess an understanding and passion for the organization's mission and goals, as well as the ability to ascertain how top prospects' social aims map to those goals. A general zeal and affinity for philanthropy is also hugely helpful. Finally, on the analytical side, make sure your designee has the ability to search through a wide range of research resources and the ability to track detailed information in your database, all combined with an interest in continuing education on the topic.

Hopefully, you can find one person who possesses all these attributes, and if you want to get even more specific, APRA offers a handy resource for assessing the skill sets needed when hiring research professionals (see Resource Review), which is free to members or available for a fee. Otherwise, you can hire for the position and integrate these needs into your job description or, if that's not an option, select your top candidates and weigh them against these criteria, but be sure to factor in how much capacity they have available. Finally, many small-to-medium-sized nonprofits find it more efficient, both from a budget and an overhead standpoint, to outsource this function and hire a consultant, firm, or freelancer.

2. Start with Your Inner Circle

What do you already know about your donors, and are you starting this effort from ground zero, or do you already have some donor and prospect research in place? When starting any fundraising campaign, you'll typically want to *begin with donors who are closest to your organization*, and already give regularly. The most important tool here will be your database and the information you've collected and tracked to date. (See more in Chapter 6 on databases.) Based on your existing donors' interest and connection to your cause, are they giving at capacity, or is there room to upgrade them?

Once you have a strong grasp on your "inner circle" of donors, you'll want to expand your research to people and organizations in your database that you don't know much about. Your researcher's goal will be to *rank and prioritize prospects, so you know where to focus*. Hopefully, they can do this by analyzing the data you already have: who donates annually; who is married to someone who donated; who lives in the wealthiest neighborhoods; who gives large donations to similar organizations, etc. You can also use external tools, such as wealth screening services, to identify prospects with the greatest capacity.

After you've done some homework on your other donors, you still need a ranking system to help prioritize efforts. Keep it simple, at least in the beginning. *By subjectively assigning a score of 1 to 3 for both a prospect's connection and capacity, you will streamline your efforts tremendously*. When deciding if someone's connection merits a 1, consider whether she volunteers, is a board member or is married to one, and to what extent she's shown a commitment or passion for your cause. Perhaps you're working on a cure for malaria and know The Bill & Melinda Gates Foundation are huge funders in that arena, but you give them a 2 since you haven't had any discussions to date, so you're still an unknown. But they'd certainly score a 1 on capacity, which is the size of check you think they can write if motivated. The most connected, highest capacity prospects will be ranked as a 1-1 and quickly rise to the top of your prospect list, meaning you'll focus the most resources, time, and follow up on them.

If your organization has a large prospect pipeline, you may want to get even more specific and use a rating system like the one Helen Brown and her team employ. Brown says, "When you create a ratings system, keep it simple and easy-to-understand at a glance. Systems fail when people have to pull out cheat-sheets to look up codes all the time, or when available codes run out due to growth. Here's what I recommend:"

Capacity Ratings should be real numbers.

Rating Code	Translation
5	$5,000–$9,999
10	$10,000–$24,999
25	$25,000–$49,999
50	$50,000–$99,999
100	$100,000–$249,999

Etc.

The Next Gift Amount is different from the capacity rating. Someone's capacity may be $1 million, but the next gift you might ask for could be their first gift of $25,000. You might use the same codes as for the Capacity Rating, or use the actual number rather than a range.

Rating Code	Translation
5	$5,000–$9,999
10	$10,000–$24,999
25	$25,000–$49,999
50	$50,000–$99,999
100	$100,000–$249,999

Etc.

Inclination/interest codes should be quick and easy to figure out, like a grade in school.

Rating Code	Translation
A	We are their top philanthropic priority
B	We are a priority
C	We are not yet on their radar
D	We are not a priority
E	Do not solicit (add date and reason why in accompanying text box)

Readiness codes help keep you on schedule and forecast end-of-year totals:

Rating Code	Translation
6m	Will be asked in the next six months (add date)
12m	Will be asked in the next year
18m	Will be asked in the next 18 months
24m	Will be asked in the next two years
Camp	Will be asked in the campaign
Ask	Ask has been made, awaiting response
Ask Accepted	Awaiting gift
Ask Declined	No gift. A "reason why" text box can be useful here.
Stewardship	Gift arrived, donor to be thanked

3. Support the Ask

Now that you've identified your top fundraising prospects within your database, it's time to do more in-depth research. Your researcher can use both free and fee-based tools, including searching the Web, to find information like the prospect's connection to the broader cause (e.g., he's volunteered or donated in this area, has a family member affected by your issue), if he is married and has a family, where he lives and works, where he went to school, and any professional affiliations he may have. Perhaps the researcher will uncover information like the selling of a business, a big donation to a like-minded organization, family or inherited wealth, foundation affiliations, and memberships in exclusive yacht or country clubs. Your researcher can also *use free tools like Google Alerts* (http://google.com/alerts) *to keep tabs on any major activities or life events* by simply setting up an alert with the prospect's name.

Simply put, *the more information you gather on top prospects, the better prepared your fundraising team will be to make and maximize their asks.* This intelligence adds context to any interactions, helping you or your fundraiser to better know the prospect, develop a relationship, and create a suitable strategy.

4. Keep an Eye on Top Prospects

Sustained fundraising success is dependent on your stewardship of existing donors, particularly your biggest supporters. Tools such as Google Alerts, mentioned in the last tip, will help you stay informed and provide critical, up-to-date information to your fundraisers that enables them to strengthen relationships and adjust strategies accordingly. You also want to *track all activity on key donors in your database* so that you can identify patterns of behavior and plan appropriate follow-up; that means notes from every call, meeting, and bit of relevant research finds its way into the person's profile for future reference. It's also helpful to **track the lead fundraiser associated with every prospect**; that way, anyone who wants to communicate with that donor knows whom to speak with regarding any questions or updates.

If you have the capacity to go a bit deeper into tracking key prospects and donors, **implement a "moves management" system to keep track of where major donors are in the fundraising cycle**. This can be as simple as adding an extra column to your Excel spreadsheet or a new field in your database to track their status, but using a consistent key is crucial. At the very least, **list every major prospect's stage as identification, cultivation, ask, or stewardship** (e.g., I, C, A, or S). Finally, add a field for next steps, and then set alerts in your calendar or from your database so you're notified when it's time for the next follow-up.

5. Expand Your Pipeline

Now that we've covered the donors and prospects you know about, let's move on to sharing some tips for adding new prospects. This is key to creating ongoing sustainable revenue for your organization, so you should **allocate the resources needed to ensure constant prospecting, with at least monthly activity**. For individual donors, **start by creating a donor model,** meaning you identify characteristics that your existing or ideal donors have. For example, perhaps you are looking for donors interested in ALS who live in San Francisco, have the capacity to give five-figure gifts, and have donated at least $100,000 to similar organizations. You can then use subscription-based databases, such as DonorSearch, LexisNexis, NOZA, ResearchPoint, and more to find prospects who meet these criteria. (See Resource Review below for links.) If you have the capacity, you can even use multiple databases to cross-reference and narrow your focus on certain prospects. You can also buy a third-party list, but there are wide ranges of lists, and thus a wide-range of quality. For prospect research on foundations and corporations, Foundation Center has a subscription-based online directory that's fantastic. (More in Chapter 19.)

6. Stay Informed

Donor and prospect research is a dynamic industry, and advances in technology make it important to stay on top of trends and new tools. If you can afford the approximate $200 membership fee, it is wise to **join APRA, the Association of Professional Researchers for Advancement**. They offer regular webinars and ongoing educational opportunities, information on trends and new tools, and a great annual conference. They also have regional chapters that focus on educational opportunities and professional development, many of which produce events that are open to the public. Take a look at the Resource Review at the end of this chapter for more tools that will help you keep your saw sharp and succeed in prospect and donor research.

Conclusion

In order to maximize fundraising success, it's critical that you know how to conduct research on your existing donors, as well as how to identify and prioritize new prospects. Having the right person in charge of this task will ensure that you find accurate, detailed information that's communicated clearly to your frontline fundraisers, allowing them to build stronger relationships and create suitable strategies. Your number one tool in this endeavor will be your database, where you will track key information and activity, rank your donors and prospects, and keep track of their place within the fundraising cycle. There are external tools like the Internet, wealth-screening services, and subscription-based databases that can advance your efforts and help you find even more major prospects, but again, all of this takes time and attention, which means it must be made a strategic priority, instead of being viewed as a burden or distraction. After all, without key information on your donors and prospects, your fundraisers are operating in the dark.

Do's and Don'ts

Do. . .

> . . . assign someone on staff to spearhead your prospect and donor research efforts, or work with a seasoned consultant who can provide you with strategic support.

> . . . focus the majority of your research resources on the top 5 to 10 percent of your donors and prospects.

> . . . create a system, however basic, that enables you to rank and prioritize donors and prospects.

Don't. . .

> . . . assume your researchers can find information that prospects want to keep private.

. . . fail to debrief and communicate key information with frontline fundraisers before they go on donor or prospect calls.

. . . let a month go by without spending some time and energy on adding new prospects to your fundraising pipeline.

. . . use information that is not available publicly unless the donor has divulged it.

About the Expert

Helen Brown is a development veteran of nearly thirty years and is the president of the Helen Brown Group. She co-authored the book *Prospect Research for Fundraisers: The Essential Handbook*. Brown works with a variety of clients to establish, benchmark, and re-align research departments; identify major gift prospects; and train researchers and other fundraisers through on-site and web-based training services. She was previously a board member of the Association of Professional Researchers for Advancement (APRA) and president of the New England Development Research Association (NEDRA).

Resource Review

The Helen Brown Group (www.helenbrowngroup.com)
    Find a great library of articles, case studies, and resources on prospect and donor research.

Filla, Jennifer J., and Helen E. Brown. *Prospect Research for Fundraisers: The Essential Handbook*. John Wiley & Sons, 2013.
    A practical guide for fundraisers to get the most out of their prospect development efforts.

Hogan, Cecilia. *Prospect Research: A Primer for Growing Nonprofits*. Jones and Bartlett, 2004.
    An essential how-to for those new to prospect research who want to learn the basics of the profession.

Cannon, Christopher M. *An Executive's Guide to Fundraising Operations Principles, Tools and Trends*. John Wiley & Sons, 2011.

Provides fundraisers with easy-to-understand approaches to evaluate and address fundraising operations needs and opportunities. This guide simplifies and focuses on the analysis of problems and needs, allowing a quick return to fundraising.

Birkholz, Joshua. *Fundraising Analytics: Using Data to Guide Strategy.* John Wiley & Sons, 2008.

This book provides step-by-step instructions for understanding your constituents, developing metrics to gauge and guide your success, and much more.

MacDonell, Kevin, and Peter Wylie. *Score! Data-Driven Success for Your Advancement Team.* CASE, 2014.

This book provides explanations of basic issues, such as obtaining data, what to ask for, and what operations to perform once the data is in hand. It also includes examples of useful and common analyses to give the reader the "feel" of what data analysis is all about.

Association of Professional Researchers for Advancement (APRA) (www .aprahome.org)

Great resource for continuing education; be sure to check out their quarterly newsletter, blogs, webinars, and their annual conference, almost all of which are squarely focused on prospect and donor research for nonprofits. Their "Body of Knowledge" is a helpful resource, available free to members, that defines standard competencies for those in the functional areas of prospect research, data analytics, and prospect management (www.aprahome.org/p/cm/ld/fid=493)

New England Development Research Association (NEDRA) (www.nedra.org)

If you are based in America's Northeast, this is a great regional organization that produces an annual conference and offers a wide range of helpful resources and links.

The California Advancement Researchers Association (CARA) (www .caresearchers.org)

Similar to NEDRA, but intended for nonprofits based in the Western U.S.

Association of Advancement Services Professionals (AASP) (www.advserv.org/)

Wonderful resource offering articles and information on prospect and donor research, as well as an annual conference.

DRIVE (http://thedriveconference.com)

This is a big annual conference focused on data analytics, which is a crucial component to successful prospect and donor research.

Prospect Research Databases

- DonorSearch (www.donorsearch.net)
- LexisNexis (www.nexislexis.com)
- NOZA (www.nozasearch.com)
- iWave/PRO (www.iwave.com)
- ResearchPoint (www.blackbaud.com/howto/researchpoint.aspx)
- WealthEngine (www.wealthengine.com/markets/nonprofits)

Listservs are great forums for exchanging ideas, challenges, and questions with peers:

- Prspct-l (general prospect research focus) www.aprahome.org/p/cm/ld/fid=15
- Prospect-DMM (data analytics focus) https://mailman.mit.edu/mailman/listinfo/prospect-dmm

Donor Databases and CRM

"Information is the new oil."

—Cheryl Contee

Introduction

Fundraising is the lifeblood of your nonprofit, so it's critical that you invest in a constituent relationship management (CRM) tool to serve as your donor database. As donor profiles change, you need 21st century tools to help you understand your supporters and reach them in personal ways. You need to know what their interests are, how they give, and how to best engage and solicit them. *Segmenting your supporters and communicating with them in customized ways will help you maximize response rates.* This powerful technological tool can also provide a dynamic way to give donors real-time feedback on the impact their donations make possible, and enable you to analyze your efforts and make more informed, strategic decisions. For example, how is your direct mail program performing compared to your email campaigns or events, and how are you tracking against your key performance indicators?

A CRM database allows you to store crucial donor information, including contact info and gift history, and can also send communications, integrate with social media, track organizational data like finances, volunteer activity, and much, much more. This helps you better manage relationships with constituents and supporters. For example, a CRM database can track information, like the number of clients you serve, and help you collate that data in one simple view, like a dashboard that can be accessed via the Internet, or even your cell phone. Imagine meeting with funders or donors and pulling up your organizational dashboard on your mobile device, showing them how you are meeting your goals, sharing real-time statistics on impact and organizational performance, and clarifying how you're really making a difference with their money. (See more on dashboards and tracking impact in the next chapter.)

There are many systems on the market today that are well suited to nonprofits, most notably Salesforce and NetSuite.org, both of which are donated freely to nonprofits and can address all your data warehousing needs. If, for some reason, you choose to use multiple systems, remember to ensure that they're all connected and "talk to each other." This is usually done through an API, or application programming interface.

To learn more about how nonprofits can use CRM platforms to power their donor databases and fundraising efforts, I talked with Suzanne DiBianca, president of Salesforce Foundation, and Peggy Duvette, director of social impact at NetSuite, who broke down the formula for success into five simple tips.

Critical Skills and Competencies

1. Pick the Right Platform

There are a lot of options for CRM platforms on the market, and step one is taking the time to do your homework and determine which will work best for your organization. In order to ease this process, develop your requirements and a clear understanding of the problems you're trying to solve. Read articles and reviews from third parties (see Resource Review below), and talk with other nonprofits that do similar work and are of similar size. Find a platform that your entire team will be comfortable using, as any database or CRM is only as powerful as the information that is entered.

Choose a platform that will suit you five years down the road, while also meeting your current needs. Of course, cost will be a determining factor, including setup and customization costs plus ongoing fees, but make sure you are also considering your return on investment, such as increased donations.

The biggest companies in the field today are Blackbaud, Salesforce, and NetSuite. Salesforce is the most popular tool for nonprofits and gives away ten free licenses, plus they have a great hub called The Power of Us, where customers can collaborate, share best practices, and see solutions. NetSuite offers five free licenses to organizations to support their donor relationships, financials, and volunteer program. Blackbaud is an expensive but powerful tool best suited to larger organizations with multi-million-dollar budgets.

2. Identify an Owner

You need someone on your team to take ownership of your CRM and be its champion. Ideally, this is a systems-focused person who understands and enjoys data collection and analysis, but he or she should also be enough of a "people person" to work well with all departments of the organization, including development, marketing, volunteer management, finance, and others.

Once selected, this person should first *create a timeline, budget, and strategy for implementation* of the platform (factoring in all the steps below), and be responsible for integrating and customizing it for your organization, or at least overseeing the volunteer or firm that does. He or she will be in charge of collecting and inputting data, as well as guiding other members on the team to contribute.

It will be your champion's job to engage the end-users of your CRM as early as possible, facilitating adoption. Your champion will also oversee troubleshooting, reporting, and analytics, and be able to track key metrics and create organizational dashboards, which can happen automatically with time. Remember that your point person will need support, training, and access to further educational opportunities, such as conferences and webinars.

3. Find and Clean Your Data

Once you have a CRM champion in place, focus on maximizing the value and utilization of this tool. Based on your goals and objectives as an organization, *identify the key performance indicators that will help you gauge performance*. Remember, beyond tracking fundraising results, you'll also want to monitor programs, finances, volunteer efforts, and more. To figure this out, you'll likely want to talk to leaders and front-line staff across all departments, possibly in a group setting. Be sure to include your executive director and board, as those are two key audiences for the reports you'll generate, so knowing what information will be most helpful is critical.

Once you've clarified what information you want to track, find out where this information currently exists and how it will be used moving forward. Once you know where all your data lives and are ready to migrate or input it into your database, you need to "clean" it. This means ensuring that it's accurate and current, eliminating duplicate entries, and that data on all key donors, volunteers, and staff and board are included.

LinkedIn is a great tool for filling in missing blanks and, if you have the budget, which can sometimes come from "capacity building" grants from foundations, you can hire a systems implementer. These are consultants or firms like Exponent Partners that specialize in helping organizations gather, clean, and input their data, as well as integrating and customizing CRM platforms for you.

4. Invest in Training and Documentation

Once your CRM platform is in place, your champion must introduce it to each department and all key personnel, providing them with training and guidelines for usage, including a data entry protocol to ensure consistency. To maximize benefits, your entire organization has to be comfortable with your platform and integrate it into their workflow. For most users, it's sufficient to only train them in basic functionality, but for department heads and more advanced users, your champion should spend time training them to do things like running reports and creating dashboards, which are reports that integrate a range of metrics to provide a bird's eye view of the organization or a program or department. Once created, these dashboards can be automatically generated by your CRM and emailed to relevant team members, providing helpful insights regularly.

Your champion should also create a frequently asked questions (FAQs) document to reduce time spent answering common inquiries, and he or she should update this document over time as FAQs are identified. Your champion should also create a simple user manual that outlines the various processes you've put in place, clarifying their value and offering important how-to information. Most platforms provide numerous training videos and free webinars that your champion can also selectively share with your team over time.

5. Stay Current

To ensure that you get the most out of your platform, you'll need to keep it maintained and up-to-date. This means having an ongoing process for keeping your data clean and staying abreast of new features and software updates. CRM providers often release new training videos or webinars, usually for free, and these will help your champion ensure you take full advantage of this powerful technology. Most providers also produce annual conferences that are great places to learn new ways to more effectively leverage your platform, as well as meet and learn from other users.

Conclusion

Selecting and implementing a CRM platform is a lot of work, but it is a long-term investment that will enable you to raise more money and run your organization more effectively and efficiently. Having more visibility into your operations and key data at your fingertips offers benefits most nonprofits can't even imagine. Your success will start with tracking basic information, such as donor contacts and giving history. And once you start tracking more detailed information like areas of interest, how key donors like to give, and real-time insights into your programs' effectiveness, you can build relationships and communicate with supporters and prospects in much more powerful, personalized ways. Beyond the tremendous fundraising and external benefits, your CRM platform will also bolster organizational capacity, giving you access to key information and dashboards that will facilitate key strategic decisions and help you keep your finger on the pulse of your organization and its impact.

Do's and Don'ts

Do. . .

> . . . interview similar nonprofits to obtain their feedback on particular platforms before deciding which CRM is right for you.

> . . . test out CRMs you are considering to ensure they are user-friendly and easy to use.

> . . . ensure your systems are all integrated and able to seamlessly share information.

> . . . select a champion to "own" your CRM and have him or her train key personnel on how to use it.

Don't. . .

> . . . pick a platform or tool just because it is free; make sure it's right for you.

> . . . rule out platforms because of cost without factoring in your return on investment.

> . . . fail to clean your data on an ongoing, regular basis.

> . . . input all of your data into a new system at once; start with a small sample and test.

About the Experts

Suzanne DiBianca is the president and co-founder of the Salesforce Foundation. DiBianca is a recognized leader in the area of integrated corporate philanthropy and in helping nonprofits take advantage of modern technology to maximize impact. DiBianca sits on a number of boards and advisory councils, including the World Affairs Council's Global Philanthropy Forum and Goodwill Industries.

Peggy Duvette is the director of social impact at NetSuite, a leading CRM/ ERP cloud platform, and oversees the NetSuite.org donation program, which offers NetSuite technologies for free to nonprofits around the word. She is a leading voice in the area of technology and social impact. Her focus at NetSuite is helping small and mid-sized organizations advance social impact though the grant program. Previously, she served as executive director of WiserEarth.

Resource Review

The Nonprofit Matrix (www.nonprofitmatrix.com)
> This is a directory of digital tools and services for nonprofits. Check out their directory of CRM platforms to decide which is right for you at www. nonprofitmatrix.com/database-crm/

Salesforce Foundation (www.salesforcefoundation.org)
> The Foundation offers ten free licenses of their CRM platform to nonprofits and higher education organizations, with discounts beyond that. Salesforce's annual conference in San Francisco, Dreamforce, offers a

dedicated track for nonprofits. Also, check out their nonprofit video case studies at https://www.youtube.com/user/SalesforceFoundation

NetSuite (www.netsuite.org)
NetSuite is a leading ERP/CRM cloud platform that offers five free licenses to nonprofits and social enterprises to support donor relationships and financials. NetSuite also helps organizations build capacity through their pro bono volunteer program, an initiative that partners NetSuite employees with grantees to facilitate adoption and build technology capacity.

Blackbaud (www.blackbaud.com)
This public company offers a variety of tools for nonprofits to manage their data, including the donor database platform, Raiser's Edge, and the CRM platform, Luminate. Their platform is best suited to larger nonprofits with millions of dollars in annual revenue.

The Connected Cause (www.theconnectedcause.com)
Find tips, resources, and helpful articles on nonprofit technology, including: "Best Practices in CRM for Nonprofits": http://theconnectedcause.com/best-practices-crm-nonprofits/

Idealware (www.idealware.org)
This site is dedicated to helping nonprofits make smart software decisions, with a focus on open source technology. Find reports, blogs, and articles, including "Ten Common Mistakes in Selecting Donor Databases (and How to Avoid Them)": www.idealware.org/articles/ten_common_mistakes_in_selecting_donor_databases.php

NTEN (www.nten.org)
NTEN helps nonprofits use technology more effectively. Check out their annual conference NTC, and find great resources and articles on their site, such as "Selecting a Nonprofit CRM System? Start with the Strategy!": www.nten.org/article/selecting-a-nonprofit-crm-system-start-with-the-strategy/

TechSoup (www.techsoup.org)
The world's largest provider of technology to nonprofits, TechSoup offers steep discounts on all kinds of IT to nonprofits and libraries, as well as providing great resources and articles on their site and a free webinar series.

CauseVox (www.causevox.com)
This is an online fundraising and crowdfunding platform that also offers great resources and articles on their website, including "5 Must-Know Tips in Selecting a Nonprofit CRM": www.causevox.com/blog/nonprofit-crm/

7

Measuring Impact
Data, Stories, and Organizational Dashboards

"If you can't measure it, you can't manage it."

—Peter Drucker

Introduction

Making a difference is the reason the nonprofit sector exists, and as we've shared in many of the chapters in this book, *fundraising success revolves around your ability to make—and relay—impact.* Donors, especially younger ones, want to know where their money is going and what it's accomplishing, and are increasingly demanding metrics to prove it. If you can't clearly, compellingly show donors and prospects the difference their donations have made, they won't support your work. Furthermore, you need to know whether you're putting your organization's valuable resources and staff time toward something that's having the impact you intended, or whether a change of strategy is needed or can create even greater impact. That means it's critical you're able to set and demonstrate progress toward goals and objectives, which is only possible if you measure progress. When you do, your donor cultivation and stewardship efforts will thrive; plus, you can leverage these insights to refine your efforts, magnifying impact and creating efficiencies.

Said another way, measuring impact serves two connected purposes. First, it provides valuable insights, data points, and stories you can share with the outside world, enlisting their support. Second, evaluation helps you gauge your performance internally, against past performance, other organizations, and the sector as a whole, enabling you to make better strategic decisions.

In order to excel in this arena, you need to *create a culture that values collecting both data and stories*. That means tracking key programmatic and operational metrics like number of youth served, meals delivered, money raised and spent, and so forth, as well as individual examples of the lives you change or specific success stories of your projects. Then you'll organize this information for both external communications and internal audiences. For example, the stories you collect provide great content for your fundraising and marketing emails, while key metrics can be integrated into useful dashboards and reports to share with staff and board members.

To learn more about evaluation and measuring impact, I talked with Steve MacLaughlin, director of analytics at Blackbaud, who provided a great framework for any cause looking to gauge, convey, and maximize impact.

Critical Skills and Competencies

1. Identify Key Performance Indicators and Secure Stories

In all my years working with nonprofits, the simplest yet most transformative question I've come across is: "What does success look like?" I share it at almost every group meeting, especially when planning new programs and initiatives, as well as when launching fundraising campaigns. Think about your mission and the impact you hope to generate, whether it's creating a vibrant arts scene in St. Louis, helping people escape poverty in Mexico City, combating climate change, or whatever your goal. Typically, these goals don't manifest out of thin air; *key performance indicators (KPIs) are useful metrics tracked to gauge your progress*.

These will vary depending on the strategy you employ to achieve your goal, also known as a "theory of change." If your mission is to fight homelessness in Detroit and your approach is doing that through vocational training, programmatic KPIs might include the number of participants in your job-training program, or how many people secured employment. ***When combined with powerful individual stories, KPIs help you convey impact to your donors and prospects***, enabling you to better cultivate and retain them. Moreover, KPIs provide a road map for how your work advances your vision and mission.

KPIs are also helpful in assessing organizational effectiveness. If you aren't running an efficient organization, solving problems will be a huge challenge, even if your strategy has great merit. Some examples of useful operational KPIs include board member attendance at meetings and committee participation, monthly expenses and income by department, cash reserves and number of months this can sustain you with no additional income (also known as "runway" or your "rainy day fund"), and the existence of strategic plans for departments such as fundraising, technology, HR, or others. Similarly, identifying KPIs for fundraising is also very useful, including number of prospects, calls and meetings with prospects per month, proposals submitted, donor renewal rates, and so forth.

Remember that not everything that counts can be measured; and not everything that's measured counts. Don't go overboard and drive yourself crazy tracking a thousand things. Instead, ***identify the select few KPIs that are most meaningful and insightful, and watch those religiously***.

One final note here: while collecting data is great, don't forget to ***collect personal stories to document your impact and humanize your work***. Talk to the people you serve, and ask how you've affected their lives. Have the people who run your programs or volunteer share their personal stories and connections to the cause. Even brief videos or audio recordings from a phone can be powerful, as can short blogs where one person's voice shines through. Remember: ***people don't give to organizations; they give to people***. Stories are critical to your ability to share your story in a way that reaches people's hearts. That includes success stories, but also those that demonstrate the need. As evaluation guru Lovely Dhillon puts it, "Although we all aim to change the world, it starts with the little steps—the quality of life enhancements that we make for just one person, and how we make their life just a little bit better."

Outputs Versus Outcomes

When assessing impact, it's important to know the difference between outputs and outcomes. An ***output*** is a quantifiable action taken, such as number of emails sent, number of new followers on Twitter, number of clients served, or meetings held. Outputs

(*continued*)

(continued)

are basically a list of things you've done. On the other hand, ***outcomes are not about what you did, but what happened as a result***. Basically, *outputs are the "what," while outcomes are the "so what?"* Outcomes demonstrate you're making progress toward your goals and mission, delivering the change you seek. For example, if you aim to increase college access for youth of color like the Posse Foundation, college enrollment and graduation rates for their participants are two concrete outcomes. Outputs help deliver those outcomes, and in this case could include number of mentors recruited, hours of academic support provided, etc.

It's crucial to understand this difference, and many nonprofits confuse the two and erroneously think that measuring outputs is enough, when you really want to measure the *difference* you're making. It doesn't matter that you fed 100 people last year and 1,000 people this year if those 1,000 are still suffering from malnutrition. That is, ***outcomes force you to look at your strategies and the differences they actually make*** and force you to assess: "Is our theory of change working? Are we making the difference we intended to make?"

2. Develop a Plan to Measure Progress

Now that you have clarity on what success looks like, how can you tell if it's actually happening? This requires a plan and strategy for collecting data and evaluating your KPIs. Nonprofits are typically stretched thin and trying to make due with insufficient resources—including time and personnel—so if you don't set up systems and prioritize collecting information and regularly assessing impact, you'll be overwhelmed trying to go back and collect a bunch of data all at once. That is why ***it is critical that data collection be integrated into the way you do your everyday work***.

Tools such as databases and CRM platforms (see Chapter 6) can streamline this process and also provide a valuable central repository for storing it. You can distribute a daily, weekly, or monthly survey to staff, volunteers, clients, and even board members to collect key information. Think about how often you want to measure certain metrics: How often do you want to know things are going well, or how quickly do you need to know when they are going badly? Tie all these inputs together and ***create daily, weekly, monthly, quarterly, and annual reports, sharing progress as represented*** *by your KPIs*. Use these reports to think through how much you can improve outputs and outcomes if you invest more resources, helping you prioritize efforts. For example, when we increase our email list by 1,000 names, we raise $500 more a month through email solicitations, or with $1,000 a month of additional spending, our soup kitchen can serve 5,000 more meals. Some of these return on investment and output calculations can even find their way into your live event or the donate string on your donate page, as detailed in Chapters 12 and 15, respectively.

3. Integrate Your Evaluation and Strategic Plans

What plans already exist in your organization? Do you have a strategic plan, a fundraising plan, an operating plan? Start with these in mind when creating your evaluation plan, since *integrated plans and strategies, all driving toward the same goals and outcomes, ensure alignment and maximize impact*. Your overall strategic plan is the starting point for all planning efforts, especially evaluation. Do the metrics and indicators you've identified lead to your overarching goal? Your evaluation plan should assess both progress on specific programs, as well as the impact on your overall mission and goals. Also, your strategic plan should provide the resources and time for integrating learning culled from measurement and evaluation activities.

4. Tear Down the Walls

It's critical that you *foster collaboration and partnership between the people running your programs and those conducting evaluation and analysis*. They need to work closely and articulate the importance of their work to one another for the good of the organization. Program staff need to be included in the creation of your evaluation plan, as they are on the front lines, collecting information and witnessing impact. They provide a great reality check for determining how realistic proposed data capture strategies are, and they can generally share great insights into the clients you serve. Get them on board with your strategies, such as surveys, collecting stories, and counting activities. Make sure they understand the connection between data collection and the funding that makes their work possible. Ask them open-ended questions about how they'd assess your impact, and on the changes and trends they've seen over time. Smart nonprofits capture and share these stories and trends, both at internal staff meetings and to the public through newsletters, funding proposals, and other means.

5. Look to the Past to See the Future

If you've already tracked information and collected historical data, you're in a great position to forecast. For example, through simple analysis perhaps you can determine how many major donor meetings you need to have in a month to secure five gifts, or raise $50,000. These insights can dictate future activities and priorities, helping you fine-tune your fundraising strategy, but also programs, operations, and more. Look at a previous time period—ideally, the same month in a previous year—and simply do the math. Measure how many major donor meetings were conducted and how many gifts were received as a result. If you make these changes and your results don't match expectations, then re-think your activities and strategies. Perhaps you're not identifying the right prospects, not sending the right people to donor meetings, or perhaps there's another reason. If you don't have historic experience or data to rely on as a baseline, ask other nonprofits or do research online. In this case, you'll want to be as conservative as possible in your estimates, setting realistic expectations and avoiding being unpleasantly surprised.

6. Benchmark Yourself

Assessing your impact and progress toward goals isn't just about looking at your own performance. It's also incredibly valuable to look at similar organizations, either based on their area of focus, location, staff, or budget, perform. How do you compare to your peers? Compare your fundraising efforts and specific KPIs with other groups to identify growth opportunities and establish your strengths. *The best way to identify industry benchmarks is through aggregate industry research*, including that conducted by Blackbaud, Giving USA, and M+R. Generally speaking, it's not appropriate to ask peers for sensitive information like donor retention rates, number of major donors, or conversion rates, but if you have a close friend inside, sometimes he or she will share otherwise sensitive information. What's more accepted and realistic is assessing your performance based on these third-party reports, figuring out the specific metrics where you're lagging, such as donor retention, and then reaching out to ask peers for advice on how they succeed in that area.

7. Rock the Dashboard

As mentioned earlier in this chapter, you've enlisting the input of your board and staff to identify your KPIs. Now take this to the next level and ask key groups—including program staff, your board, and various departments—which five to seven KPIs are the most helpful when assessing the health and impact of the organization. Is it revenue raised per week, clients served per month, annual employee retention, or something else? *Prioritize and*

showcase your most important KPIs in an organizational dashboard,
identifying a red, yellow, and green range for each.

For example, we should be serving at least 900 clients a month, but this may
dip to 800 in off months, but it certainly should never fall below that. Once you
know 0 to 799 is red, 800 to 899 is yellow, and 900+ is green, this information
is integrated into a monthly report automatically generated by a CRM or
created quickly by someone on staff and shared at every program staff meeting,
along with a select few other KPIs. If the various KPIs are all green, then it's
a quick way to tell things are going smoothly and you can move on to your
intended agenda; a yellow, or especially a red, indicator likely means you should
take a second to discuss why something is off, and what to do about it.

Use this dashboard at regular staff and board meetings to assess your
organizational health as a group, and proactively identify and address any
potential "red" flags. Whether it's a delay in completing work, problems securing
foundation grants, or a slowdown at your shelter, sometimes a visual, data-driven
tool is helpful in bringing important trends to light. This color system lets staff
and board take one look at a dashboard and know where to focus their efforts.

Case Study: charity: water

Since 2006 charity: water has raised over $170 million and brought
clean drinking water to 5.2 million people. They've completed more
than 16,000 projects, enlisting the support of over 700,000 donors.
A large part of their success comes from their ability to collect data,
measure their impact, and share this with donors and prospects.
When you give a donation to charity: water, you know *exactly* what
your money went toward, and you can often literally see the faces
of the people your contribution helped. This is why people keep
giving to them, and how they're able to continue their work to bring
clean water to the world. Kaitlyn Jankowski, supporter experience
manager, shared the four secrets to their success:

1. Collect Specific Data
charity: water uses technology and partnerships to gather very
specific information from their projects and share it with their
donors. A large chunk of their data collection happens on the ground
through local, trusted partners who oversee the implementation
of their projects. To set these partners up for success, they created
protocols to ensure partners collect the most important information,
including village demographics, photos, stories, and project costs,
plus they provide support and guidance on data collection. They

(continued)

(continued)

bolster this process by collecting as much data as possible internally; they also leverage outside auditors to visit their partners and field projects, alongside a program compliance team, to ensure the data collected is reliable and accurate.

2. Communicate Honestly and Consistently
Throughout the 21-month lifespan between the time a donor contributes to when he or she sees the actual completion of a typical project, donors receive three specific communications that convey the information gathered, plus detail the impact of their donations. They're notified when their money reaches the area—at which time they receive an update directly from the local partner—and once the project is complete, when they receive a summary with GPS coordinates, photos, details on the number of people served, exact project costs, and more.

Part of charity: water's commitment to transparency is also being willing to share bad news when it occurs. To them, ***authenticity dictates being in full communication***. For example, charity: water knows on average it costs $30 to bring clean water to one person, but in Rwanda costs ran to $65 per person. They seized the opportunity to educate their donors on the specific political and geologic obstacles faced, communicating in an honest way that only solidified their role as an issue area expert, but never hid what some groups might feel is embarrassing news. One year, on the anniversary "live drill" where people log on to witness live video of villagers rejoicing at the water spurting out of the ground, they couldn't hit water. charity: water was honest and let their supporters know that they tried and failed, but made it clear they were committed to coming back and doing what it took to serve this community. It's important to be transparent with the people who make your work possible. If things don't go as planned, let them know, and ensure them that you are doing all you can to remedy the situation.

3. Use Data Externally and Internally
In addition to supporting fundraising efforts, monitoring and sharing this specific information enables charity: water to keep tabs on operational efficiencies. The same data points they share with donors form the key performance indicators used internally to assess their efforts. These data points, and others, are at the top of their organizational dashboard and are used by staff and board to gauge progress toward goals and outcomes.

4. Collect Stories
One of the most powerful ways charity: water communicates its impact is through sharing personal stories of the transformation that occurs in someone who gains access to clean drinking water.

(continued)

These can be harder to collect and unearth, but because they are so important to recruiting and retaining donors, charity: water decided to **dedicate resources and staff time specifically to collecting stories**. They send team members to communities to get to know the locals and gain their trust. They host village or town meetings and ask open-ended questions like: "What does your life look like, now that you have easy access to clean water?" or "What does having access to clean water mean to you?" or even "Has this project impacted your life and community?"

When their staffers come across a great story, they make sure to gather details such as names, specific locations, and other personal details that provide important texture for donors, adding dimension to the account. They **gather photos and videos to bring stories to life**. Finally, charity: water uses these site visits to ask questions that can help them refine their efforts internally, including: "How has this project disappointed you or let you down?" or "Has the project ever broken, and if so, what happened?" charity: water thrives because they look for both success stories to share with supporters, as well as stories that inform their future work and help them improve. Ultimately, they want donors to feel good about being generous and experience as much joy as possible after they give. Their goal is *never* to guilt people into giving, but rather to inspire them to do so.

Conclusion

Measuring the impact of your organization is absolutely critical to raising money and to running your organization more efficiently. Thankfully, the technology available today allows us to do it in easier and more insightful ways than ever before. This work is transformative for organizations and is the basis of your existence as a nonprofit—it is how you know you're achieving your mission and running a healthy organization. With this information at your fingertips, you can prove to foundations that their investment is worthwhile, inspire donors to give you more money, recruit new supporters to join you, and make smarter strategic and tactical decisions for your organization.

Do's and Don'ts

Do. . .

. . . identify a set of key performance indicators that can help you assess your effectiveness toward achieving your overall goals.

. . . select the most important KPIs and integrate those into dashboards that help key departments and groups make smarter decisions and proactively identify problems.

. . . evaluate your overall organization at least once a quarter and host a group discussion to discuss strategies for improvement.

. . . set learning goals, questions, and hypotheses annually, even though they may last several years.

. . . include evaluation costs into your foundation proposal budgets.

Don't. . .

. . . determine outcomes and outputs without first consulting your strategic plan.

. . . fail to engage program staff from the beginning of the evaluation process.

. . . keep bad news to yourself; communicate with donors and supporters transparently to build an authentic relationship.

About the Expert

Steve MacLaughlin is director of analytics at Blackbaud and has spent more than 15 years building successful online initiatives with nonprofit organizations across the world. MacLaughlin serves on the Nonprofit Technology Network (NTEN) board of directors and is a frequent blogger, authored a chapter in *People to People Fundraising: Social Networking and Web 2.0 for Charities*, and was co-editor of *Internet Management for Nonprofits: Strategies, Tools and Trade Secrets*. MacLaughlin is also a frequent speaker and keynote speaker at a wide range of nonprofit technology and fundraising events.

Resource Review

Foundation Center–Tools and Resources for Assessing Social Impact (TRASI) (trasi.foundationcenter.org)
This database contains approaches to impact assessment, guidelines for creating and conducting an assessment, and actionable tools for measuring social change.

Urban Institute–Outcome Indicators Project (www.urban.org)
This resource supports nonprofit performance tracking by suggesting outcomes and indicators, new measurement approaches, and enhancements to existing systems. Visit their site and search for "Outcome Indicators Project."

Kanter, Beth, and Katie Paine. *Measuring the Networked Nonprofit.* Jossey-Bass, 2012.
This book offers the tools and strategies needed for nonprofits looking for reliable and measurable data from their social media efforts. Using the many tools presented in this great text will not only improve a nonprofit's decision making, but will produce results-driven metrics for staff and stakeholders.

Grantcraft (www.grantcraft.org)
This website provides materials that offer insights and approaches to improve the effectiveness of social sector organizations, including several guides on evaluation and assessment.

Innovation Network–Point K Learning Center (www.innonet.org)
Offers a useful set of tools, including an Organizational Assessment Tool, Logic Model Builder, and Evaluation Plan Builder, all of which support nonprofits in designing and implementing program assessments.

Root Cause–Building a Performance Measurement System (www.rootcause.org)
This guide provides a practical, five-step process for developing a performance measurement approach to support nonprofits as they select metrics, design reports, and communicate impact.

W. K. Kellogg Foundation–Evaluation Handbook and Logic Model Development Guide (www.wkkf.org)
This workbook provides a framework for approaching nonprofit program evaluations that support program performance. The guide introduces the logic model tool to nonprofits seeking to strengthen program design and delivery, and disseminate results. Go to their homepage and search "evaluation handbook."

Chaney Jones, Sheri. *Impact and Excellence: Data-Driven Strategies for Aligning Mission, Culture and Performance in Nonprofit and Government.* Jossey-Bass, 2014.
This book is the culmination of a robust study into the most successful data-driven strategies for today's nonprofit and government organizations. It focuses on five strategic elements to success based on proven principles, with solutions that are easy to implement and often lead to sweeping change. Each chapter includes discussion questions and action items to help leaders implement key concepts in their own organizations.

Nonprofit Hub (www.nonprofithub.org)
Find helpful resources, including the article "Nonprofit Storytelling: Seven Tips for Sharing Stories About Your Work."

Getting Attention (www.gettingattention.org)
Find case studies, tools, and resources on Nancy Schwartz's blog and check out the article "6 Story Types to Tell."

Blackbaud (www.blackbaud.com)
Leading online fundraising platform, which leverages their vantage point of processing more than $16 billion in giving to produce a wide range reports and resources. Most notably, this includes their Index (www.blackbaud.com/blackbaudindex), a monthly view of overall fundraising and online giving trends across the nonprofit sector, and their Charitable Giving Report (www.blackbaud.com/charitablegiving), an annual review of both overall and online giving trends by size and sector in the United States.

American Evaluation Association (www.eval.org)
A global organization of 7,000 members dedicated to improving evaluation practices and methods, increasing evaluation use, and promoting evaluation as a profession.

Giving USA (www.givingusa.org)
The gold standard in charitable giving data for the past 50+ years; published annually.

Money for Good (www.hopeconsulting.us/moneyforgood)
Series of valuable research reports on donor behavior.

Morino, Mario. *Leap of Reason: Managing to Outcomes in an Era of Scarcity* (4th ed.). Venture Philanthropy Partners, 2011.
This book inspires leaders in the social and public sectors to take bold action to create more meaningful, measurable good for those they serve. It's become a widely shared resource for those seeking measurable change, informing board retreats, strategic-planning efforts, staff-development initiatives, and university management classes across the United States and in more than two dozen countries around the world.

Crutchfield, Leslie R., and Heather McLeod Grant. *Forces for Good: The Six Practices of High-Impact Nonprofits* (2nd ed.). Jossey-Bass, 2012.
This updated book examines a proven framework that helps nonprofits shift from an organizational mindset to a relational one, from a more industrial era model of production, where the nonprofit produces goods and services for customers, to a networked model, where the nonprofit's mission is to catalyze social change by inspiring others to action.

Part
III

Individual Donors

Chapter 8

Grassroots Fundraising
Building Your Donor Pyramid

"Nothing changes without individuals, but nothing lasts without institutions."

—Jean Monnet

Introduction

The movement for civil rights in the United States didn't happen overnight. Dedicated leaders and volunteers worked tirelessly for years to achieve equality for all. And throughout the struggle, Dr. Martin Luther King, Jr., and the dozens of other community and church leaders involved recognized that to have power, strength, and longevity, they needed to build a broad and stable base of support. This same principle applies to your fundraising efforts. *Without a large base of individual donors, your fundraising pyramid can collapse*; diversification is the key. Grassroots fundraising means that *your organization isn't supported by just one foundation*, corporation, or wealthy individual; it means that you have the power of many, and the aggregate total of their time, money, and support adds up to real change.

Grassroots fundraising doesn't necessarily mean having a large number of small donors. It's really about having a large base of individual donors that you

79

can count on. And if properly cultivated and stewarded, donors who start small can grow into major donors and lifelong supporters. This strategy is especially critical to the success of smaller organizations and efforts that may not have the resources or staff to pursue government, foundation, or corporate support, since anyone can reach into their community to build a base of loyal donors.

But just as the civil rights movement took years to develop, you must be ready to make the investment in cultivating a large base of individual donors over time. There are no shortcuts with grassroots fundraising. You can't just buy a list and hope to raise money. You have to **identify people who care about your cause and inspire their connection, then their passion, and finally, their support**. You have to work hard to build trust, communicate clearly, and cultivate relationships that will result in a stream of steady income, as well as priceless advocacy on behalf of your organization. To talk about grassroots fundraising in-depth, I sat down with author and *Grassroots Fundraising Journal* co-founder Kim Klein, who started by saying, "Grassroots fundraising is the financial expression of democracy."

I asked Klein to talk about the *specific skills and capabilities that nonprofit leaders and organizations need to have in place* in order to successfully grow and activate a diverse base of support, and she listed these top seven tips:

Critical Skills and Competencies

1. Have a Compelling Plan for Change

To inspire donor support, you'll need more than just a dream of how the world should be. Taking it a step further and being able to present a clear vision of *exactly* how you'll get there—the partners, the strategy, the traction to date, etc.—are all imperative when establishing your credibility. Put simply, **donors need answers to the questions: "What do you believe in?" "What are you going to do about it?" "What have you already done?" " How can I trust your organization?" and "Does anyone agree with you?"** Having a concrete plan that includes these answers will form the primer coat of your effort to secure a large base of individual donors.

2. Set a Clear Goal

It is crucial to understand how much money you need to raise, but to do that, you need to **ask yourself: "What does success look like?" and "How many donors do we need to achieve that goal?"** Assess your prospects and look at factors such as your fundraising and campaign history, organizational capacity in terms of volunteers, and resources such as staff, databases, and equipment. And if you've never done a campaign before and you can't pick a fundraising goal based on experience, Klein says to just pick a number that feels right to you. In any case, *having a specific fundraising goal is absolutely imperative to maximizing support.*

Don't Be Afraid to Dream Big

As you're setting your campaign fundraising goal, consider setting your sites a bit higher and creating both a baseline goal and an aspirational one. Donors often prefer ambitious goals and like to see organizations with big visions. You aren't raising money to maintain the status quo; you're constantly trying to move your organization and cause forward. As Leo Burnett said, "When you reach for the stars, you may not get one, but you won't get a handful of mud either."

Consider the story of an executive director of a hospital, who was reading the *Chronicle of Philanthropy* and saw that one of her board members had given a $6,000,000 gift to the other main hospital in town. She was frustrated and upset because this board member had never given them a seven-figure gift. She went for a walk around the block, came back and contacted the board member to set up a lunch.

After dispensing with the small talk, she finally got the nerve to ask the question that she was really there to ask: "I saw the big news about your gift to St. Luke's—how wonderful!" She continued, "But I have to ask, *why didn't we get that $6,000,000 gift?"* The board member paused and then replied, "Well, nobody ever brought me a $6,000,000 idea."

Remember: If you don't swing the bat, you can't hit the ball. If you don't bring the $6 million idea to the table, no one can fund it.

---

3. Ensure 100 Percent Board and Staff Participation

No one person can recruit and engage a large base of supporters, so you need lots of people driving this effort—and not just staff. You need volunteers and, most importantly, a strong board that fully participates. As discussed in

Chapter 3, *each of your board members should make an annual "capacity" gift*, meaning the largest gift he or she can comfortably make and one of that person's top three philanthropic contributions of the year. If they aren't prioritizing the organization in their philanthropic investments, they shouldn't be on the board, and this expectation needs to be clearly, explicitly set from the get go in a Board Member Agreement—again, see Chapter 3 for more on that.

The point is, you need to be able to tell other potential donors that 100 percent of your board gives because they deeply believe in what you're doing; after all, if they don't give, why should this donor? Beyond their own personal contributions, it's also crucial that the board play an active role in fundraising. Board members should help you identify prospects, make introductions, attend donor meetings, make direct asks of peers when appropriate, host house parties, and participate in thank you letter writing and phone calls to key donors. In addition to the board, all staff members must participate in the organization's fundraising efforts, and they should be trained on how to contribute, from sharing information to their networks, to identifying fundraising prospects.

4. Invest in a Donor Database

A successful fundraising effort is dependent on your ability to track critical information about your donors, such as their contact information, how much they give, their giving preferences (via email, direct mail, annually or monthly, etc.). Using a donor database will allow you to track this information as you receive it and to use it strategically in your fundraising campaigns. You need to invest not only in the database, but also in training multiple people to regularly use it. Details on selecting a tool and building out your database can be found in Chapter 6, but one quick word on how this intersects with your grassroots fundraising:

If you learn something useful about a donor that will help you build the relationship, put it in the database. You can't rely on memory alone to keep track of these important bits of information. The next time you have a meeting with a key donor, you'll be able to check your notes and prepare by reviewing how much they've given, which appeals they've supported, and, hopefully, personal information that will help show them that you truly care—did they mention family during your last meeting or other organizations or causes they are dedicated to?

Think through the kind of information you can collect on your donors beyond the basic contact and giving information. Are you interested in age, race, gender, marital status, length of time in the community, etc? Tracking donor information also allows you to analyze your donor base and target your asks or shift your strategies accordingly. But remember to be systematic and thoughtful about the information you record; focus on updates that are relevant and helpful in the fundraising process, instead of trying to track every minor detail.

5. Know Your Donors

Once you have a database to track critical donor information, you can begin to strategically communicate and fundraise. When new donors join, you can coordinate a batch of personalized thank you letters. When grassroots donors tell you they don't want paper mail, you can ensure that they only receive electronic communications. If a donor only wants to give once a year, you can make sure that you only solicit the person annually. *Personalizing communications to donor segments dramatically improves results.*

You can even pull information out of your database so a solicitation letter references programs they supported previously and their last gift date and amount ("Your recent gift of $x on x/x/xx allowed us to accomplish. . . With another gift of $X today, we'll be able to. . . ."). *If you are sending an annual appeal to monthly donors, it is critical that you acknowledge their monthly donations before asking for an additional donation* (more on annual appeals in Chapter 11.) You need to show your donors that you pay attention and that every one of them is valuable to you. Even small donors want respect, they want their names spelled correctly, their giving histories tracked and acknowledged, and to be communicated with in the ways they prefer.

6. Ask Regularly

Too often organizations are under-asking their most faithful donors. *Unless a donor specifies otherwise, it is completely acceptable to ask three or four times per year.* If properly thanked and kept informed of the impact of their donations, donors can be extremely generous. Klein suggests using diverse asks on key donors to keep things interesting. Consider a phone call or inviting them to an event, in addition to traditional asks like mail and online appeals. If you aren't asking your donors often enough, you are missing out on huge fundraising opportunities. And from time to time, don't be afraid to humbly and respectfully invite your existing donors to consider increasing their support. As you stretch and take your efforts to the next level, they may want to join you!

7. Show Impact and Gratitude Often

Donors have a right to know that their money is being well spent. They aren't likely to give you money again if you can't show them how their past support was put to good use, in ways they care about. *People donate with their hearts first and then with their heads*. Don't underestimate the value of sharing stories and statistics with your donors—show them what their funding made possible. And thank them. A *lot*. We can't emphasize this enough. *Donors want to know that you respect and appreciate them*. You need to make them feel like they're part of your work, instead of treating them like ATMs, or abandoning them when you get a big gift or grant. Be sure to *send prompt, personalized gift acknowledgements to all donors regardless of size*, and make sure that you space out your requests so that not every communication is an ask.

Conclusion

Grassroots fundraising isn't just about the money—it's about building a powerful base of support. With grassroots fundraising you get more than donors; you get people who help you accomplish your work—you get a choir. Building a broad base of donors is hard work and requires time and energy. You must be willing to invest in the process and into building relationships. But if you do, it will pay off with huge rewards.

Do's and Don'ts

Do...

> ... take the time to spell out a clear vision and goals for your fundraising campaign.

> ... thank your donors every time they give, and in addition express gratitude two or three times a year to communicate the impact their support is having.

> ... create an aspirational goal that you don't necessarily share with all donor prospects.

> ... ensure all board members make a personal capacity gift every year.

> ... send prompt, personalized gift acknowledgements to all donors, regardless of size.

Don't. . .

> . . . treat your donors like ATMs; put the relationship above all.

> . . . be afraid to invite donor support three or four times a year.

> . . . abandon small donors when you get a big gift or grant.

About the Expert

Kim Klein, principal of Klein & Roth Consulting, is an internationally known trainer, speaker, and author of five books, including of *Fundraising for Social Change* and *Reliable Fundraising in Unreliable Times*. Klein co-founded the *Grassroots Fundraising Journal* in 1981 and was its publisher for 25 years.

Resource Review

Grassroots Institute for Fundraising Training (GIFT) (www. grassrootsfundraising.org)
> Great resource for finding articles and practical information on grassroots fundraising; they also produce the *Grassroots Fundraising Journal*, the annual Money for Our Movements conference, and provide training and consulting services.

Grassroots Fundraising Journal (http://bit.ly/1CX3dDM)
> A bimonthly print and digital publication that features articles with practical strategies covering all areas of individual giving, including special events, direct mail, major donor programs, membership campaigns, and more.

Nonprofit Quarterly (https://nonprofitquarterly.org/)
> A print and online publication that provides articles on a variety of nonprofit topics. Check out their webinars, and sign up for the daily digest.

M+R Lab (www.mrss.com/lab/)
> A free collection of articles and advice from a group of experienced nonprofit consultants; includes case studies on a wide variety of topics and causes.

The Agitator (www.theagitator.net/)
> A great online blog from industry experts Tom Belford and Roger Craver that provides information and advice on nonprofit fundraising and marketing strategies.

Klein, Kim. *Fundraising for Social Change* (7th ed.). Jossey-Bass, 2016. Comprehensive overview offering a step-by-step strategy for identifying, securing, and stewarding grassroots support.

Money for Our Movements: A Social Justice Fundraising Conference (http://bit.ly/P9mwoP)
A biannual conference that provides fundraising skills training geared toward social justice activists: concrete examples and models, debates and plenaries, and networking opportunities.

Articles with Good Reviews of Database Options

Finding the Right Donor Database for Your Nonprofit: www. nonprofithub.org/volunteer-management/finding-right-donor-database-nonprofit/

Top 15 Nonprofit Donor Management and Fundraising Software Report: http://bit.ly/1Ncq3iG (register to download the free report)

A Few Good Donor Management Systems: www.idealware.org/articles/few-good-donor-management-systems

Chapter

9

Major Donors
Building Relationships, Making the Ask, and Stewardship

"Fundraising is the gentle art of teaching the joy of giving."
—Henry A. "Hank" Rosso

Introduction

Did you know that in 2014, 80 percent of the $358.38 billion in charitable contributions to U.S. nonprofits came from individuals? The single largest contributor to the 7.1 percent increase in overall giving, according to Giving USA, "was an increase of $13.88 billion in giving by individuals—58 percent of the total change between 2013 and 2014." And even in countries where the government provides the lion's share of support to NGOs, *tapping into the massive potential of individual supporters is absolutely critical to your success.* Now that we've provided some tips for building out the base of your donor pyramid in our last chapter, let's move on to looking at how to engage major donors who can transform your work and your organization.

As we noted in Chapter 8, all individual fundraising programs require a lot of time and effort. They require an organization committed to relationship-building and keeping people involved; they require staff, board engagement, and strong stewardship. But if done well, the payoff is big. Donors who are engaged and treated well can become life-long supporters. They can also be great sources of new donors by connecting you to others who support your cause. To learn more about why major gift fundraising is so crucial to nonprofit success, I spoke with well-known fundraising consultant and author of *Beyond Fund Raising*, Kay Sprinkel Grace.

The key to successful individual fundraising and securing major gifts is stewardship. According to Grace, think of your supporters as "donor investors" or "partners for positive change" instead of simply donors. And most importantly, after you receive the gift, realize that *this* is when the real work begins. "This is the most important, yet most neglected piece of the fundraising process." She argues that our lack of stewardship is leading many nonprofits to a donor hourglass, versus a pyramid: at the top are a few people making very large gifts, and at the bottom are a lot of people making small gifts. The middle of the hourglass gets narrower and narrower if you fail to properly steward your base and ensure those relationships blossom. Without stewardship of existing donors, your only option is to constantly bring in new donors, which only gets harder over time.

With that said, let's dive into the tips and tools Grace shared when outlining the most important factors necessary for building and maintaining a thriving major donor program:

Critical Skills and Competencies

1. Prospect Constantly

It's unfortunate, but many organizations neglect their donor pipelines unless there is a campaign or crisis. To be successful in securing major donors, you must *constantly* be looking for new supporters of all sizes. Not all donors stay with you for a lifetime, and in fact AFP's 2014 *Fundraising Effectiveness Survey Report* claimed an average 57 percent churn rate for donors annually. This means that you need to be vigilant in adding new leads into your pipeline, replacing slightly more than half your donors every year in order simply to stay afloat.

Prospecting for major donors involves looking for people with shared values, a passion for the issue(s) you focus on, and, one hopes, a personal connection to your work or team. First, look at annual reports and donors lists of organizations similar to yours. When you go to the opera, the symphony, the theater, or museums, look at their donor lists, too. You'll probably find a lot of crossover between them, since these are clearly patrons of the arts—make sense? You can do the same thing by reviewing published lists of supporters from other groups that overlap with your work in some way. You should be on the lookout for useful donor lists constantly and—as outlined in Chapter 5 (Prospecting and Donor Research)—run them through your own database and wealth screens, vetting people based on existing contacts and demonstrated interests.

It is absolutely crucial that you involve your board in major donor prospecting. Take their contact lists once or twice a year and run them through your database to find even more connections. Your board should not only be sharing names with you, but also reviewing prospect lists and helping prioritize leads. Your board should be talking to people about your organization, and then reporting back to you when they've identified prospects. But the key to tapping this resource is making it both easy, and expected. *Dedicate a few minutes at each board meeting for members to write down the names of a few new people they've identified as prospects.* Be sure to also create a development committee on your board, so that a few dedicated members can help you screen and prioritize prospects and keep fellow board members accountable and engaged. And finally, take the time to meet or talk with each board member individually to create their own custom fundraising strategy and provide them with any support, training, and materials needed to secure their full participation.

Tracking Major Donors in Databases

When inputting major donor prospects into your database, be sure to track their names, addresses, and any known connections to your organization. You should also be tracking information on their known connections (to people, organizations, other funders), their interests, and other organizations they're affiliated with or have given large donations to. It's especially helpful to *assign values to major donor prospects for both how closely they are connected to your organization and area of work, as well as their giving capacity*. A simple subjective range of 1 to 5 in both of these fields will enable you to easily sort and identify your top-priority prospects.

2. Realize Your Organization Is a Means to an End

In order to secure large gifts, you need to engage your donors on a long-term basis. Grace talks often about the importance of transformational versus transactional giving. When your organization focuses on donations as transactions, you fail to appreciate that *your nonprofit is a channel that exists to connect people with resources to the change they want to see in the world.* Or as Grace is fond of saying, "***People don't give to you; they give through you.***" Always remember that you are an investment vehicle through which donors and funders help solve community challenges and enrich life experiences.

In transactional giving, an organization thinks only of what it is doing *to* the donor: identifying, qualifying, cultivating, soliciting, acknowledging, and so forth. With transformational giving, an organization instead focuses on the impact that donor has *on the issue*, recognizing it is merely a conduit for change. Again, this is the concept of the "donor investor" Grace started out with, and this subtle yet powerful shift creates an infinity loop between donor and organization.

A transformational donor stewardship loop has replaced the traditional stewardship model:

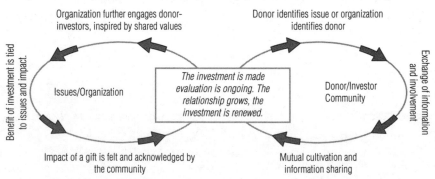

Just remember one of Grace's signature sayings, "***People don't give to you because you have needs. They give to you because you meet needs.***" Transformational giving calls for mutual identification, mutual stewardship, and getting to know *one another*. It's about realizing the coin has two sides. So in addition to asking a donor to give to your organization, ask what your organization can do for the donor. Just remember JFK's famous "Ask not what your country can do for you" speech if that helps!

3. Prepare Your People

Most people don't want to ask for money because they don't know how and are afraid of rejection. Realize *it's your responsibility to equip and train your staff, board, and volunteers* and to prepare them for success. And again, when done right, a prospect should always feel comfortable saying no. As nonprofit professionals, we have a responsibility to give our people messages that are easy to articulate and to help them practice. *Equip your board and volunteer network with facts, figures, and, most importantly, stories, and results will follow*.

In *The AAA Way to Fund Raising Success*, Grace developed a framework that she calls the "Triple A", and it's used with hundreds of organizations across the world, especially in the United States, Australia, Italy, and the Czech Republic. The basis of the framework is that there are three roles: Ambassador, Advocate, and Asker. *Not everyone on your team is going to be confident or comfortable with asking, but that doesn't mean they don't play important roles in fundraising. Everyone on your team, particularly board members, should be trained as effective Ambassadors.* Ambassadors know the organization's message and are enthusiastic spokespeople. If they're not enthusiastic, they shouldn't be on your team—passion is a prerequisite for participation. Advocates play another important role. While Ambassadors make friends, Advocates make the case. Advocates are not only conversant on your organization; they know your issue well and can participate on a deeper level by doing things like public speaking, recruiting new board members, and making phone calls to elected officials. They are also coached in how to skillfully handle objections. Finally you have the Askers. Askers are also Ambassadors and may be Advocates as well, but must also be confident and well trained if they are to feel confident. Take the time to map out your opportunities for involvement, present those opportunities to the entire team, especially board and staff, and use this framework to allow each member of your team to establish his or her most confident role in the fundraising process.

4. Master the Ask

Fundraisers like Grace follow a framework created by the late Hank Rosso. *There are four main steps in making an ask: the opening; involvement; the presentation; and the close*. The opening should be very brief, keeping chitchat to a minimum, thanking people for their time and conveying excitement and gratitude. And *never, ever apologize for taking their time*. The involvement phase of the ask is where you engage the donors and ask open-ended questions to get them to talk about their relationship to the organization and their passion for the issue. This step is *critical* and cannot be skipped. You need to ***listen before you ask***. (This is sometimes called the "appreciative inquiry process"; see Resource Review for more information.) Be sensitive to their needs, and if they push the conversation forward quicker than you'd prefer, don't linger—remember that *the donor's needs come first.*

Now that you know more about what they care about and why, you are better prepared for your presentation. This is where you talk about the vision, plan, and programs of your organization and the impact a large gift would have on your cause. This is where questions will be asked and answered. And finally comes your close, where there is an explicit, direct ask. That means you ***request a specific amount of money, map it to their connection to the cause, and clarify exactly what it will make possible***, for example: "Thanks so much for your interest in our vocational training program! Would you consider a gift of $500,000 to help launch the initiative and serve 500 homeless people next year?" *After making the ask, it is crucial that you stay quiet.* It is critical that the next person to talk is the donor.

There are a few answers you might hear. If it is "yes," that's great! If you get a "maybe" or "I need to think about it," you can respond with something like "I understand. We are asking you to make a significant commitment. Do you need further information, and *can we set a time when I can get back in touch with you?*" If it is "no," you should absolutely try to find out what "no" means, but never, ever say "Why?" because it puts people on the defensive. This is another place where silence will serve you. You want the donor to elaborate and, if you are silent after the "no," the donor most often will explain his or her reason. Maybe it is the amount of the ask, in which case you can reply, "I understand. What amount would you consider giving at this time?" Maybe it's that the timing isn't right, in which case your reply should be "I understand. When would be a better time?" If it is truly a "no" because he or she hasn't aligned with your approach or efforts, then simply thank the person and say something like, "Well, naturally we're disappointed. May we keep in touch, and perhaps look forward to a time when you feel more connected?" Of course, it goes without saying that you should definitely follow up on whatever you commit to; tomorrow's major donor may be the one who told you "no" at today's meeting. Finally, it's extremely important to thank those who have taken the time to meet with you, even if they turn you down.

A final note on asking: make sure that *in addition* to large gift, special project, and program funding, you also ***ask all major donors for annual unrestricted*** *donations*. Donors making gifts at certain levels often designate them for specific programs and projects. However, you should also invite major donors to give smaller, unrestricted annual gifts to keep them connected to your organization and in support of its overall work. It is a way to safeguard their investment. Typically, a large gift commitment may be *a three-to-five year pledge*. It is critical that your donors understand the importance of supporting the infrastructure of the organization annually as well. If you are engaging your donors on a regular basis and making them feel a true part of your organization, these asks will be easy. If they say their contribution includes both annual and special project support, be sure to understand the donor's intent regarding the distribution of the gift inside the organization.

Of course, these requests need to be handled respectfully and, just like any ask, it's simply an invitation that may certainly be declined—Grace suggests thanking donors for the gift they've already committed to, and then using language like: "I invite you to consider strengthening your investment by also supporting the current programming of our organization. Would you consider a smaller unrestricted contribution of $X to provide us with general operating support?" You can also invite them to support a capital, endowment, or annual campaign, if appropriate. But at all costs *avoid securing a large gift and then circling back in a couple months to ask for more*, as that's almost always viewed as disrespectful and unappreciative; the key is making these additional asks on the spot.

5. Value Every Donor

Grace believes that stewardship is the most important, and the most neglected, step in the fund development process. Too often fundraisers spend all of their time and energy bringing in gifts, and too little on keeping their donors on board. Remember *it's much easier to keep an existing donor than it is to bring on a new one!* Donor retention is much higher among repeat donors than with first-time donors. After all, they've already demonstrated their support and made contributions. The key to effective stewardship is building and maintaining relationships with your donors. *Thank your donors at least three times a year and give them at least quarterly updates on the impact their gifts are making possible*. Send occasional notes with program updates and *make thank you calls for gifts of all sizes*.

Unfortunately, many organizations have created an arbitrary internal benchmark about when they start stewarding donors. Who are we to judge the amount of a donation? $50 or $100 may be a "stretch" for the family or person who donated it. Maybe a $10 donor will eventually leave you a large estate gift. *Every donor should be treated as a major donor prospect worthy of stewardship.* Whether they give $1 or $1 million, each should get a personal touch. Donors give from the heart, and their gifts are an indication that they are looking for a relationship. Sending generic printed receipts to low-level donors does not show that we care and value their contributions. Personal touches, such as a handwritten thank you on a gift acknowledgement or a quick thank you call go a long way in bringing a donor further into your organization's fold. In other words, ***if you don't properly thank the little gifts, you'll never get the big ones***. Also, don't confuse automatic electronic acknowledgements generated after online gifts with a true thank you letter. The first is only an acknowledgment; the second is the real thank you that may launch a long relationship.

"Who does not thank for little will not thank for much."

—Estonian proverb

Grace recalled an anecdote that's similar to many I've heard from veteran fundraisers:

> "I had a donor in my very first job that would send one or five dollar bills every month. One day, I called her and said, 'I am so touched by these gifts.' 'Well,' she said, 'What I do is that every month, whatever I have left over, I send it to you.' I was so moved because I didn't know of any other donors with this kind of incredible commitment and personal connection, and I made sure that this woman was invited to our tea parties and major donor events. It turned out that she owned a piece of property that had become quite valuable. She left the organization that property when she passed, resulting in a sizable gift that had a major impact on our work."

Let's end with one final tip that makes showing appreciation to each and every donor much more feasible. ***Stage an annual (or more frequent!) thank-a-thon*** where you enlist staff, volunteers, board members, and, when possible, beneficiaries of your programs, all of whom call donors to simply thank them for their support. The key to success for these is that *there is no ask*, no event invitation, nothing—you're just calling to recognize their contribution and let them know it made a difference. Donors usually expect an ask on these calls and are almost always delighted to receive your gratitude, and it's a great way to remind your board and staff both of the crucial role donors play, as well as the impact your organization has in the community. And, of course, donors will certainly remember this when making their next contributions.

Conclusion

Always remember to think of your organization as a conduit instead of an endpoint. Donors aren't giving to you because your organization has needs; they're giving to you because you are meeting a need and creating change. When you realize that donors aren't giving to you, but through you, then the asking becomes an honor rather than a burden. Share your passion for your cause with pride and people will be inspired to join you. And realize you don't have just donors—instead, you have *donor investors* who give because they care, and who keep giving because you show them that you value their support, and that it makes a difference in ways they care about. As Grace says, "They are your partners for positive change." That's their ROI. And as you express gratitude and communicate impact through ongoing stewardship, you will reap the rewards of loyal and generous supporters.

Do's and Don'ts

Do. . .

> . . . ask your board for a contact list of potential major donors once or twice a year, plus invite them to share new prospects at every board meeting.

> . . . provide opportunities for Ambassador, Advocate, or Asker roles to everyone on your staff and board.

> . . . arm volunteers with stories to share with potential donors.

> . . . ask major donors to make unrestricted annual donations, even if they're smaller.

> . . . stage an annual thank-a-thon and recognize the contribution of every donor.

Don't. . .

> . . . only steward donors above a certain gift amount.
>
> . . . send more asks than program updates.
>
> . . . ask donors to meet your organization's needs; instead explore how you can advance their goals for impact in the community.
>
> . . . don't be the first to speak after making an ask of a major donor.

About the Expert

Kay Sprinkel Grace is a well-known fundraising consultant, founder and principal of Transforming Philanthropy, and author of six books, including *High Impact Philanthropy* and *Beyond Fundraising*. In 2013, the Lilly Family School of Philanthropy at Indiana University awarded her the Henry A. Rosso Medal for Lifetime Achievement in Ethical Fund Raising. On a personal note, she's one of my heroes and has been inspiring and educating nonprofit fundraisers around the globe for decades.

Resource Review

Grace, Kay Sprinkel. *Beyond Fundraising: New Strategies for Nonprofit Innovation and Investment* (2nd ed.). John Wiley & Sons, 2005.
This is a basic fundraising book that covers mission, vision, values, annual and capital giving, planning and conveys Grace's unique philosophy about philanthropy.

Rosso, Henry A. *Hank Rosso's Achieving Excellence in Fundraising* (2nd ed.). Jossey-Bass, 2003.
Through two editions of this seminal work, initiated by one of the 20th century leaders in philanthropy and continued through Indiana University's Center on Philanthropy—now the Lilly Family School—the basic principles of fundraising and the related leadership and management issues are presented so solidly that the book has become an essential guide for beginners and those seeking to strengthen their skills.

Grace, Kay Sprinkel. *The AAA Way to Fundraising Success: Maximum Involvement, Maximum Results*. Whit Press, 2009.
A brief and readable handbook for making sure everyone on your board (and some staff) find their "confidence zone" in resource development.

Wealth Engine (www.wealthengine.com)
A great tool for prospecting and donor research, including wealth screening.

Grace, Kay Sprinkel, and Alan L. Wendroff. *High Impact Philanthropy: How Donors, Boards, and Nonprofit Organizations Can Transform Nonprofit Organizations*. John Wiley & Sons, 2001.
Setting forth the transaction versus transformation giving model as the basis of high-impact philanthropy, this book also explores how effective marketing supports the fund development process.

The Fundraising Authority (www.thefundraisingauthority.com)
Great hub for articles and resources, as well as this helpful post about major donor fundraising.

"Major Donor Fundraising 101." The Fundraising Authority RSS. (www .thefundraisingauthority.com/individual-fundraising/major-donor-fundraising-101/)

Miller, Carolyn J. *The Nonprofits' Guide to the Power of Appreciative Inquiry*. Community Development Institute, 2004.
This book provides a variety of sample appreciative inquiry questions in many topic areas, as well as a theoretical background of its use in nonprofits and other organizations.

The Chronicle of Philanthropy (www.philanthropy.com)
This great print and online publication offers articles on the latest news affecting nonprofit organizations. Sign up for their free news feed.

Local Community Papers. If your work is focused in a particular community, regularly reading the regional paper is a great way to stay abreast of local news.

10

Direct Mail
The Ins and Outs

"Nothing ever comes to one, that is worth having, except as a result of hard work."

—Booker T. Washington

Introduction

No one knows how much of the roughly $335 billion in U.S. nonprofit contributions in 2014 was accounted for by direct mail—but anyone actively involved in fundraising today (except perhaps for digital specialists) will tell you that appeals with a stamp attached brought in *far* more than social media, email, mobile, and other new communication channels. With the possible exception of major gifts, which are generally solicited face-to-face, there's really no other fundraising strategy that's as important for nonprofit success from a purely financial standpoint.

Direct mail is a great way to build a steady stream of unrestricted revenue from individuals, as well as spread awareness and brand recognition. However, it's an expensive investment, and ***direct mail is best suited to organizations with large donor lists and budgets of at least $1 million***. If you are a national organization or have a large annual budget, and are prepared to invest at least $250,000 to $500,000 over several years before your efforts bear fruit, direct mail may have a lot to offer.

Smaller, grassroots organizations are better off focusing on online fundraising and building relationships with individual donors who can give major gifts over time, as outlined in various other chapters in the book. Depending on the size of your donor list and your organizational capacity, you can conduct a smaller direct mail program in-house by sending several letters a year to your donors, including perhaps two standalone appeals and appeals that precede or follow your online solicitations.

Direct mail is half art, half science. The greatest success comes to those organizations that respond creatively to the needs and desires of their supporters, standing out while staying on target with their message. And of course, *a strong commitment to rigorously maintaining and analyzing your donor list is a must.* If this sounds like you, then you're sure to benefit from the insights of industry leader and 30-year direct mail veteran, Mal Warwick, who outlined these seven tips for success:

Critical Skills and Competencies

1. Know Your Numbers

There are two categories of direct mail: acquisition and house mailings. Acquisition mailings recruit new supporters, while house mailings renew and raise additional donations from existing supporters. House mailings include mailings to renew annual contributions from donors or members, as well as special appeals. Either way, before you start, you must understand average response rates so you have some sort of benchmark for what to expect. *Acquisition mailings typically receive a 0.25 percent to 2 percent response rate.* This means that up to 2 percent of people will reply with a donation.

Once you acquire those donors, and properly steward them, *your investment will really begin to pay off when as many as half of your donors respond with second gifts.* Subsequent appeals will bring donations from a much larger percentage of those who give second gifts. Ultimately, your organization will derive a steady stream of revenue from the valuable minority of newly acquired donors who remain loyal for years. That's because individual *renewal mailings and special appeals are likely to yield response rates of 10 to 25 percent.* The profits from your program can rise much further over the years as you convert these loyal supporters into monthly donors, who sometimes give as much monthly as they donated overall in earlier years.

2. Prepare for the Long Haul

Direct mail is a strategic, long-term process that generates its greatest rewards over years, not weeks. *It is extremely rare for a new direct mail program to yield net revenue in its first few years*. If you are just starting, no matter what size program you have, you have to be prepared to invest a substantial amount of money and persist in the face of what looks like failure for several years. Once you have a large enough number of repeat donors, you will see a steady stream of income that not only pays for the direct mail program, but also a large portion of your organization's work. As the wise Yoda once said, "Patience you must have, my young Padawan."

3. Grow Your List

Building a large donor list is critical to succeeding in direct mail. To do this you will need to invest in strong acquisition campaigns by renting or exchanging lists of donors, members, or subscribers who seem likely to be interested in the work of your organization. Renting lists means paying a third party—typically a brokerage firm specializing in lists, but sometimes a fellow nonprofit—for a *one-time* use of their list.

Warwick recommends getting a random sampling of 5,000 names from the list to *do a test mailing before committing to renting an entire list*. This will help you determine the number and average amount of gifts you can expect from the overall list, ensuring it's a wise investment. If your donor list is large enough and your privacy policy allows for it, *consider exchanging lists with other, like-minded organizations*. In doing this, you are giving those organizations the option of mailing single fundraising appeals to your donors, and vice versa; but *be sure to document the list is for one-time use only*. List exchanges are typically large mailings and your response rate from these is not likely to be over 1 percent.

4. Trust the Data, Not Your Gut

In direct mail, being creative is not enough, and you can't rely on your intuition. There is no way to know what will work best to maximize response. After over 30 years of industry experience, Warwick still cannot consistently guess which letters and messages will succeed. As he puts it, "*Only a fool will depend on gut instinct and not read the numbers dispassionately.*" That is why it's critical to rely on the data and test, test, test.

Take small portions of each of the acquisition lists you've selected and use them to test different messages and creative approaches (different copy, envelopes, graphics, inserts, etc.). To get accurate results, you'll want to plan for at least 200 *responses* to these test "packages." This means you'll need to start with a large sample size. For example, if you are doing an acquisition mailing, and you have a list of 100,000 names, the best way to find the right message would be to take 20,000 random names from the list and split them into two groups. Mail one group message A, and another group message B. Whichever gets the higher response rate is what you'd mail to the remaining 80,000 donors. Ideally, if your list is large enough, Warwick suggests increasing your sample size and doing another round of testing before mailing to your entire list. The more you can test, the better the results you're likely to see.

5. Know Your Donors

Once you have a steady stream of active donors, it's important to **customize your communications for different subsets of them**. To do this, you must get to know them. Do they care about a particular program? How much and how often do they donate in a year? Do they give monthly, or just during your annual campaign or at your gala? As outlined in numerous chapters throughout the book (Chapters 8, 9, and 16 on grassroots fundraising, major donors, and email, respectively), knowing these things allows you to *segment your donor list and communicate with them in more personal ways*, improving response rates demonstrably. **Consider creating a giving club or patron's circle to entice donors to give at higher levels**, and provide them with public recognition.

Probably more than anything else, **the key to success in direct mail is getting to know the top 5 percent of your donors**. Pay special attention to your most loyal, generous donors, and work to move them up the giving ladder. Send them special messages and shower them with personal attention. Warwick wrote an entire book about this approach, known as "high-dollar" direct mail fundraising (see Resource Review below.)

6. Focus, Focus, Focus

When drafting a direct mail letter, you must focus your ask. If you overwhelm your reader with multiple messages and requests (e.g., sign this, call your Senator, spread the word, donate), then you will dilute your efforts, your ask will lose its power, and your letter will be tossed. Less is more.

When a donor or prospect opens your letter, you only have a few seconds to get his or her attention and convey your message. You need to *communicate clearly and get straight to the point*: ". . . here is the problem; here is what we are doing about it; will you support us with a gift of $X?"

7. Create a Schedule . . . and Stick to It

It's crucial that you *create an annual editorial calendar for your mailings*. Detail exactly when you'll send your acquisition mailings, renewals, and special appeals, so you're clear on both timing and frequency. Mapping out your mailing campaigns in advance not only helps with financial planning, but also ensures an ongoing, consistent dialogue with your members; just as with social media, it's about finding a drumbeat, not riffing an occasional solo. And, most importantly, it's critical that you stick to the schedule and don't remove mailings from your calendar.

A typical annual direct mail calendar will include at least two acquisition mailings and three to as many as ten renewal mailings for existing donors or members—depending on the size of your donor base—as well as special appeals for certain projects and programs spread throughout. Your calendar should also map to your year-end strategy, as outlined in Chapter 11, since *a series of direct mail combined with email appeals in the final days of December is likely to bring the best results*.

And while some consultants will recommend that every communication include an ask (even if less prominent or direct), Warwick disagrees. He emphasizes the importance of including "relationship building" mailings in your calendar. In order to properly steward your donors you need to keep them engaged and make them feel informed and a part of the organization. Remember Kay Sprinkel Grace's insights on this transformational giving in Chapter 9—you are a conduit for impact, not an endpoint. So thank your donors—via direct mail and all other channels—for the work they make possible without always asking for more. In the long run this will result in more loyal and generous donors.

Conclusion

Direct mail is best suited to organizations with large capacity and substantial resources. When done properly, it can result both in significant amounts of revenue and greater public awareness. Through direct mail you bring new donors into your organization, and you create loyal donors who renew their gifts year after year. It's also an entry point for many key donors who become major and planned giving donors. It may require a lot of work, a sizeable investment of cash, and years of patience, but if you follow Warwick's tips and properly thank and steward direct mail donors, you will create a steady and robust stream of sustainable revenue for your organization.

Do's and Don'ts

Do. . .

> . . . create an annual editorial calendar for your direct mail efforts, and stick to the plan.

> . . . run test campaigns on portions of your list to determine the best message to send to your entire database.

> . . . send regular program updates and thank you mailings, which do *not* include an ask.

> . . . customize and personalize your messages to distinct donor segments.

> . . . create a giving club or patron's circle to entice donors to give at certain levels.

> . . . create a special cultivation plan for the top 5 percent of your direct mail donors.

Don't. . .

> . . . get into direct mail expecting to make your money back in less than three years.

> . . . send mailings with multiple asks or calls to action.

> . . . undertake a direct mail program if your organization has less than a 50,000-person mailing list or a budget under $2 million.

About the Expert

Mal Warwick is an author, consultant, and public speaker, and founder and chairman of Mal Warwick|Donordigital. Warwick has authored 20 books, including *How to Write Successful Fundraising Appeals* (3rd ed.), and *Revolution in the Mailbox*.

Resource Review

Warwick, Mal. *How to Write Successful Fundraising Appeals* (3rd ed.).
Jossey-Bass, 2013.
Chances are, the thought of writing a fundraising appeal makes you
nervous; this book, the standard text in the field, will show you the way
to succeed.

Warwick, Mal. *The Mercifully Brief, Real-World Guide to Raising $1,000
Gifts by Mail.* Emerson & Church, 2005.
This is the only book on the topic of "high-dollar" direct mail
fundraising.

Warwick, Mal. *Revolution in the Mailbox: Your Guide to Successful Direct
Mail Fundraising.* Jossey-Bass, 2004.
Here's a guide to the science of direct mail, including how to choose
acquisition lists, how to segment your donor file, and what results you
might expect from different mailings.

The Direct Marketing Association (http://thedma.org)
Great resource for news and information on direct marketing, and be sure
to check out their great annual conference.

The Bridge Conference (www.bridgeconf.org)
This is one of the best annual conferences for direct mail fundraisers.
It provides education and research on cutting-edge trends, as well as
practical insights and user-friendly ideas.

The Agitator (www.theagitator.net/)
A great online blog from industry experts Tom Belford and Roger Craver
that provides information and advice on nonprofit fundraising and direct
marketing strategies.

Year-End, Annual Appeals, and Membership Campaigns

> "It is more rewarding to watch money change the world than watch it accumulate."
>
> —Gloria Steinem

Introduction

According to Giving USA, 72 percent of all nonprofit donations came from individuals in 2014. And one of the most popular ways for individuals to donate to nonprofits is through annual and year-end appeals and membership campaigns. These donations are not only an important source of general operating funds, but also a critical strategy for creating and sustaining a loyal base of supporters. Fundraising is about building relationships, and you can't possibly meet every single one of your supporters in person. Membership campaigns and annual appeals are great ways to connect with people on an ongoing basis and share the impact of your work and their support. Whether driven by direct mail or email (see Chapters 10 and 16, respectively), these efforts raise money for your organization and create a special dialogue between you and your donors, bringing donors closer to your work as they see the results of their support.

Network for Good's Digital Giving Index found that 31 percent of all annual giving occurred in December 2014, with almost one-third of that taking place in the last three days of the year, so having a solid year-end strategy is crucial. But whether it's your annual campaign or a formalized membership campaign, raising money using these strategies can advance your fundraising goals and create a legion of supporters ready to help you spread the word and advocate on behalf of your cause. Telling a politician that you have 40,000 members poised and ready to take action goes a long way in establishing credibility and moving your agenda forward.

While similar in nature, year-end appeals, annual appeals, and membership campaigns have unique features. Annual appeals are fundraising asks typically sent through direct mail and email to existing donors at a certain time of the year. A year-end appeal is simply an annual appeal sent at the end of the year, and both of these strategies revolve around a campaign including an initial message and several follow-ups. A membership campaign also features multiple messages, but you offer specific benefits to those who sign up and contribute.

To learn more, I sat down with Farra Trompeter, vice president at Big Duck, a communications firm that exclusively works with nonprofits, and vice chair of NTEN's board. Trompeter shared eight great tips to help you succeed in raising money with annual and year-end appeals and membership campaigns.

Critical Skills and Competencies

1. Find Your Passion

Do you remember *why* you started working at your nonprofit? What was it about its mission, vision, or programs that excited you on day one? That same passion is what motivates your donors, and it's important to tap into it when you create campaigns. Too often, fundraisers are kept at an arm's length from programs. Seeing and experiencing the work you're raising money for is incredibly inspiring, and it often inspires some of your best, most transformative fundraising ideas.

Get out in the field with program staff, see your organization's work in action, and meet the people you serve. Interview clients and unearth stories about the impact your organization is having on their lives. Recharge your batteries with the knowledge that your fundraising efforts are driving good work. Finding your passion will give you a sense of pride and honor in your fundraising that you'll convey in your fundraising appeals. *Your ability to communicate your organization's impact—fueled by a dose of personal passion—will shine through and inspire more and bigger donations*.

2. Understand Your Donors

Good communication skills are key to success in this area. Your words need to connect with people and inspire them. To do this, you need to know whom you're talking to. What do your donors care about, and what drives their giving? When preparing your appeals, think about the answers to these questions, and write as if you are writing to *one* donor, not a bunch of names on a spreadsheet.

Odds are you'll target several different types of people with your campaigns, but follow Trompeter's suggestion and *create a few "donor personas" to personalize your message and get inside the heads of your intended audience*. Give each persona a name and a story, and detail what drives their connection to your cause. Keep these in mind when you write your appeals.

Maybe you're an LGBT advocacy group writing to Bob, a 62-year-old man from Texas with a grandson who is gay. Bob made a small donation because his grandson forwarded your last campaign, but this is not his number one issue. Another persona could be Betty, the 41-year-old married lesbian with a daughter who is passionate about LGBT equality, both because of personal prejudice she's faced, but also because she wants her daughter to grow up in a world free from bigotry. The point is to connect with the donors you are writing to and to remember what matters to *them*—not just what feels critical to you or your organization.

3. Identify Membership Pricing and Benefits

As you prepare to launch a successful membership campaign, you need to identify the right benefits and pricing. Look at similar organizations in your area. If you're a theater or museum, what benefits do other local groups offer, and at what price? Next, look at your own data. *Review your average gift size and make your membership price point 10 to 20 percent above that*, so that over time you can increase this important metric. *When identifying member benefits, tie them closely to your organization and the impact you have*, not something generic. Your benefits should be connected to the mission of the organization and the reasons why people support you. For example, if you're a group that promotes youth development through sports, offer tickets to local sporting events; or if you're a museum, offer early access to new exhibits.

4. Plan Campaigns Instead of One-Time Appeals

Sending a single letter or email asking for support may generate a small level of interest, but it's never going to deliver the results of a full-fledged, strategically planned campaign that unites messages across all of your communication platforms. Create a theme for the campaign and interweave relevant stories, images, statistics, and language throughout. Write and design materials that resonate with your donors and help them appreciate the issue you're working on, why it matters, and how they can help. Explain the problem, the solution, and how the donor can play a part.

Provide a timeline and goal for the campaign, along with the impact it will enable, something like "We're raising $100,000 by the end of the year to open up a new facility" or "We're enlisting 1,000 new members in the next two weeks, and then we're taking our case to Congress!" It's crucial to *keep each message simple and include only one call to action*. Trompeter also recommends starting out by *not* asking for a donation, but instead making action-based requests, like sharing an image on social media or signing an online petition, before making your fundraising request.

5. Schedule Appeals and Updates

Plan a series of well-designed, professional communications that include reminders for those who don't donate initially, progress updates, and a final impact summary. As we detail in Chapters 10, 16, and 17, *creating a comprehensive editorial calendar is the key to running successful campaigns with consistent messaging across channels*. Having a map helps you balance the frequency and timing of your messages. Once you begin your campaign, remember that just because a few people complain about hearing from you too often, it doesn't mean that you've stepped over a line. Analyzing key metrics (see Tip 6) will help you determine the value of additional communications.

As a point of reference, *year-end campaigns typically occur over a six-week period starting in mid-November and culminating at the beginning of the next year*. A year-end or annual campaign might include one to two direct mail pieces, five to six emails, and one to three Facebook or Twitter posts per week (use the tips in Chapters 10, 16, and

17, respectively). When integrating all this into your editorial calendar, *increase the frequency of messages as you approach the deadline or end of the campaign* to create a sense of urgency and enlist help in getting your campaign across the goal line.

Sample Year-End Campaign Calendar

- *September to November:* Develop specific goal for total dollars and donors, create campaign theme and calendar, draft and design high-end direct mail appeal card and seven email messages, create low-end and high-end donation forms, produce four shareable graphics and copy for weekly social media posts.
- *November 24:* Drop direct mail appeal to existing donors, scheduled to arrive after first email appeal.
- *November 25:* Launch campaign with a Thanksgiving email message, sharing thanks and asking supporters to do the same. After message is sent, tag three donors in a Facebook post, and asked them to do the same using the campaign hashtag (see the Facebook post below).
- *December 01:* Send first email appeal announcing matching gift; post campaign artwork on homepage and via posts to Facebook and Twitter.
- *December 02:* For Giving Tuesday, promote the campaign with two posts each on Facebook and Twitter.
- *December 13:* Send second email appeal from a family member of a child with Duchenne.
- *December 15:* Send December e-newsletter featuring the campaign, a blog post about the fundraising project, and donation-centric images.
- *December 18:* Send third email appeal from a staff member about the need for research.
- *December 26:* Send fourth email appeal from a young person/ people with Duchenne (with video).
- *December 30:* Post last-chance message on Facebook and Twitter; text appeal to mobile donors.
- *December 31:* Send fifth email appeal from founder with a last chance to give message.
- *January 06:* Send out a thank-you message to all (with variations for donors/non-donors); post report-back/thank-you messages on Facebook and Twitter.

(continued)

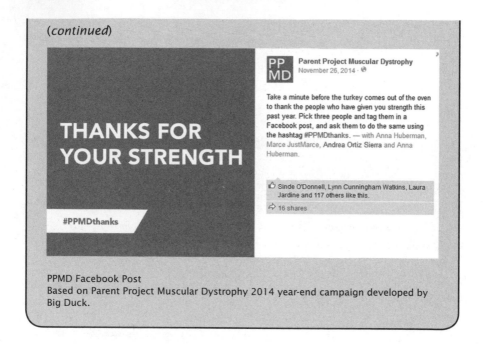

(continued)

PPMD Facebook Post
Based on Parent Project Muscular Dystrophy 2014 year-end campaign developed by
Big Duck.

6. Use Your Best Channels

To maximize the impact of your campaigns, you must leverage the
most effective channels for raising money, including email, direct mail,
and your website. Integrate all these channels into your campaign
and be consistent with your messaging. Think about where you have
an established presence and where you've been successful in the past.
Rather than focus on identifying new sources of prospects, *fundraising
campaigns like these work best when you focus on soliciting existing
donors through proven channels*. Use social media strategically to provide
depth, share stories, and update supporters on the campaign using videos,
photos, and peer testimonials, but don't rely on Facebook and Twitter
for direct fundraising appeals. Prominently feature the campaign on your
website using graphics, a lightbox or other image that takes over your
homepage, or a landing page. Customize your donation page to feature
the language and images associated with the campaign, and potentially
customize the ask string to match the campaign or donor's giving history.
And per Chapter 18, *ensure that all your channels are compatible with
mobile devices, especially the donation page on your website*. You will
leave money on the table if people aren't able to donate from their phones
or tablets, and this trend is increasing over time.

7. Make Data Your Friend

The only way to determine your success is to take time to evaluate your efforts and analyze your data. Invest in the right tools and dedicate staff resources to collecting data on an ongoing basis (see Chapter 7 for more on data capture and analysis). Look at open and unsubscribe rates to see whether you're losing people by sending too many communications. Look at click-through and response rates to make sure donors and members are taking the actions you hope for. Look at average gifts and amounts raised by each message to determine whether your campaign is effective. *Compare current campaign data to previous efforts, as well as to industry standards by looking at reports by groups like M+R, Blackbaud, and Giving USA* (see Resource Review below). During the campaign, experiment with testing components of your communications like graphics, messaging, subject line, day or time, and others to determine what works best before sending to your entire list. See Chapter 10 to learn more about testing direct mail campaigns, Chapter 15 for tips on optimize your website donation page, and Chapter 16 for tips on email campaigns.

8. Report Back

The key to keeping your donors loyal and engaged is effectively communicating the impact their donations have on your cause. *When your campaign ends, let donors know whether you reached your goal and be honest if you didn't*; donors appreciate transparency. Thank them, communicate the impact their donations are having, and be *specific* about work that you will accomplish because of their support. Send ongoing updates when you hit milestones and see successes, and remind donors that it was their contributions to the campaign that made it possible. Update the campaign page on your website or blog, and post to social media with the same information.

Conclusion

The key to successful year-end and annual appeals and membership campaigns is remembering that it isn't about your organization; it's about your loyal base of donors. Put yourself in *their* shoes, and understand why they care about your cause and why they give to your organization. When you craft campaign messages, write as if you're addressing a specific donor;

avoid generic language that doesn't connect with donors. Convey the impact their donations have on a regular basis in order to steward them and sustain their support year after year. Build membership campaigns around benefits that reflect your organization's mission, and plan campaigns with themes that are integrated across all of your best fundraising channels. Continuously improve your efforts and fundraising results by paying close attention to your data and looking at previous efforts and industry standards. When done well, these appeals and campaigns can raise the bulk of your critical general operating support and provide a dependable base of support for your work.

Do's and Don'ts

Do. . .

> . . . create an editorial calendar to map out your campaign and ensure strategic timing, frequency, and integration with any other competing messages or campaigns.

> . . . send a higher-end direct mail piece at the end of the year to existing donors to cut through the clutter, perhaps in an envelope that's not a standard size.

> . . . give prospects an action to take besides giving to engage them.

> . . . regularly survey or interview your donors to find out what they're passionate about and what member benefits or programmatic issues would be most compelling.

Don't. . .

> . . . choose member benefits that have no connection to your organization; make sure they reflect your mission and are of value to donors.

> . . . forget to send a personalized thank you message, in addition to an automated donation receipt.

> . . . ignore donors once the campaign ends; send monthly updates and provide other opportunities to keep them engaged.

> . . . fail to analyze your campaign once it's completed; take a close look at the data to see how it performed.

About the Expert

Farra Trompeter is vice president of Big Duck, a communications firm that exclusively works with nonprofits. Since joining in 2008, she's led dozens of organizations through major brand overhauls, multichannel year-end and annual campaigns, successful membership campaign launches, and more. She's a frequent speaker around the country on topics such as the link between branding and fundraising, donor engagement, and social media strategy, and she serves as vice chair on the board for the Nonprofit Technology Network (NTEN). Trompeter is also an adjunct professor at New York University and The New School.

Resource Review

Here are three helpful studies that provide industry benchmarks for email and online fundraising. Whenever you rethink your strategy, start by comparing your current performance against past results. You should also compare your data against your peers using some or all of these studies:

> M+R Annual Online Fundraising Benchmark Study: mrbenchmarks.com
> Network for Good Digital Giving Index: www1.networkforgood.org/
> digitalgivingindex
>
> Blackbaud Index of Online Giving: https://www.blackbaud.com/
> nonprofit-resources/blackbaud-index

Fundlio's Top 20 Fundraising Blogs (http://fundlio.com/blog/best-fundraising-
blogs)
   Online fundraising platform Fundlio took the time to write up great descriptions of their favorite blogs, including Big Duck's and many others from *Nonprofit Fundraising 101* interviewees. These are great resources for staying abreast of trends in the industry.
NTEN: The Nonprofit Technology Network (NTEN.org)
   A membership organization aimed at helping nonprofits master technology for social change. Their annual conference, NTC (ntc.nten.org), covers all aspects of nonprofit technology, fundraising, and communications, and also offers a sneak peak at the findings of many of the reports outlined above.

Which Test Won (https://WhichTestWon.com)
> This is a great resource to learn more about testing, where you can review the tests and results from different emails and web pages and learn which performed better. This is a great, fun tool to help you figure out what works and apply test results to improve your programs.

The Chronicle of Philanthropy (https://philanthropy.com)
> A weekly periodical that also publishes an online edition. This is a great resource for finding articles and case studies about crafting fundraising campaigns and appeals, as well as the latest trends in the industry.

The Agitator (www.theagitator.net/)
> A great online blog from industry experts Tom Belford and Roger Craver that provides information and advice on nonprofit fundraising and direct marketing strategies.

Warwick, Mal. *How to Write Successful Fundraising Appeals* (3rd ed.). Jossey-Bass, 2013.
> The thought of writing a fundraising appeal may make you nervous. This book, the standard text in the field, will show you the way to succeed.

Association of Fundraising Professionals (www.AFPnet.org)
> This is the leading association for development professionals. In addition to publishing helpful resources and providing great content for professional development, they host an annual national conference as well as several regional conferences, often referred to as "Fundraising Days," which feature leading experts and current examples.

Big Duck (www.BigDuckNYC.com)
> Their blog regularly features articles about fundraising campaigns and suggested fundraising and marketing approaches, as well as lots of great content on branding, communications, social media, and more.

Chapter 12

Event-Based Fundraising

"A mind that is stretched by a new experience can never go back to its old dimensions."

—Oliver Wendell Holmes, Jr.

Introduction

In today's digital age, much of our fundraising and relationship-building happens through technology. It is becoming less common for fundraisers to have personal interactions with donors, but these are still critical when raising funds and developing connections. Events are an important way to engage with donors and create an experience that not only brings awareness to your cause, but also inspires a sense of community among supporters and generates much-needed funds. They're also an important way to engage with Millennials and younger audiences. Eventbrite found that over 75 percent of the Millennials they surveyed would rather spend money on a desirable experience—such as an event—versus simply donating, and over two-thirds said events make them feel more connected to a cause. It's crucial that your nonprofit effectively engage your next generation of donors, and events are one key to doing this.

Events require a significant amount of time and effort and aren't often an organization's primary source of funding. However, when done right the benefits you reap with a successful event far outweigh the resources you invest in it. Events can play a key part in cultivation and stewardship strategies, making critical differences in your efforts with major donors, foundations, and important allies like partners and board members. Live events will help you reap additional donations from key supporters and inspire new ones to join you. They're key marketing opportunities and great ways to get your cause and story in front of more people, and events provide a focal point for people to rally to your cause.

There are endless types of events, but all of them should reflect your organization and fit within your fundraising strategy. If your goal is to identify and cultivate a small group of high net worth donors, think about having a small event at the home of a board member or major donor. If you're a small, grassroots organization fighting economic injustice, you probably don't want to throw an expensive and fancy gala. Whatever your strategy, events provide an opportunity to inspire people in ways that other forms of communication simply cannot.

To learn more about maximizing the fundraising potential of nonprofit events, I sat down with Tracy Kosolcharoen, marketing manager and nonprofit lead at Eventbrite, and Daniel Lurie and Jen Pitts at Tipping Point Community. They shared ten great practical insights and tips to help you bring more money in the door.

Critical Skills and Competencies

1. Identify Specific Goals

What is the primary goal of your event—raising money, identifying new donors, spreading awareness, or promoting your cause? According to Lurie and Pitts, *the key to success is a clear purpose that drives and focuses all of your efforts*. Once you've identified your primary goal, you need to set additional, specific event goals, like number of attendees, tickets sold, money raised, and so forth. Take the time to think through the impact of your event. What will you accomplish, and *why* are you doing this? You need to be able to clearly communicate the purpose and impact of your event in marketing materials and to the supporters who join you in person.

Think about your key stakeholders—donors, board, volunteers, staff, vendors, and more—and ask yourself: What do we want the experience to be like for them? Remember, *your event begins long before the actual day*; it begins the moment you start talking to people about it.

2. Create a Calendar and a Budget

Create a calendar and work backward from your event date. List all necessary tasks (such as creating marketing materials, securing volunteers, selling tickets, securing sponsors and auction items, solidifying logistics like venue and catering) and assign deadlines and people responsible for each item. Create a *conservative* budget that estimates the revenue you expect, plus all related expenses. Use past events as a baseline if possible, justifying any increases in expectations, and keeping those to 10 to 25 percent, unless there's a significant change in format. If this is your first event, think through how many tickets, tables, and sponsorships you can realistically sell. And be conservative when it comes to your expenses as well, especially around items like beer and wine that you hope to have donated.

Once you have a reasonable budget, including both projected revenue and expenses, compare those two numbers. *If you don't project raising at least twice as much as you spend, then don't call it a fundraiser*. That's not to say you shouldn't do the event, but think of it as a "friend raiser" or networking event to manage expectations. Keep people accountable to the budget and your deadlines by holding regular meetings to assess your progress.

3. Recruit Key People

Your next step is mobilizing the human resources needed to succeed. These people, including staff, board, volunteers, and key supporters, will be critical to maximizing your fundraising results. *Recruit an event committee at least six months out*, so that you have a team of people helping to focus and drive your efforts. Key duties and roles include recruiting and managing volunteers, coordinating logistics, promoting ticket sales, securing auction items, and most importantly, enlisting speakers, performers, in-kind and media partners, and sponsors and table captains. If you have enough people on your committee, divide their roles and assign responsibility for these.

As detailed in Chapters 3 and 4, when engaging your board or volunteers in fundraising, the key to success is making it as easy as possible for them to support you. Again, think "low touch, high value" and *create toolkits with sample emails and social media posts and images to facilitate outreach*. This is helpful to drive ticket sales down the road, and to securing sponsors, table captains, and partners when you're starting out. And as we discuss in Chapter 17, Social Media and Crowdfunding, "seeding the tip jar" helps drive support, so tap this inner circle of supporters to secure initial ticket sales, event hosts, and sponsors *before* engaging the public.

Ensure expectations are clearly communicated to everyone you recruit, and that you leverage them strategically so they feel engaged and see the impact of their contributions.

4. Secure Sponsors

If your event strategy includes securing corporate, individual, or foundation sponsorships, ***begin outreach at least six months in advance***. Securing sponsors requires time and cultivation, and many institutions need months to budget for this support.

Think through what you are asking of sponsors, and what you are offering in return. Having a solid sponsorship package that outlines the various levels and associated benefits will be key in driving results. Even if you're soliciting people and foundations, ***the most effective event sponsorship proposals typically follow the corporate framework outlined in Chapter 23 and include an option for table captains***, also known as event hosts. Table captains typically buy eight to ten tickets and receive recognition at the program, plus entry to a VIP reception beforehand if you include that in your agenda. Often, their guests will pay for their tickets anyway, resulting in twice the revenue. And as discussed in Chapter 25, pursue in-kind and media sponsorships using your corporate proposal as a template, and then make a few edits to customize it for this audience.

When reaching out to sponsorship prospects, start with past event sponsors and your biggest supporters. Thank them for their patronage and remind them of the impact they've made possible before inviting additional support. For example, with the $100 million Tipping Point Community raised over the past ten years, they've impacted nearly 500,000 people living in poverty. In addition to these big numbers, they often personalize impact by sharing individual stories of those who've benefited from their work.

Finally, remember that providing sponsors with a great experience is key to securing their support in the future. Nurture these valuable relationships, and make sure to fulfill and over-deliver on any promises you make. And take the time to figure out what's most important to these key partners so you can be sure to meet their needs. For example, ask sponsors what information they'd like to know about your audience, and then integrate relevant questions into the registration process or follow-up surveys.

5. Build a Strong Event Page

All-in-one event registration platforms like Eventbrite allow you to easily build an integrated event page to sell tickets and promote your event. *Your goal with the event page is to maximize your conversion rate*, meaning the percentage of people who visit the page who actually sign up to attend.

The first step to improving your event page's conversion rate is leveraging your prime content areas, including the upper-right-hand corner of the page, the middle of the page "above the fold," and in your navigation bar. "Above the fold" is an old newspaper term, meaning people see it without needing to scroll down or flip the page. These key areas are where you want to share the what, where, when, and how of your event, and *be sure to focus on only one call to action*. Ideally, create a button that says "Sign up now," "Order Tickets," or "Register."

Once people click on the button, *offer group registration options and provide people with opportunities to donate if they are unable to attend*. Use a tool like Eventbrite to ensure your event page is compatible with mobile devices, able to be integrated with your database or CRM, and that it enables people to easily share the event information through email and social media. *It's critical that you use a platform that prompts people to invite their friends to attend immediately after registering*. Just as with online fundraising, making it easy for people to invite their social networks to follow their lead after they donate or sign up drives huge results; in fact, Eventbrite discovered that 67 percent of event shares happen after registration and that *every Facebook share is worth $4 in ticket sales*. Social media shares can also drive "FOMO," or fear of missing out, since people considering attending can see which of their friends registered and be motivated to do the same.

One final note on the registration portion of your event page: keep it simple and ask only for necessary information. Eventbrite's research established a clear, direct correlation: *the more fields in your registration form, the lower your conversion rate*. Part of this is due to load time—the Aberdeen Group found that a one-second delay decreases conversion rates by 7 to 10 percent. You can always collect more details later, so focus exclusively on securing the information you need to register people. If you really want to know what music people want, secure input on the direction of the event, or figure out which conference sessions people plan to attend, send a follow-up email after people sign up.

6. Promote Your Event

Now that you have your team and plan in place, as well as your event registration page, it's time to spread the word. Start by leveraging your existing networks and outlets, including social media, public relations, your newsletter, mailing list, etc. Eventbrite found that *email is the most effective way to recruit event attendees*, followed by social media, particularly Facebook and Twitter. *Coordinate and plan all your outreach in an editorial calendar*, as detailed in Chapter 17.

Remember that you're not in this alone: engage your events committee and volunteers, possibly including a social media marketing committee, also outlined in that chapter. Recruit any event speakers or VIPs to this team, reminding them the commitment is limited to just five minutes a week and providing outreach toolkits to make emailing and posting as easy as cut and paste. Ideally, give each person or partner on your event committee a unique tracking link or URL so you can easily gauge which team members proved most valuable as you plan future events.

Collectively, all this outreach drives excitement and momentum. This is crucial since typically *people need to hear about an event six times before they sign up*. Beyond the peer-to-peer and organizational marketing, don't forget that media sponsors are another great way to generate tremendous exposure, as detailed in Chapter 25. Finally, if you have a Google Grant, leverage AdWords to drive traffic to your event page, and add keywords there to maximize search engine rankings.

7. Understand the Ticketing Lifecycle

According to Eventbrite, most nonprofits *launch ticket sales six to eight weeks out*, which they've identified as a best practice. Kosolcharoen recommends you *provide a 10 to 20 percent early bird discount for the first two weeks* to drive initial registrations, since *40 percent of events sell less than half their tickets until the week of the event.* This results in tremendous stress; plus it complicates planning and logistics, such as catering orders. Anything you can do to combat people postponing their registrations will help on many levels, but be sure that you're covering your costs before offering any discounts.

Use social media to build momentum and encourage early signups with things like hashtags, which allow you to track and encourage conversations around your event, and which can result in your event trending on social media. Use free tools like Twubs or Hashtag.org to look these up and ensure no one else is using them, or simply search on Twitter itself. We talked about FOMO earlier; Eventbrite found that 80 percent of Millennials experience and are driven by this phenomenon. To capitalize on it, ***offer incentives through contests promoting your hashtag, price discounts, or reserved seating to drive ticket sales.*** Invite people to tweet about your event in exchange for a chance to win tickets, or hold a contest where the person with the most retweets or shares gets to meet a VIP or keynote speaker.

8. Create an Agenda

Well before event day, it's very helpful to ***map out a detailed timeline, or "Q2Q," for your program***, including time for both preparation and breakdown. Map out a realistic agenda and leave in cushions, because things almost always run late. Here's a typical sample agenda for a donor event, including a few tips for each component:

- Welcoming Reception (cocktails, appetizers, and time to mingle; Jazz or other light background music; if you have a VIP Reception, it typically happens here in a private room)
- Food Service (dinner or lunch with sit-down service for more formal events; it's ideal to wait until plates are cleared before starting the program to avoid background noise)
- Welcoming Remarks (two-to-three-minute welcome from a key board member, MC, or sponsor; this can also be accomplished via a short video)
- Client Testimonial/Mission Moment (a client shares the impact of your work on his or her life, personalizing your work; can also be a brief partner report speaking to your effectiveness and the impact of a compelling program/project. Either way, this can also be accomplished via a short video)
- Live Auction (use an experienced auctioneer if possible; secure minimum bids ahead of time to ensure responses and kick-start momentum; packages revolving around unique prizes that money can't buy, like lunch with a celebrity, are ideal)
- Presentation from Executive Director (outline the history and impact of the organization; share the event's purpose and fundraising goal and the overall impact it will make possible)

- The Ask (pass around donation envelopes and have volunteers poised with mobile devices to collect donations—see insert below for detailed process and tips)
- Announce the Results (thank the audience and let them know how much was raised and what these funds will allow you to accomplish)

This may sound like a lot to get through, but in fact, you're best off keeping your program as short as possible. After years of experimentation, Tipping Point Community recommends you *keep the spoken portion of your program to 15 to 45 minutes*. If you're hosting a small, casual event—especially one where people remain standing—keep it to no more than 15 to 20 minutes. If it's a larger, more formal event like a gala or luncheon, keep your presentation to less than 45 minutes. If you talk for too long, you'll lose people's attention. *Give your speakers and presenters clear guidance and provide them with key messages and talking points* in advance. And definitely take the time to rehearse with them before the big day.

9. Maximize Your Ask

There are lots of ways to raise funds on site at your event, including silent and live auctions, "fund a need"s, and of course, making an ask. If one of your main event goals is fundraising, then—unless there's a compelling reason—*it's crucial you explicitly and directly invite people to donate* and support your good work. There are different approaches for doing this, including the one detailed below by one of my personal heroes, Van Jones. Not surprisingly, after raising more than $100 million, in large part via their annual benefit, Tipping Point Community has dialed in their unique recipe for success.

As with many nonprofits, the CEO and founder, Daniel Lurie, has traditionally been the spokesperson who makes the big fundraising ask. Tipping Point creates an exciting, dynamic environment that evokes peer pressure and friendly competition to maximize giving. After sharing the overall work of the organization to date, and the impact its current campaign will unlock, he tells the audience that the group's board underwrites all operating expenses—so every dollar raised goes directly to the cause—and, when possible, shares a matching or challenge grant to inspire giving.

In partnership with an auctioneer, Lurie then invites attendees to stretch themselves as much as they can, with gifts ranging from $25 to more than $1 million. Over the years, Tipping Point has experimented with using glow sticks as bidding paddles, asking everyone to bid at once using event technology like LUMI, and visibly opting in at various pledge levels. Of course, there are donation envelopes on the tables for people to complete, as well as volunteers poised to assist donors with giving. Pitts cautions double-checking your cellular and Wi-Fi connection before experimenting with various technologies and mobile phone–based giving transactions. Finally, just as with auction items, Lurie advises securing some gifts in advance if you plan to invite support at various levels, which helps inspire others to follow suit and match giving.

Van Jones' Live Ask Recipe

In all my years of fundraising and running in nonprofit circles, I've been to lots of galas and fundraising events. Hands down, I've never seen anyone better at making an ask at a live event than Van Jones, CNN correspondent and president and co-founder of Dream Corps. I sat down with him to learn a few of his secrets, and he graciously shared his formula for unlocking support.

Establish credibility. Speak to your past impact and the strengths as an organization. Focus on your accolades and accomplishments, versus the needs or challenges of your organization. Frame your work and progress as powerfully as possible; remember that *people want to be part of a winning team, not bail out a sinking ship*. It's also helpful to share a quick story to put a face to your work; perhaps you talk about Martin, the 15-year-old who dropped out of school, but whom you helped to get back on track, and who is now a successful college student.

Humanize your work. Notwithstanding the last comment, it's still important to authentically share the passion and dedication needed to drive impact. Have one of your staff members share the obstacles you've overcome along the way, including those he or she faced in their personal role. Jones finds this often to be even more effective than talking about the people in need, since your audience can identify with them as peers, and they believe in and want to support their good work.

As Jones says, "It's getting people to think about, 'How can I help this person, who's doing something every day that's hard and that I believe in, but the fact is, I'm not doing it myself? Look at the sacrifice this person is making; their time, their life, their energy. What can I do to help them be more effective?' These are your good, hard-working peers who need you to chip in." Instead of merely sharing the same pitch as

(continued)

(continued)

every other organization, with an exclusive focus on the need, the numbers, and maybe some anecdotes, don't be afraid to pull the curtain back on how difficult—and even scary—the work can be and what keeps you going. *Be vulnerable* and share your emotional roller coaster, and let the audience know how much is riding on the event as you head into the next day, the next week, and the next month. ***Help attendees realize that what they do in the next few moments is going to really make a difference for the people you serve, and also on your staff's ability to help them***.

Communicate the need. Now that people understand the human impact of your work on both staff and clients, it's time to share the event goal and help your audience understand the increased impact their support will make possible. Be clear about what you're raising money for and *exactly* how it will make a difference. Communicate a specific overall dollar amount and impact, and clarify what specific gift amounts can enable, similar to the gift string concept outlined in Chapter 15.

For example, "With your support, we aim to raise $10,000 tonight, which will allow us to help 50 at-risk kids, just like Martin. Every gift of $200 empowers us to provide a mentor and after-school programming for a child in need. For every $1,000 we raise, we can expand our programs to a new school, and every $2,500 underwrites our expansion into another low-income community like West Oakland." If you have a projector, display these levels of giving and associated impact on the screen, using compelling photos to visually enforce each.

Make the ask. Before diving into the ask, make sure you express gratitude for the support your attendees have already provided simply by registering or sponsoring the event. Remind them that their presence is a demonstration of their commitment to the cause. Then start your ask and ***make it clear you're excited to invite their support, and let them know you are also a donor*** by saying something like, "I now have the honor of inviting you to *join me* in supporting this crucial work." Be real and authentic, and remind them that their support will help create more success stories like the one they just heard. ***Have volunteers pass out donation envelopes and pens, but tell the audience not to fill them out yet***.

Once everyone has an envelope, take a breath and ask the audience to take a moment to reflect on everything they've heard.

Let silence do some of the work, since getting your attendees to be fully present is critical. Jones says this is the part of the program where you have to "stop the show." You've talked about the work, the impact, the stories, and about the passion of the staff, but often many attendees are likely trying not to get "shaken down" too badly and want to get out of the event as cheaply as possible. *Stopping the show is the key to fighting this lowest common denominator.* To do that, you ask for the attendees' presence, in the form of handing them the donation envelope, but telling them not to fill it out, but instead to reflect for a moment.

Instead of immediately asking them to complete the form, *invite your audience to think about a donation amount that they'd be proud to announce* if they had to come up on stage and read it out loud. As Jones shares, "Can you honestly say that this number, given what you now know—how important this is to people doing this work—is a number you'd be proud to stand up and yell out? If it's not, you should pick another number, because I might call on you! Then, once they pick that number they're proud of, push it one step further and say, 'OK, what if you went one level higher? Could you pay your bills? Is everything going to be OK? Who's willing to go one click higher? Just raise your hand. We don't even care what the click is, it's just who's willing to go one level higher?'"

Just as your organization is stretching as it seeks to expand its impact, invite them to stretch with you. To Jones' point, ask them to think about their intended gift amount, and then to contemplate the difference it would make in their lives if they were to add a zero, or check the next box over. What kind of sacrifices would they need to make? And then invite them to consider the impact that additional contribution would make possible for your staff and the people you serve. And then, finally, invite attendees to complete their envelopes.

Your goal when doing all this isn't to inspire your most loyal donors; they're likely already committed to supporting your work to the full extent possible. Rather, you're looking to untap the potential of the 75 percent of your attendees who, with proper motivation, can go from giving nothing to writing a check for $500, or even $5,000.

Close the ask. Once you've secured the presence of your audience, had them contemplate their donation amounts, invited them to stretch with you, and asked them to fill out their

(continued)

(continued)

donation forms, you'll need to fill a few minutes. Jones likes
to use this time to share a personal story, whether his own or
that of another donor who stretched financially and witnessed
the impact it unlocked. Often he'll invite a board member up
to talk briefly at this point, which provides a public forum of
recognition for one of your major donors.

Either way, the message you're looking to convey here is
that this isn't about them; it's about donating to the cause with
humility. Your speaker should communicate why he or she is
taking a stand, underscoring the hard work and commitment
of the staff, the tremendous value the organization offers
the community, and gratitude to the supporters—like your
attendees—who make it all possible. Once people have filled
out their forms, thank them for their incredible support, and
encourage the volunteers to start collecting the envelopes.

10. Follow Up and Debrief

Your event doesn't end when everyone goes home. Seize the opportunity to
maximize the experience and ride the wave of goodwill created. ***Thank people
as soon as possible after the event for their attendance and donations,
ideally with calls and hand-written notes*** from your executive director or
key board members. Make them feel celebrated. Share the goals you reached
and the impact their contributions will make possible. Per Chapter 23, send
sponsors impact summaries and ask about their experience, looking for clues
on how you can improve in future years. You can even send a post-event
survey using tools like Eventbrite or SurveyMonkey to collect key data
points, input, and overall approval ratings. ***Debrief with your staff and key
volunteers*** to get their input on what went well and what needs work in the
future. Capture all of this and reference it closely when planning future events.

Conclusion

Of all the ways to raise money while building relationships with your
supporters, events are one of the most powerful. No other form of fundraising
allows you to give people a *shared*, in-person experience that can inspire
generosity and loyalty. A well-organized and professionally executed event can
deliver new donors, increase the giving of existing supporters, create a strong
sense of community and impact, and rally people and partners to support your

cause and take action. When done right, your events will create a positive, long-term memory for people that serves as a keystone in your relationships. To maximize your success, make sure that your event is focused, well planned, and properly promoted, and that it leverages key resources, including your existing support network, sponsors, and partners, and an event registration platform. And remember: things *always* go wrong at events, but your audience rarely notices. They only see what happens in front of the curtain, so provide them with the best experience possible, and you will reap the rewards.

Do's and Don'ts

Do. . .

> . . . send out a save the date as soon as you confirm your date and venue.

> . . . select an event registration platform that integrates with social media, your CRM, and other key technology platforms.

> . . . use unique tracking links or discount codes so you can analyze which partners, volunteers, and campaigns drive ticket sales.

> . . . have your keynote speaker or a supportive celebrity or VIP send out your event invitation to drive response rates.

> . . . have a Twitter wall at your event so people can read and contribute tweets branded with your event hashtag.

Don't. . .

> . . . start or end your event late; it demonstrates disrespect for your attendees' time and is unprofessional.

> . . . let the verbal program of your event run longer than 45 minutes.

> . . . let anyone speak at your event without first giving him or her talking points and rehearsing.

About the Experts

Tracy Kosolcharoen is marketing manager at Eventbrite, an organization that helps nonprofits use technology to improve event strategies and increase fundraising and awareness for their causes. Prior to spearheading nonprofit events at Eventbrite, Kosolcharoen managed marketing at American Express and OpenTable.

Daniel Lurie is the CEO and founder of Tipping Point Community, a San Francisco–based nonprofit that raises money for the fight against poverty. Previously, Lurie worked for the Bill Bradley Presidential Campaign, Accenture Consulting, and the Robin Hood Foundation. In 2013, Lurie chaired the successful Bay Area Super Bowl bid to host Super Bowl 50. He serves on the board of directors for Single Stop USA, the Mimi and Peter Haas Fund, and the Levi Strauss Foundation.

Jen Pitts is the managing director of communications, events, and development at Tipping Point Community, which raises about half of their $21 million budget from their annual event. Prior to Tipping Point, Pitts spent four years working in communications, events, and special projects at the Robin Hood Foundation.

Resource Review

Eventbrite (www.eventbrite.com)
   Eventbrite is a leading event registration platform, with a special focus on serving nonprofits. Check out their Event Academy at www.eventbrite.com/academy to find fundraising, sponsorship, and volunteer management resources, including case studies, templates, and a valuable blog.
Ortiz, Claire. *Twitter for Good: Change the World One Tweet at a Time.* Jossey-Bass, 2011.
   This is a great book that breaks down how nonprofits can leverage social media to promote their causes and events.
Kingston, Kathy. *A Higher Bid: How to Transform Special Event Fundraising with Strategic Auctions.* Jossey-Bass, 2015.
   This book offers a fresh approach to fundraising and walks you through how to make a benefit auction one of the centerpieces of your next fundraising event.
The Nonprofit Times (www.thenonprofittimes.com)
   Find a variety of helpful resources on nonprofit issues, and check out their article "9 Rules for Event Planning."
Grayson, Harriet. *Special Events Planning for Non-profits.* Ocean Breeze Press, 2015.
   This book is a guide to creating, designing, organizing, implementing, and evaluating special events for nonprofits.

Network for Good Blog (www.fundraising123.org)

Find a lot of helpful resources on nonprofit issues, including planning, implementing, and evaluating the success of events. Check out their article "Planning and Executing a Successful Nonprofit Fundraising Event" and the whitepaper "Analyze This: A Nonprofit's Guide to Event Fundraising Analytics," which highlights key metrics and best practices that drive event fundraising success.

Nolo (www.nolo.com)

Find helpful templates, contracts, and worksheets on a variety of topics, including nonprofit events, and check out their article "Special Events 101 for Nonprofit Fundraising." Attend other fundraising events of like-minded organizations. This is a great way to learn best practices, see pitfalls to avoid, and find inspiration.

Chapter 13

Runs, Walks, and Rides
Community-Based Fundraising

"Without a sense of caring, there can be no sense of community."
—Anthony J. D'Angelo

Introduction

According to Running USA, 20 million adults in the United States participate in competitive runs. And they estimate that three times as many adults run recreationally, meaning approximately one-fifth of the U.S. population. You'll hear me say this in other chapters, but it's worth repeating since it's so important: *you have to meet your donors where they're at*. To build a base of individual supporters, typically you need to reach out to and engage the masses, and community-based fundraising events like runs, walks, and rides are a great way to do this.

Runs, walks, and rides are not only great ways to reach large audiences; they're also a great platform to bring people together and create a powerful sense of community, pride, and accomplishment. Humans associate with one another through shared experiences. Participants in your events will associate their feelings of community with you, leaving a lasting impact and providing you with valuable future fundraising opportunities.

To learn more about organizing successful community-based peer-to-peer fundraising, I sat down with Jeff Shuck, founder and CEO of the nonprofit consultancy Plenty. Shuck believes that in today's technology and social media–driven world, more and more of our daily lives are influenced by our peers. We check out restaurants on Yelp, buy things based on recommendations from people we've never met on Amazon, and see news stories from our friends' Facebook newsfeeds. *Our world has become peer-driven and to succeed, fundraising efforts need to follow suit.* Runs, walks, and rides are opportunities for you to share your pride in raising money with others, who in turn take it into their communities. Not only will they raise money from their peers for you, but they raise awareness of your cause and inspire others to join them.

To guide you on your efforts to produce successful runs, walks, and rides, Shuck shared an insightful seven-point plan, which also has implications for all forms of community-based peer-to-peer fundraising.

Critical Skills and Competencies

1. Prioritize and Focus

The first thing you need to ask when organizing a run, walk, or ride, is: "What is our primary purpose for doing this?" Is your top priority raising money or awareness, bringing in new supporters, or something else? Of course, you can accomplish more than one thing with your event, but *unless you decide on your number one priority, you won't be able to properly focus your efforts*. If your priority is raising awareness, you should focus on creating shareable marketing materials and asking participants to get the word out. If your priority is raising money, you should focus on providing fundraising materials and useful templates and coaching to participants. Whatever top priority you identify, be sure to focus your calls to action around it. *Don't overwhelm participants by asking them to do multiple things at once*.

2. Specify Your Audience

In general, the more people you engage in your event, the more money you'll raise. But be smart about recruitment. Don't make the mistake of defining your audience too broadly or trying to educate an entire city. *Start with people who are most connected to your cause as your core base*, and let them help you expand and reach new audiences. The more focused you are at first, the more people you'll eventually engage, since engaging your core audience deeply will result in powerful peer marketing. Plus, the more specific and targeted you are with your outreach, the more you'll get out of your social media and marketing efforts.

3. Ask Away

They say, "If you don't ask, you don't get." You need to explicitly *ask* people to participate in your run, walk, or ride, and you need to invite them to fundraise on your behalf. This sounds basic, but many organizations fail to be specific and forthright in their requests. Shuck says *the fundamentals of a good event ask are threefold: talk about the need you're addressing, specify the impact their support will make, and finally, make a direct, explicit ask.* Remember, if *it doesn't end in a question mark, it's not an ask*. For example, ask: "Will you support our cause?" instead of saying: "I hope you can help us." This sounds simple, but a question mark increases response rates.

The majority of giving for runs, walks, and rides happens online nowadays, so *your donation page is your main platform for making your ask.* Pay close attention to the language you use on the form, and make sure the donation levels or "gift string" you suggest don't sell you short. See Chapter 15 for more about donation forms and how to calculate suggested giving levels.

You will have two primary opportunities to ask people: when you ask them to sign up and when you ask them to recruit friends and raise money.

Ask People to Sign Up

Before you launch your event, get your board, staff, and key allies to sign up. This is the "seed the tip jar" notion discussed in Chapter 17 on crowdfunding. Once you've signed up the people in your inner circle, use every tool at your disposal to spread the word: social media, newsletters, website, emails, advertising, direct mail, media partners, etc. Focus on your core audience, and ask those who sign up to encourage their friends to follow their lead. *Provide registrants with templates and sample language for social media and email outreach and send reminders asking them to follow through.* There are many platforms on the market that will help facilitate this (see tip 7.)

Ask People to Donate

How you frame your fundraising asks is critical. Don't ask people to raise $1,000 for you; that sounds daunting. Instead, ask them to email five of their closest friends and family and ask for contributions to meet their fundraising goal of $1,000. Provide registrants with encouragement, guidance, and tools, such as communications templates, so they can easily make fundraising requests of their peers. Make sure they have the ability to customize these templates and that they understand the importance of personalizing each ask they put out. And remember to continually communicate, encourage, and inspire your participants with updates on the overall campaign and celebrate their successes. Personalize your communications with them and thank and congratulate them when they make progress toward meeting their individual fundraising goals.

4. Separate Logistics and Fundraising

There are two kinds of events: good events and bad events. Your goal, obviously, is to hold a great event that leaves your participants with fond memories, not nightmares. Make sure you take care of the basics, pay attention to the details, and carefully think through all logistics: securing permits, having good food and entertainment, staying on schedule, ensuring adequate facilities like restrooms, being handicap accessible, and so on. Ensure you *have a dedicated person responsible for event logistics who is separate from the person in charge of raising money, recruiting participants, and supporting their fundraising efforts*. Don't make the mistake of having the same person in charge of both the logistic and fundraising aspects. These are equally important parts of your event, and *both* need someone with the right experience and skillset focused and dedicated to ensuring its success.

5. Provide Good Service

Good stewardship is essential to successful fundraising, and the same is true for successful events. Think through all the problems people may have, leading up to and at the event, and prepare resources and answers for them in advance whenever possible. Where do people go if they have questions the day of? If I am injured on the course, is there someone there to support me? Who do I call about fundraising questions before the event? What happens if I don't know how to use the donation platform? What if I need to cancel my participation for some reason? Taking good care of your supporters goes a long way in ensuring a great experience and leaving these key allies with a positive impression of your organization. Remember, fundraising is about building long-term relationships, and cultivating and stewarding donors is a crucial part of that process. And this applies beyond simply putting out fires; *take the time to recognize your VIPs and top performers publicly and personally*, like the ones who raise the most money or recruit the largest team. These are the folks you want to drag on stage and thank them in front of a huge audience, and the ones your executive director needs to write hand-written letters to after the event.

6. Capture Everything

Your event participants, and the supporters they recruit, are valuable fundraising prospects. They are likely supporting you because of a close personal connection, but now that they've given, you have a chance to turn them into long-term donors. To do this, you'll need to communicate in a clear, compelling way, demonstrate appreciation for and the impact of their gift, and steward them over time. But that's next to impossible if you don't **secure their contact information in a database or CRM** (see Chapter 6 for details).

Thankfully, as outlined in Chapter 12, many of the leading event registration platforms integrate seamlessly with your CRM, facilitating this data collection and analysis. But however you're collecting information, be sure to capture people's email and mailing addresses, how much they raised and/or donated, and any other useful data points around their engagement. Did they share marketing materials or hold an event of their own to raise money or spread awareness? If so, add those notes in! **Use tools like surveys to gather more detailed information and feedback from participants**.

Not only do you want to capture information from your participants, but you should also collect event insights. **Host a post-event debriefing meeting with all staff and volunteers involved and talk through what was successful and what needs improvement next year**. Review your fundraising and attendance results and discuss whether they met your goals or fell behind. What factors contributed to this? It's important to learn from both your successes and disappointments and to honestly evaluate your efforts and the resources you dedicated to them.

7. Use Technology

In the previous tip, we listed some examples of the types of technology used to capture event data: survey tools, databases, CRMs, and event registration platforms. We've moved on from the days when nonprofits had huge wads of cash in shoeboxes at events.

There are numerous event management and peer-to-peer fundraising platforms available that make things like signing up attendees, accepting registration fees and donations, sending customized communications, and providing participants with fundraising and communication templates infinitely easier, more efficient, and more effective.

There are options for every type of event and organization. Some are lightweight and affordable; these are best for nonprofits doing small-scale events, and others are better suited for organizations running large or regular events. Some platforms only provide the basics, while others will guide you through your fundraising efforts and offer more sophisticated tools for engaging and interacting with participants. Take the time to find the right tool for you, and see the Resource Review below for a list of options and resources for evaluating platforms.

Case Study: Kyra Millich, Volunteer Fundraiser

Kyra Millich is an avid fundraiser and passionate participant in runs, walks, and rides. She raised just over $25,000 for the Leukemia and Lymphoma Society and the National Multiple Sclerosis Society. She was one of the top fundraisers at these popular events, even though she had little to no fundraising experience, and this is in large part due to her ability to share her personal passion and turn adversity into positive experiences that benefit others. After suffering a from the heartbreak of a failed relationship in 2003 and later being diagnosed with relapsed MS in 2013, Millich used these events to empower herself and do something meaningful about the issues she cares about. I asked Millich how she was able to excel and, in particular, what advice she'd give to nonprofits looking to foster engagement with their participants. She shared four simple tips.

Help People Overcome the Fear of Asking
It's important that your participants are proud to fundraise. Help them understand that they aren't asking their friends and family to donate to *them*; they're asking their loved ones to support a cause they care deeply about, like fighting a disease or finding a cure. Take a lesson from fundraising icons like Kay Sprinkel Grace and Lynne Twist and **teach your participants that they're simply the channel through which people give, and the vehicle that inspires them to make change**. Keeping these things in mind helped Millich feel confident, empowered, and proud to raise money for worthy causes.

Ask for More Than Money
Taking the time to think about what resources her friends and family had to offer beyond cash donations was crucial to Millich's success. For example, friends helped her secure wine, food, and venues for fundraising events, where she hosted a live auction and took bids

for a free session with an executive coach, a one-on-one yoga class, and even a date—all contributed for free by her friends. Some in her network also volunteered to ensure the success of her events. And most of these same friends became donors themselves! Help your participants think creatively about fundraising strategies and ways they can leverage their connections to raise more money, and suggest concrete examples that other participants put to work.

Make Them Storytellers
Millich found the communication templates and sample messages extremely helpful when conducting her outreach, as many times putting the right words to a fundraising appeal, or trying to articulate a disease concisely, can be challenging. These templates made her feel more comfortable and provided her with useful information about the cause. Ultimately, though, Millich is clear that it was her customization of these templates and inclusion of her personal story that led to her success. Teach your participants how to personalize materials and templates and briefly share their stories, especially regarding their personal connection to the cause. Once again, examples are very helpful here.

Be There
From making sure that participants know how to contact you for answers or advice, to providing materials and guidance, to going the extra mile and sending representatives to key participants' personal fundraising events, being there for your participants will help them feel supported and able to move past challenges and successfully reach the finish line. Always follow up with a thank you to all participants, even if it's simple words of encouragement and appreciation, and inspire them to stay involved.

Conclusion

Holding community-based fundraising events like a run, walk, or ride is an extension of your mission into the community. Make sure it's something you are proud of. This is a valuable opportunity to recruit new supporters and evangelists while raising money and awareness for your cause. Runs, walks, and rides are a unique way to foster connections between people and your cause and can provide your supporters with a sense of pride, accomplishment, and community. By paying attention to the details and properly servicing and stewarding your participants and the supporters they recruit, you will leave everyone with a great experience and wonderful memories that will have a lasting effect on your organization and its reputation.

Do's and Don'ts

Do. . .

> . . . use mobile devices to allow people to register and pay on-site the day of the event.

> . . . collect information on the supporters your fundraisers and participants recruit.

> . . . have an information station at the event for participants and attendees.

> . . . give participants the name, number, and email of a key staff contact for questions and support.

> . . . have your entire staff either working or participating in the event.

Don't. . .

> . . . have the same person in charge of the logistics and fundraising aspects of your event.

> . . . let your event get behind schedule.

> . . . launch your event registration to the public before getting key supporters signed up.

About the Expert

Jeff Shuck is founder and CEO of Plenty. For almost two decades, Shuck has been a motivator and thought leader in the nonprofit space. His specific areas of focus include nonprofit strategy and brand positioning, experiential and peer-to-peer fundraising, mission-based leadership, segmentation and forecasting, network modeling, and constituent analytics.

Resource Review

Plenty (www.plentyconsulting.com)
> Shuck's consulting firm has an active blog with a focus on runs, walks, and rides. They also publish an annual report on the topic and offer free webinars.

Running USA (www.runningusa.org)
  Running USA is the industry association for North American running
  events.

Idealware (www.idealware.org)
  Find articles, reports, training opportunities, and helpful resources such
  as the blog post, "A Few Good Tools for Peer-to-Peer Fundraising."

Peer-to-Peer Professional Forum (www.peertopeerforum.com)
  They hold the leading Run/Walk/Ride annual conference, which usually
  takes place in Atlanta or Orlando.

TechSoup (www.techsoup.org)
  Find a lot of helpful resources on their site, particularly the article, "A
  Few Good Online Event-Registration Tools."

Nonprofit Technology Network/NTEN (www.nten.org)
  Find lists and reviews of different technology platforms on their website
  and check out their annual Nonprofit Technology conference (NTC),
  where you can dive deeper and learn more about best practices and
  available technologies.

Event Management Solutions and Software

Eventbrite (www.eventbrite.com)
  Eventbrite will help you post and customize your event page, collect
  registration fees online and at your event via mobile devices, get the word
  out, and track your progress in real time. This is an affordable solution
  with dynamic offerings for nonprofits, and it integrates seamlessly with
  your CRM.

Classy (www.classy.org)
  Formerly StayClassy, this is an online and mobile fundraising platform
  that is great for runs, walks, and rides. They also have a very useful blog
  and offer free webinars for nonprofit leaders.

Convio TeamRaiser (www.blackbaud.com/TeamRaiser)
  This online event fundraising software is dynamic and well suited for
  large organizations or organizations that do regular walks, runs, and rides.

Cvent (www.cvent.com)
  Cvent provides online solutions for events and surveys. They provide
  mobile support and have custom solutions for nonprofits.

14

Fundraising Across the Generations

Millennials, Baby Boomers, and More

"If we do not plant knowledge when young, it will give us no shade when we are old."

—Lord Chesterfield

Introduction

Today, over half the world's population is under 30. Wherever you work around the globe, your successful long-term fundraising strategy depends on recognizing that there are generational differences in how people approach their philanthropy. Unfortunately, most nonprofits today are currently fundraising with a "one size fits all" or "cookie-cutter" approach, and not balancing their focus on younger and older donors. *To maximize fundraising results, you need to know who your donors are and adjust your strategies accordingly.* Your most generous donors today won't be around forever, so you need to equally focus your efforts on developing relationships with the next generation of contributors.

Effectively fundraising across the generations requires a multi-pronged approach that balances a focus on retaining your older, more generous donors (Baby Boomers and Seniors), while also making a long-term investment in building new kinds of relationships and cultivating younger donors (Gen-Xers and Millennials), who will contribute more as they age into their prime giving years. This *balance is the key to long-term sustainability*. You don't want to overvalue younger, newer donors at the expense of your loyal, older donors or vice versa.

To learn more about how to effectively engage different generations, I sat down with Alia McKee, principal of Sea Change Strategies, who was the primary research partner on the 2015 *Next Generation of American Giving Report*, and Derrick Feldmann, president of Achieve and lead researcher for the Millennial Impact Project. Before we dive into the seven tips and insights they shared on this crucial issue, let's review a few facts for context.

Note that while the data shared in this chapter is U.S.-specific, the insights and ideas apply to NGOs and charities worldwide, as the generations tend to behave similarly around the globe.

The Generations: What Fundraisers Need to Know

Millennial (Born 1981–1995)
- Millennials represent 11 percent of total U.S. charitable giving. *
- They are the largest generation: 80 million.**
- They spend a lot of money: $300 billion on consumer discretionary goods in 2014.*
- They're philanthropic: $16 billion of the $300+ billion donated in 2014.*
- They "get" marketing: the most marketed to generation in history.***
- They are inherently social: most likely generation to spread your message through social media.**
- They don't respond well to fundraising phone calls.
- For them, *the pinnacle of support is sharing your cause with their social network.*

Gen-X (Born 1965–1980)
- Gen-Xers represent 20 percent of total charitable giving.*
- Along with Millennials, Gen-Xers are far more likely to give online.
- Combined with Millennials, Gen-Xers represent 31 percent of all dollars donated (an aggregate total that exceeds giving by Seniors).*

- Sixty-two percent of Gen-Xers (and 70 percent of Millennials) feel more excited about a product or cause when their friends agree with them about it.*

Baby Boomer (Born 1946–1964)
- Baby Boomers represent 43 percent of total charitable giving.*
- At 78 million, they fall just below Millennials as the second largest generation.*
- Boomers report donating an average of $1,212 to between four and five charities each year (that's more than twice the average contribution for younger donors).*
- *2013 marked the first time that Boomers were just as likely to give online versus via direct mail.**

Senior (Born 1945 and earlier)
- Seniors represent 26 percent of total charitable giving.*
- Seniors give more on average than either Millennials or Gen-Xers, and support a wider array of charities.*
- Seniors are still most responsive to direct mail and telemarketing.
- Along with Boomers, nearly half of Seniors say that *monetary donations represent their most impactful contribution* to a nonprofit, compared to just over a quarter of younger donors).*
- In general, Seniors want to hear from someone of high authority in the organization.

Source: The 2015 Next Generation of American Giving Report
**Source: 2010 U.S. Census*
***Source: The Millennial Impact Report (see Resource Review below for a link)*

Critical Skills and Competencies

1. Track the Age of Your Donors

Knowing how old or young your donors are is the first step in fundraising across generations. You can *do this with data appends to your database or by collecting the information through offering incentives* like birthday gifts, messages, or extra content. You can also send out a survey using a tool like SurveyMonkey to collect key demographic information, including age. Most importantly, you should be talking to your key donors and learning about them, and then capturing this information in your CRM or database so you can segment your donors and prospects accordingly. (See Chapter 6 for more information on databases and CRMs.)

2. Listen

American culture values talking and eloquence, but in fundraising, listening to your donors and prospects is more important. Take the time to *find out what your generational cohorts are looking for, what kinds of messages are most compelling to them, which media and devices they want to use to communicate with you, how often they want to hear from you, and what they are willing to do besides donate*. Again, you can collect this kind of information in a survey, and incentives always help. You can analyze your results by age group and compare your findings to third-party research to gain insights about how to best communicate with your donors (see studies listed in Resource Review).

3. Identify Goals for Each Generation

Having goals for each generational segment will allow you to create specific tactics to achieve them. For example, if you want to increase your Boomer donor retention rate by 15 percent, you need to know what messages are most compelling to them and create a strategy to achieve your goal. If your goal is to increase new Millennial and Gen-X donors by 10 percent, then you can look at donor recruitment strategies, such as robust online engagement and volunteer programs. (Read more in tip number 5 below.)

4. Diversify Your Giving Channels

As outlined in Chapter 10, direct mail is far from dead, but it won't last forever. *Millennials and Gen-Xers are far more likely to give online*. According to the *Next Generation of American Giving Report*, *as of 2013, for the first time Boomers are just as likely to give online versus via direct mail*. Seniors are still more responsive to direct mail and telemarketing, while Millennials don't respond well to fundraising phone calls.

Your investments in particular fundraising strategies will pay off better if you focus them on the appropriate generation. However, before thinking social media is the best fundraising tool, consider that only 6 percent of people across generations gave that way, versus making website and mobile contributions. Every chapter in Part 4 provides insights on these various channels, but for now, it suffices to say that social media is best utilized as an engagement tool. Rather than ask for money, you should be asking people to spread the word and promote your cause and organization.

5. Know What Your Donors Want

Different generations respond to different approaches. In general, *Seniors want to hear from someone of high authority* in the organization and are more likely to trust the nonprofit to direct funds as needed, rather than needing to know exactly where their gifts go. Nearly half of Seniors and Boomers say that monetary donations represent their most impactful contribution to a nonprofit, compared to just over one-fourth of younger donors according to the *Next Generation* report.

Younger donors, especially Millennials, want to see their impact clearly. A young donor once told McKee: "It's not enough to tell me you are doing something good. I want to *see* it." They believe they can make the biggest difference by volunteering and by spreading the word to their networks. So **it's critical that you give younger donors and prospects meaningful things to do besides donating**, and have robust online engagement and volunteer strategies. And remember: regardless of age or generation, *no donor ever stops giving because he's thanked too much*. Make sure you clearly communicate how all donations map to impact. Millennials in particular want more updates throughout a campaign, rather than only at the end, so be sure to leverage email and social media to share these frequently.

6. Recognize the Power of Peers

If you want to engage younger donors, incorporating social media into your fundraising strategy is key. If they donate, they will likely tell their networks, creating an opportunity to not only enlist a donor, but also an evangelist, advocate, and fundraiser. The *Next Generation of American Giving* study found that 70 percent of Millennials and 62 percent of Gen-Xers feel more excited about a product or cause when their friends agree with them about it, as compared with 45 percent of Boomers and 40 percent of Seniors. *Younger donors are extraordinarily connected to their friends and are influenced by what their friends like.* You can **employ social media and crowdfunding to harness the power of peer influence**, simply by showcasing how many other young people are involved with what you're doing.

As outlined in Chapter 17, crowdfunding campaigns can be a particularly great way to engage and excite Millennials. In fact, according to the *Millennial Impact Report* 78 percent of Millennials have participated in peer fundraising campaigns, and many have actually run one themselves.

Moreover, it's typically their first exposure to fundraising, so you're leaving an indelible mark on future donors, plus their personal connections and stories help other new donors emotionally connect with your impact and work.

7. Create a Ladder of Engagement

Donor relationships are a journey, not a destination; your goal is to guide people from inaction to action, and that happens over time in myriad ways. Think of a ladder: you start at the bottom where your donor just learned about you, and then you move them up a rung by persuading them to visit your website. You move them further up when they share content on social media, come to an event, and then perhaps make a donation. *Map out the desired touch points and contributions you seek from supporters, and create a strategy for moving people from one rung to the next*, engaging them further at each step. Fundraising should only be one part of your goal; devote equal focus to getting them to take action, including signing petitions and telling their peers and social networks about you. Just like the donor pyramid discussed in many other chapters, the bigger the base, the more support is generated. This strategy will help you identify your strongest community ambassadors, who are ripe to move up the ladder and support you in other ways.

Conclusion

The long-term viability of your organization—in particular its fundraising success down the road—is dependent on your next generation of donors. Think of the major donors you have today. Will they be your major donors 20 or 30 years from now? By implementing the tips above you can balance your efforts between retaining your older, loyal donors and recruiting and engaging younger ones. Fundraising is a time-consuming and challenging task, and fundraising across generations may seem overwhelming. But if tackled over time, it doesn't have to be. Take it step by step. Start with collecting the necessary data, and ease into customizing your communications and approaches. Set goals and create strategies and tactics that you know you can implement, and hold yourself accountable to those goals. You'll gather critical insights that will help you to better create relationships and raise more money from all donors, ensuring your organization continues to thrive and deliver the impact you know to be possible.

Do's and Don'ts

Do. . .

. . . balance your desire to recruit tomorrow's donors with your need to maintain healthy relationships with today's loyal supporters.

. . . survey your donor base and find out how old they are, how they want to hear from you, and what they're willing to do besides donate.

. . . showcase peer involvement with social media and crowdfunding campaigns, especially when looking to recruit younger donors.

. . . make an effort to communicate more regularly with younger donors.

Don't. . .

. . . expect that the boom in online giving means that social media is a great place to raise money; think of it more as an engagement tool.

. . . quit sending direct mail or doing telemarketing, especially to Seniors.

. . . bother using telemarketing on younger donors.

. . . limit the ways people can contribute to your organization to only making a monetary donation.

. . . assume one message will work for all of your donors.

About the Experts

Alia McKee is a veteran online communications and fundraising strategist and principal of Sea Change Strategies, a boutique research and fundraising strategy consultancy that helps nonprofits transform their approach to fundraising by building deep relationships with donors and prospects, and the primary research partner for the 2015 *Next Generation of American Giving Report*. Alia is a noted speaker, author, and blogger, and her work has been featured in *Forbes, The Chronicle of Philanthropy*, on NPR, and more.

Derrick Feldmann is president and founder of Achieve, a research agency that helps causes and companies address their most pressing issues through research and data-driven awareness and fundraising campaigns. Feldmann is a sought-after speaker, researcher, and advisor and is the lead researcher for the *Millennial Impact Project*, a multi-year study of how the next generation supports causes.

Resource Review

The Next Generation of American Giving Report (www.blackbaud.com/ nonprofit-resources/generational-giving-report)
  This study shares a lot of practical tips for maximizing fundraising results across the generations.

The Millennial Impact Report (www.themillennialimpact.com/research)
  This annual study looks on how Millennials engage with causes directly, at the workplace, and with peers. With more than five years' of research, this is the most comprehensive study offering great insights for nonprofits looking to engage younger donors and allies.

MCON (www.mcon.events)
  This annual conference is affiliated with *The Millennial Impact Report* and provides a broad array of tips and tools for collaborating with next generation donors and supporters to create movements.

The Millennial Alumni Study (www.themillennialimpact.com/research)
  This study, done for *The Chronicle of Philanthropy* in 2014, looks at how Millennial alumni engage, work with, and view donating to their alma maters. The findings of this study help university fundraisers lay the groundwork for post-graduate relationships.

Sea Change Strategies (http://seachangestrategies.com)
  A consulting firm focused on helping nonprofits maximize fundraising results by getting to better know their donors and build deep relationships with them. Check out their whitepaper The Missing Middle: Why Neglecting Middle Donors Is Costing Non-Profits Millions.

Blackbaud BBCon (http://bbconference.com)
  Blackbaud's annual user conference frequently offers sessions on generational giving.

The Bridge Conference (www.bridgeconf.org)
  This annual direct marketing conference features discussions around generational giving and philanthropy.

Non Profit Crowdfunding Bill of Rights (www.kimbia.com/need-feedback-crowdfunder-bill-rights)
  This is an effort to define a set of standard expectations that legitimate crowdfunding and peer-to-peer campaigns should adhere to in order to ensure a well-managed, transparent, and effective experience.

Pew Research Center (www.pewresearch.org/topics/millennials)
Find a wealth of data and research done on the Millennial generation.

Saratovsky, Kari Dunn, and Derrick Feldmann. *Cause for Change: The Why and How of Nonprofit Millennial Engagement.* Jossey-Bass, 2013.

Written by Millennials about Millennials, this book examines strategies for engaging Millennials as constituents, volunteers, and donors and focuses on how organizations can realign themselves to better respond to this group of 80 million current and future supporters.

Case Study: LiNK (Liberty in North Korea).
This human rights organization raised over $500,000 from Millennials—learn about it at www.achieveguidance.com/2015/03/12/peerfundraising/

Part IV

Online Fundraising

Chapter 15

Maximizing Website Donations

"The Internet could be a very positive step towards education, organization, and participation in a meaningful society."
—Noam Chomsky

Introduction

According to M+R's 2015 *Online Fundraising Benchmark Study*, online revenue and the number of online gifts increased by 13 percent in 2014. Compare that to the 2 to 3 percent annual growth of overall nonprofit fundraising, and factor in the low barrier to entry for small, grassroots organizations, and you'll quickly grasp why online giving represents a huge opportunity, and why it's now an essential part of any successful long-term fundraising strategy.

People of all ages and generations have embraced the Internet as an essential part of their lives, including identifying and supporting the causes they're most passionate about. It's your responsibility to meet supporters where they're at, which is increasingly online. And this is especially true for reaching your next generation of donors: Pew Research recently found that 24 percent of teens now "live" online (see Resource Review). No matter what age donor you're courting, your website is likely the first place potential supporters will go to learn more about you, so ensuring a solid presence there is vital to fundraising. A great website will inspire people to donate to you, plus provide valuable, real-time data that will help you analyze why and how people give, allowing you to fine-tune your message and content.

To learn more about maximizing online giving, I sat down with Caryn Stein, vice president of communications and content at Network for Good, and editor of the Nonprofit Marketing blog. She outlined five solid tips that provide any nonprofit with a great starting point for raising the big bucks in a digital landscape.

Critical Skills and Competencies

1. Stay on Message

Your message is your message, no matter what medium you use to share it. It's imperative that you *integrate your website and online fundraising activities with your overall fundraising strategy and marketing plan*. What kind of people are you trying to reach, and what do you want them to do? Just as you should do with any marketing effort, think about how your website engages people and drives them to action. Do the look and feel of your website and online communications match the rest of your materials? Donors will find you through many channels, and you don't want them to feel a disconnect when doing so. Stay consistent and ensure your website and online marketing strategies are in line with your overall fundraising strategy.

2. Keep It Simple

Again, your website is the most likely place potential supporters and others will go to learn more about your work. In fact, Google's ThinkMobile report found that 54 percent of people rely on nonprofit websites to research organizations, compared to just 48 percent for search engines or social media, and 44 percent who base decisions on conversations with family, friends, and colleagues.

Moreover, while social media is a great platform to engage people, *the majority of online gifts come through the "donate" button on your website*. To build a strong online presence, you need a website that clearly illustrates who you are, what you do, why it matters, who supports you, and where the money goes. It doesn't have to be fancy or expensive; instead, it needs to be simple, focused, easy for donors to use and the nonprofit to update, reflective of your message, look and "brand," and ideally integrated with your social media and mobile presence. (More on those topics in Chapters 17 and 18.) As Stein says, "When I come to your nonprofit's website, I need to feel an instant emotional connection and immediately get what you do through images, colors, and fonts."

3. Make It Easy to Donate

Online attention spans are very short, and *you only have a few seconds to grab a potential donor*. Make sure your message is clearly communicated in an inspiring way on your website, and give people clear pathways to donate. It needs to be easy and fast for people to give online. *Each page of your website should have a prominent donate button* that directly leads to your donation page, and *it should never take more than three clicks to complete a donation from any page in your website*. On that page, quickly reinforce the emotions and the messages that drove them there.

Ideally, at the top of the page use an image that conveys your impact, featuring close-ups of people or animals, if appropriate. Minimize or eliminate text and "close the exit ramps," meaning remove any extraneous navigation routes so people can't click away. *Keep your donation form simple and reduce the number of required fields as much as possible*— you can always circle back for more information later, but the more you streamline the giving process, the more money you'll raise.

The exception to this rule is adding an option for recurring giving, meaning you *enable donors to give monthly, quarterly, or annually in addition to providing a one-time option*. This significantly increases the lifetime value of donors and keeps them connected to your cause, plus $10 a month may be easier for people to give, instead of a $120 contribution. Just make sure to lay out this giving option in a way that's simple and straightforward.

4. Suggest Gift Amounts

Follow the best practice of giving donors suggested donation amounts when they contribute. Anchor this "gift string" off of your average online gift. Your first option should be slightly less than your average, with your second option slightly over, and then the third and fourth options go even higher. This instantly increases online giving, since most people don't want to donate at the smallest amount. For example, if your average online gift is $35, then your options could be $30, $45, $75, and $100. Of course, *always leave a blank field for people to fill in the donation amount of their choice*.

Stein explained how suggesting donation amounts affects donor behavior through an anecdote from the book *Switch* (see Resource Review): An art museum placed a see-through donation box on-site, and when the box was empty, people walked right by it. When the box had coins in it, people gave coins. When the box had dollars in it, people gave dollars. People are unconsciously more comfortable following peer examples, which is why telethons like NPR typically answer the phone by saying something like, "Thanks for your call. The last woman who called in pledged $100. Would a gift that size work for you, or would you prefer to donate $200?"

If you fail to provide a gift string with default donation amounts on your website, you can create "analysis paralysis" for would-be donors, leaving supporters confused as to what's appropriate and potentially even resulting in them leaving without making a gift. Don't miss the opportunity to provide guidance on how much people should donate.

5. Optimize Your Presence

Once you have your donate button in place, the next step to maximizing website donations is having a tool in place to analyze traffic. Stein recommends Google Analytics (see link in Resource Review), which is free for nonprofits and easy to use. With that in place, you can test various things on your site and donation page to maximize results. Personally, I devised *a three-step experiment that reliably helps nonprofits double their online giving within one or two months*:

Optimize Your Donate Button

When Network for Good, a group that's raised over $1 billion for nonprofits online, wrote the online giving chapter in my last book, they shared a fascinating story. At one point they changed their donate button from gray to red, *instantly* resulting in a 30 percent increase in online donations! Now, I don't know if red is your color, or if your button should be round or square, or even what font you should use to make it stand out, but I do know that the answer typically isn't obvious. *Testing colors, sizes, and fonts—one at a time in the traditional A/B split methodology—will unearth the ideal donate button for you*. Take a few weeks to play with different options, and use Google Analytics or another tool to *figure out which combination maximizes the percentage of visitors to your site who click the button*. And remember: your donation button shouldn't necessarily blend in. Use different colors or fonts to make it stand out on your website. Your eye should be immediately drawn to it.

Test Suggested Donation Amounts

We already shared some thoughts on the importance of presenting a "gift string" when people reach your donation page, along with an approach for figuring out initial default donation levels. But that's just a starting point. Identifying *exactly* which suggested amounts maximize online contributions is a great use of your resources. Spend a few days or even a couple of weeks— depending on how long it takes you to attract at least 100 visitors to your donate page—with one set of donation amounts, and then assess your *average online gift*, as that's the metric you'll want to optimize against. Once you've ascertained that number, then experiment with two or three other default sets, at the end of which you'll know the optimal gift string for you.

Experiment with Impact

As Kay Sprinkel Grace shared in Chapter 9: "People don't give to you, they give *through* you." What does a $25 donation accomplish for your organization? Does it provide school supplies for one child, job training for a homeless person, or simply pay for an hour of staff time, which you can use to mentor a college student? Now that you've identified your optimal gift string, associate some kind of impact with each default donation level to communicate and concretize the incremental difference a donor can make at that level. ***Host a staff, board, and volunteer brainstorming session and come up with three or four impact examples for each donation amount.*** Start with no impact conveyed to set a benchmark—again the metric to look at here is average online donation size—and then run a series of tests swapping out the impact examples to see which ones perform best.

I've invited thousands of nonprofits all over the world to run this test and have yet to find a *single* one that was unable to double their online fundraising revenue after completing the experiment. If you are the first, I'd love to hear from you and learn from your experience. Feel free to email me directly at Darian@DarianHeyman.com.

Case Study: Mercy House

Mercy House is a $3.8M nonprofit that's provided housing and support to the homeless since 1989 in Santa Ana, California. In 2013 they partnered with CommitChange, a nonprofit fundraising platform who leveraged rapid A/B testing to **increase online giving by 110 percent in just six months**. Through their

(continued)

(*continued*)

experiments, they saw the most impact when implementing these three changes:

Break it Down: CommitChange helped Mercy House *break the donation process down into four steps—recurring versus one-time; amount; info; and payment*. Simplify each step, instead of asking for everything at once. This is increasingly important as more donors give through mobile devices, where long forms are especially overwhelming.

Promote Recurring Giving: The first step outlined above was selected very intentionally. Recurring giving options were only selected by about 2.5 percent of donors at first, but this exploded to 11.7 percent after the first screen of the donation process was dedicated *solely* to this choice, making it a much more prominent option.

Stay Consistent: Even though you're using a third party to power donation processing, remind donors what they're supporting and keep the look and feel consistent. *Ensure your logo is visible throughout the donation experience and integrate the design with your website*, so people don't feel a disconnect. This simple change directly led both to more people giving and to larger contributions.

Streamline Donations: Instead of a typical donate page, when visitors click the "Donate" button on any page at MercyHouse.net, a new window opens up exclusively dedicated to the donation process. This change improved their conversion rate and, on top of that, CommitChange discovered that *for every field eliminated from the donation experience, 2 percent more donors give*!

One last note: the learning never ends. Online giving climbed an *additional* 73 percent after another six months. Visit https://www.commitchange.com/ca/santa-ana/mercy-house-living-centers to learn how.

Conclusion

In the same *Online Fundraising Benchmark Study* referenced in the introduction, M+R also found that nonprofit website traffic grew by 11 percent in 2014. The point is that more and more people are using the

Internet to connect with, and support, organizations working on causes they care about. However, a visit to your website, or even to your donate page, is a far cry from money in the bank. Surprisingly, M+R found that only 13 percent of visitors to a nonprofit donate page actually completed making a gift. This means that it is critical that you build a website that is compelling, easy to navigate, and that inspires people to donate. People need clear pathways to your donation page, and once they're there, make it quick and easy to contribute, and dial in your exact formula using the tips above to maximize online donations. If you are new to online fundraising, don't be afraid to dive in and start small. Add a prominent donate button to your site and analyze your results through tools like Google Analytics. Keep your efforts simple and focused, and you will see results.

Do's and Don'ts

Do. . .

> . . . ensure the imagery and messages on your website are consistent with the rest of your marketing and fundraising plan.

> . . . add a prominent donate button to every page on your website, and double-check that it never takes you more than three clicks to complete a donation.

> . . . ensure your website is mobile-responsive (more in Chapter 18)

> . . . add a recurring gift option to your donate page and suggest default donation amounts.

Don't. . .

> . . . require people to set up an account in order to donate.

> . . . complicate your donation page; ask only for crucial information and streamline the giving experience.

> . . . assume older donors aren't giving online; even if they don't, chances are they are still looking at your website.

> . . . use a donation processing engine that sends donors to another website, especially one that looks different from yours and creates a disconnect in the giving experience.

About the Expert

Caryn Stein is vice president of communications and content at Network for Good, where she oversees the development and distribution of their vast fundraising training resources and is the lead editor of The Nonprofit Marketing Blog. Stein has fifteen years of digital marketing experience and has helped hundreds of nonprofits improve their online fundraising campaigns by combining the best practices of the design with compelling storytelling.

Resource Review

Network for Good (www.networkforgood.org)
  Find free online fundraising content, a great blog and newsletter, and a free webinar series.

Beth's Blog (www.bethkanter.org)
  This is a great blog on online giving, social media, and measurement.

The Nonprofit Marketing Guide (www.nonprofitmarketingguide.com)
  Find a wealth of content on how to optimize your communication with donors and prospects.

Nonprofit Tech for Good (www.nptechforgood.com)
  A blog and other resources on online giving, including free webinars and a nonprofit newsletter.

NTEN and NTC (www.nten.org)
  Get help leveraging technology to achieve your goals, and check out the Nonprofit Technology Conference, an annual gathering of leading nonprofit technology professionals.

TechSoup (www.techsoup.org)
  Find great resources on online fundraising, as well as access to a vibrant online community, free webinars, and nonprofit discounts on a wide range of technology.

Krug, Steve. *Don't Make Me Think! A Common Sense Approach to Web Usability* (2nd ed.). New Riders, 2006.
  This is a highly accessible book that offers great tips and tools for simplifying your website.

Heath, Chip, and Dan Heath. *Switch: How to Change Things When Change Is Hard*. Broadway Books, 2010.
A great read about the psychology of why people do the things they do, including donating to nonprofits.

Pew Research Center Internet Science Tech RSS. "Teens, Social Media, and Technology Overview 2015." April 8, 2015. www.pewinternet. org/2015/04/09/teens-social-media-technology-2015/

Brooks, Jeff. *The Fundraiser's Guide to Irresistible Communications: Real-world, Field-Tested Strategies for Raising More Money*. Emerson & Church, 2013.
This book offers tips for nonprofits looking to develop killer language that drives people to donate.

Wired Impact (www.wiredimpact.com)
This is a great blog about online giving, and how to ensure your site is on-brand and highly functional. They also offer design services to nonprofits.

Google's Nonprofit Hub (www.google.com/nonprofits)
Find a variety of offers for nonprofits, including free access to Google Analytics, a powerful website optimization tool, and Google Grants, where you can receive $10,000 a month to spend on Google AdWords.

Here are four helpful studies (also listed in Chapter 16) that provide industry benchmarks for online fundraising:

- M+R 2015 Online Fundraising Benchmark Study:
  mrbenchmarks.com/2015-archive.html
- Luminate Online Benchmark Report from Blackbaud:
  https://www.blackbaud.com/nonprofit-resources/luminate-online-benchmark-report
- Blackbaud Index of Online Giving:
  https://www.blackbaud.com/nonprofit-resources/blackbaud-index
- Network for Good Digital Giving Index:
  http://www1.networkforgood.org/digitalgivingindex

Chapter 16

Fundraising with Email

"The more you say, the less people remember."

—François Fénelon

Introduction

If you want to be successful in raising money from individuals, you need to reach them where they are—online. *The majority of online fundraising happens through email*, and having solid strategy is key to your success. According to Blackbaud, fully *90 percent of online giving is driven by online appeals*—especially email—but also website promotion (see Chapter 15) and disaster giving, compared to just 9 percent from peer-to-peer activities like run/walk/rides (Chapter 13) and 1 percent from social media (Chapter 17). Having a solid email and online strategy is only becoming more important over time; the number of people giving online and the amounts raised have consistently outpaced overall giving growth by about 400 percent the past few years. (See the Resource Review for links to a few studies with great statistics.) The good news is that this isn't rocket science, and with a few tried-and-true tips and tools, you can start raising big bucks via email in no time.

Beyond raising money, email is also an extremely useful and inexpensive tool for connecting with your donors and prospects on a regular basis. People on your email list signed up for a reason, so you have a wonderful opportunity to build a strong connection and inspire them to support your work. Moreover, because email is a technology-based medium, everything can be measured and tested.

In order to identify the keys to success with email-based fundraising, I talked with Kivi Leroux Miller, author and founder of NonprofitMarketingGuide. com. Miller plays close attention to email marketing and fundraising trends and helps smaller nonprofits and those new to online fundraising make sense of it all. She broke everything you need to know down into seven succinct steps, so let's get into them.

Critical Skills and Competencies

1. Plan Ahead

Instead of acting on impulse, *to succeed in fundraising through email, think in terms of four-to eight-week campaigns*, and then be realistic about how many campaigns you can successfully execute in a given year. Have a strategy session with your colleagues and key volunteers to discuss how email can help support your communications and fundraising campaigns. Consider the capacity of your organization and fundraising department and *make sure that you create a plan that you can execute on*.

As outlined in the social media and direct mail chapters, it's key that you *create a communications calendar*, also known as an editorial calendar, that outlines all of the emails your organization will send so your marketing, advocacy, and fundraising emails don't get crossed or undermine one another. The last thing you want is a donor receiving a fundraising appeal the same day he or she receives an e-newsletter or request to call his or her congressman.

We've talked about an editorial calendar in multiple chapters now, which speaks to how incredibly useful they are to underpin your communications strategy across media—if at all possible, *integrate your various editorial calendars into one master document, so you can ensure a strategic approach to all outbound communications*. This will enable you to coordinate both the timing and messaging of everything you send out, giving fundraising appeals the space they need for action before another message is sent out, regardless of medium.

2. Build Campaigns

Avoid sending one-off emails; instead, *create email campaigns centered around a particular story or topic with a timeline and goal attached*. A typical email campaign consists of at least three emails over six to eight weeks. Start with a launch email that tells a quick and appealing story, efficiently explains the need, and asks for a donation to your cause. Be sure to *identify a specific amount you need to raise*, so you can follow up with update emails saying how you've progressed toward your goal. You can send weekly follow-up fundraising emails if you have the capacity, as long as you're careful to *segment out those who have already given* (more on this in point 6, below).

As discussed in Chapter 14, especially when it comes to youth, *peer influence drives behavior*. But no matter what the age of your base, it's always effective to use statements like "In the last 24 hours, 326 supporters have donated $12,539, moving us past our halfway mark!" *Use testimonials and personal stories from beneficiaries of your work to show the impact of donations*; facts and statistics can also be powerful in moderation. Ultimately, your goal is to ensure people that their investment in your work truly makes a difference.

Miller also talks about the importance of what she calls an "engagement email." The idea is simple: *use email to ask people do something other than donate*. Perhaps it's an appeal to call their local congressperson or sign a petition if you're running an advocacy campaign, or to share information with their social networks if you're crowdfunding. Almost always, there are things people can do to support your campaign besides—or hopefully in addition to—donating. And *when engaging youth, remember that the pinnacle of engagement for Millennials isn't donating; it's sharing your good work and leveraging their social capital* (more on this in Chapter 14).

Finally, don't be afraid to declare victory! To close out your campaign, be sure to send a thank you email to your entire list to let them know you hit, or ideally exceeded, your goal and remind them of the difference their donations and support will make.

3. Build Your List

You can't raise money through email if you don't have a robust list of email addresses to market to. And as you might imagine, *the bigger your list, the more money you'll raise*, but in fact, there appear to be some diminishing returns as you grow your database.

According to M+R's 2015 *Online Fundraising Benchmark Study*, an organization with a 50,000-person email list raises an average of $6,000 per fundraising email; organizations with 250,000 email addresses raise about $13,000; and larger organizations with million-person lists raise $25,000.

So gathering email addresses is critical. ***Collect email address through your website, at events, through social media requests***, and any other ways you can think of—a short brainstorming session can deliver many great ideas to build your list. Beyond contemplating where to collect emails, think about how to motivate people to sign up, too. At the very least, you should entice people to join your list by letting them know about the valuable information they'll receive: volunteer opportunities, advocacy updates, and stories of the impact their support has on your cause.

One important note when building your list: ***sending unsolicited email— spam—doesn't work and reflects poorly upon your organization.*** Make sure people "opt in" to your email list, meaning they sign up and give you permission to market to them. It's simple: don't send communications to people who haven't given you their email addresses, and make sure those who do know that you'll be emailing them over time.

4. Craft Killer Emails

OK, now you have a list, a communications plan, and a campaign (or several). How can you ensure your emails will be read and drive people to action? Sending email is very different from writing a letter, so always ***remember these three key things to make your messages pop***:

- *Keep it reader-centered*: Most people are inundated daily with too many emails. It's not the Sunday paper; people go through their inboxes *quickly* and decide whether they will delete, keep, or take action on an email. To keep your message out of the trash, you need to **grab them with a compelling subject line that's personally relevant and to the point**. Experiment with the length of your subject lines, but make sure that you have at least a few attention-grabbing or highly relevant keywords within the first 30 characters, and then get your message across quickly and efficiently.

- *Make it a fast read*: People want to understand your email and get your message as soon as they open it—*you have about three seconds to grab their attention*. They're likely only skimming the content; **use tight headlines, two- or three-sentence paragraphs, and bolded key points to communicate your message**. Your *one* call to action must be focused, explicit, clear, and repeated two or three times; *don't bog your message down with competing asks*. Ideally, include a graphic, such as a prominent donate button that's surrounded by white space.

- *Keep it easy on the eye*: Many emails are modeled after website templates, but this simply does not work. Unlike a website, your message has to scream through an email. ***An ideal email uses only one font, only one column, and has no sidebars***. (If you do have a sidebar, use it only for links.) And remember, according to Marketing Land, *over 60 percent of emails are opened on a mobile device*, so your design needs to work on screens of all sizes. (See Chapter 18 for more on mobile fundraising.)

Email Cheat Sheet

After working with hundreds of nonprofit clients, online fundraising platform CommitChange has witnessed first-hand the tremendous role emails play in driving online donations. After reviewing thousands of campaigns and messages, they've created a framework of questions they recommend nonprofits review whenever crafting a fundraising message:

- Have I defined my target outcome and the potential reasons why people would resist taking action?
- Am I using the minimum number of words? Can I cut anything?
- Have I clearly defined the motivations of my target audience?
- Can I segment my audience into smaller groups to improve communication and results?
- Does my email include a clear call to action, or is it muddy?
- How long does this take to read? Can I make it more scannable? Have all the "clever" ideas and wording been cut already?
- Am I using power words, or is my language abstract and technical?
- Can I include any relevant imagery to break up my email text?
- Am I tracking my links? If not, use Google URL Builder or bit.ly.
- Is there any way I can provide additional value in this email?
- Does my email talk more about the recipient than the sender?
- Finally, does this email sound authentic or automated?

---

5. Leverage Data with A/B Tests

If you have the capacity, it's a best practice to do A/B testing on your emails, especially important ones like annual appeals. (See Chapter 10 for insights on A/B testing with direct mail.) Instead of "spraying and praying," ***take a few small random samples of at least 1,000 emails each from your list*** *and run a test campaign*. Send different versions of your email to each segment, testing three key elements: subject line, copy, and imagery.

Instead of guessing which subject line will get folks to open the email and read further, test out a couple of options. Whichever generates the highest "open rate" (what percent of people open your email) is your winner. It's equally easy to test copy and imagery—again, just send different versions of the email with *only* the copy or imagery changed, and then use the click-through rate (the percent of people who click on one of the links) to determine the winner. Finally, after you test each element, put the optimal combination of the three elements together, blast it out to your entire list, and watch the results roll in!

6. Use Today's Technology

There's nothing more annoying than receiving a request to do something you've already done. This makes people feel like you aren't paying attention, or worse—you're incompetent. Either way, it undermines your ability to effectively engage supporters in the future. As such, it's critical that during email campaigns you carefully *suppress people from subsequent emails who have already taken action during the campaign* (and if someone slips through the cracks and complains, be sure to reach out and apologize). It is possible to circle back and invite people to step up and support you once again, but those messages have to be carefully and gracefully crafted, clearly communicating that you appreciate what they've already done.

Having a database and sophisticated email marketing platform like Constant Contact, MailChimp, Vertical Response, iContact, or Campaign Monitor makes this easy and automatic. (See Chapter 6 for more about managing donor lists through technology.) Using an email platform will also help you easily craft professional emails without a graphic design expert on staff, process and collect donations, ensure your messages are responsive to readers who view email on mobile devices, and immediately process any unsubscribe and communication preference requests.

7. Pay Attention to the Numbers

Like any fundraising strategy, email marketing requires both careful analysis of your efforts, plus an ongoing refinement to your approach based on what you learn. The good news is that, since email is a technology-based medium, if you're using a platform like those just mentioned, this process is easy and intuitive and will help ensure you maximize your success. Keep a close eye on statistics like open rates, click-through rates, and "response rates." (What percent of people take the action you request on the back end, that is, donate, sign a petition, share information, etc.?)

According to M+R, *an ideal open rate is over 20 percent, a good click-through rate is at least .5 percent, and a good response rate is 3 percent*. To analyze the effectiveness of your email program, use these numbers and the industry standards from the studies listed in the Resource Review.

Conclusion

In today's digital age, email has become an everyday tool in our lives. It is how people communicate today, along with social media, mobile devices, and other recent inventions. And just as with those other media, *the key to fundraising success is meeting people where they're at*. Given that, there can be no doubt that email must be integral to your overall fundraising strategy. You need to build a robust list and get your messages and fundraising asks into people's inboxes. That's the only way to communicate your message via email and raise money. But remember, that's just the beginning: once you show up in someone's inbox, he or she must read the message and take action, so keep your messages brief, compelling, focused, and well-designed. In today's attention economy, if you want to break through the clutter and rise to the top of an inbox, you need to be thoughtful and craft direct and concise messages that are relevant and make people care.

Do's and Don'ts

Do...

- ... use an email platform and database; it's worth the time and expense.

- ... map out your four- to eight-week email campaigns in advance, and look at how these integrate with your other marketing efforts.

- ... conduct A/B testing on important fundraising email messages.

- ... keep your email subject lines compelling and relevant, with a focus on the first 30 characters.

Don't. . .

> . . . add people to your list without them explicitly signing up.
>
> . . . include more than one call to action in any email.
>
> . . . send an unintentional email requesting action to people who have already given you their support.

About the Expert

Kivi Leroux Miller is president of NonprofitMarketingGuide.com and the award-winning author of two books, *The Nonprofit Marketing Guide: High-Impact, Low-Cost Ways to Build Support for Your Good Cause* and *Content Marketing for Nonprofits: A Communications Map for Engaging Your Community, Becoming a Favorite Cause, and Raising More Money.* She is a certified executive coach who has worked with and trained thousands of nonprofits and charities in all 50 U.S. states, across Canada, and in more than 30 countries.

Resource Review

Here are four helpful studies that provide industry benchmarks for email and online fundraising:

- M+R Annual Online Fundraising Benchmark Study: mrbenchmarks.com/2015-archive.html
- Network for Good Digital Giving Index: www1.networkforgood.org/digitalgivingindex
- Luminate Online Benchmark Report from Blackbaud: https://www.blackbaud.com/nonprofit-resources/luminate-online-benchmark-report
- Blackbaud Index of Online Giving: https://www.blackbaud.com/nonprofit-resources/blackbaud-index

The Nonprofit Marketing Guide (www.NonprofitMarketingGuide.com)
  The beginner's guide for marketing in the social sector, and a place where communication directors learn more about the field, how to love their jobs, and can find professional development opportunities. Check out

their free downloads, including "Getting Started with Email Acquisition Campaigns," and their free email course, "15 Days to More Engaging, Inspiring E-Newsletters."

Gunelius, Susan. *Content Marketing for Dummies.* John Wiley & Sons, 2011. This book shows gives you step-by-step guidance on how to create a content marketing strategy, identify and create content that will keep your customers coming back, distribute it online, and measure the results.

Which Test Won (https://WhichTestWon.com)
This is an A/B testing portal where you can review different emails and web pages and learn which performed better. This is a great, fun tool to help you figure out what works and what doesn't in email messaging.

NTEN: The Nonprofit Technology Network (www.nten.org)
A membership organization aimed at helping nonprofits master technology. Their annual conference, NTC (www.nten.org/ntc/future), covers all aspects of nonprofit technology, including email-based fundraising.

Find blogs, whitepaper downloads, and other great information about email and online fundraising at these sites:

- Network for Good (www.networkforgood.org)
- Razoo (www.razoo.com)
- Blackbaud (www.blackbaud.com)
- Bloomerang (https://bloomerang.co/)

MailChimp's Blog (http://blog.mailchimp.com/)
The blog for this email provider features great tips and research on email marketing.

The Chronicle of Philanthropy (https://philanthropy.com)
A weekly periodical that also publishes an online edition. This is a great resource for finding articles and case studies about email fundraising.

Social Media and Crowdfunding for Your Cause

"We've entered a world where everyone is smarter than anyone."
—Anonymous

Introduction

Social media is changing the way we interact with each other and with the causes we care about. People of all ages and generations are using social media to connect with nonprofits in unprecedented ways: identifying new causes to support, tapping their social networks to raise money on their behalf, and actively engaging them in dialogue. Facebook is now the equivalent of the world's third largest country—almost a billion and a half people logged on in the last 30 days, including 71 percent of American adults, according to Pew Research—and it's not just "the kids" who are tuning in. In fact, women over the age of 45 are Facebook's fastest growing audience.

By embracing social media and meeting people where they're at, nonprofits can take advantage of the huge opportunities the digital landscape provides to attract and engage supporters, while generating tremendous exposure for your cause. Without a robust social media strategy and audience, your organization will never have its own ALS Ice Bucket Challenge, which tripled a nonprofit's annual budget in just eight weeks, nor a Kony2012 video, which reached 100 million viewers on YouTube faster than any video in history and was produced by a small nonprofit in San Diego. Moreover, you will miss out on a vital opportunity to deeply engage younger generations who will become future donors.

Perhaps most exciting, *social media presents an opportunity to turn your donors into fundraisers*. After all, professional fundraisers are fond of saying, "The most powerful form of ask is a *peer ask*." And what is social media, other than the most powerful peer-to-peer-based communication platform in history? Moreover, with the rise of crowdfunding (an online campaign to raise individual donations toward a larger goal) as a viable fundraising tactic, nonprofits need to understand how to harness the power of people online and turn them into donors and advocates.

To learn more about effectively using social media and running successful crowdfunding campaigns, I sat down with Beth Kanter, renown #nptech blogger, trainer, and author of *The Networked Nonprofit* and *Measuring the Networked Nonprofit*, and John Haydon, digital marketing expert and author of *Facebook Marketing for Dummies*.*

Critical Skills and Competencies

1. Start with the Basics

Having a simple and well-designed website is the first step in preparing yourself to embrace social media (see Chapter 15), and you'll certainly want to link to any social media platforms you're active on from your site. Once you have that dialed in, you can turn your attention to unlocking the power of social media. The first platform you'll likely want to focus on is Facebook, since it's by far the most popular outlet, plus 96 percent of nonprofits are already there, according to NonprofitMarketingGuide.com's *Nonprofit Communications Trends Report*. Catch up first, and then you can lead the pack. After Facebook, Twitter is the second most popular social network, but you may want to concentrate on others, depending on your goals and

---

* Author's Note: In addition to the chapter below, please read the appendix immediately following this chapter for tips on maximizing your efforts across specific social media platforms.

audience; for example, Pinterest is great for nonprofits targeting women, which is two-thirds of their audience, and for groups with compelling photos or infographics. ***Read the appendix immediately following this chapter for tips on specific social media platforms***.

Regardless of which platform(s) you're active on, success doesn't just happen; you have to plan for it. ***Create a monthly editorial calendar to map out your social media and crowdfunding campaigns***. This is a simple spreadsheet or calendar used to plan the timing of your posts and to coordinate messaging. Instead of only having one staff member handle your social media posts, engage multiple people to distribute your expertise and let individual voices and perspectives shine through. Remember, *people don't give to organizations; they give to people*. That said, coordinating efforts can be difficult without a simple tool to plan who is going to post what, where, when. Simply knowing that I'm posting a blog about our annual gala on Thursday at 12 noon, and then Laila is posting our auction items on Facebook that afternoon, and so on gives everyone the basic information needed to efficiently support the organization's efforts.

Note you can free scheduling tools like Hootsuite to pre-plan posts, so you don't have to actually log on during evenings, weekends, and holidays. An editorial calendar will help you manage multiple social media contributors efficiently and avoid duplicated efforts. Simply organize a monthly group meeting to plan out your content and document everything in the calendar, and then everyone knows what's expected of them. Of course, you can also add in timely posts if there's an exciting announcement or relevant article that pops up, but this gives you a baseline.

The most important thing when launching your social media strategy is to commit dedicated resources and ensure a constant stream of new content. Not doing so results in what I call the "empty store phenomenon," and sadly, it's far too common. Just as you wouldn't open up a store on Main Street with no plans to keep the shelves stocked, so too should you never launch a social media presence without a plan and commitment to stocking your presence there with content. You can actually hurt your cause by establishing a substandard, dormant presence, so if you're unable to commit, then hold off.

Once you've built a sizable and engaged social media audience, you are better positioned to experiment with crowdfunding. Before starting a crowdfunding campaign, you need to organize and create your campaign media: key messages including sample social media posts, shareable content like infographics, photo and video footage of projects and programs, photos of your team, testimonies from program beneficiaries, and whatever else helps convey your work.

P.O.S.T. to Social Media

Kanter shared a helpful framework to help you plan successful social media and crowdfunding campaigns:

P Is for People You Are Trying to Reach
What do they care about, and what do you actually want them to *do*? How can you engage this audience? ***Create an archive of compelling photos, videos, and surveys as you prepare your launch***. After mastering your presence on Facebook and Twitter, find out which social media platforms the majority of your donors and prospects are on, and focus your efforts there, but again, remember to go deeper versus wider, and don't dilute your efforts by establishing a mediocre presence on too many platforms.

O Is for Objectives
Whether establishing a social media presence or launching a crowdfunding campaign, ***the key to your success is clearly communicating the outcomes of your work and spelling out the impact of donations***. It's not about getting more "likes" on Facebook; your objectives should map directly to your mission. Start with a S.M.A.R.T. (Specific, Measurable, Actionable, Realistic and Timely) goal, not something generic like "Help us raise as much money as possible to build as many playgrounds as we can." Rather, be concrete, for example, "Help us raise $15,000 in the next 50 days to we can build a playground for the 637 children at Mission Elementary School. Research shows that schools with playgrounds have 27 percent higher attendance rates." Again, remember to ensure these objectives integrate with your overall fundraising and marketing goals; social media and crowdfunding campaigns are simply another channel for advancing your work and spreading your message.

S Is for Social
As Kanter says, "Crowdfunding is really the marriage of fundraising and social media. It's about engaging people and raising money." In order to inspire people to give, you need to engage them with your *story*. And if you're trying to create a "viral" message—meaning that you hope that those who read your message will pass it along—it's critical that your story be

shareable. ***The secret to going viral is composing a message that is compelling, concise, and credible***.

Short videos under three minutes, even more than photos, are key to creating appealing content that helps you make the case for raising money. In fact, crowdfunding platform Razoo says that *campaigns with a video raise an average of 800 percent more money!* And ***before you publicly launch a crowdfunding campaign, be sure to privately invite your inner circle of donors, board members, and supporters to contribute***; that way when the floodgates open, people won't see an empty thermometer. See Chapter 15 for more on this "seeding the tip jar" concept. Additionally, as outlined in Chapter 4, it's helpful to ***recruit a "social media marketing committee" before you launch***. These well-connected supporters agree to share your social media posts and actively engage with your content through likes and comments, magnifying exposure. When your campaign launches, these tips will help the public see that you've made progress in inspiring people to contribute both financially and emotionally, and others will be much more likely to contribute and engage.

T Is for Tools
There are a variety of tools available to help nonprofits manage their social media presence and crowdfunding campaigns:

Social media platforms include Facebook, Twitter, LinkedIn, Pinterest, Instagram, and many others.

Crowdfunding platforms include CommitChange, Indiegogo, KickStarter, Network for Good, StayClassy, Razoo, causes (now Brigade), Causevox, CrowdRise, Fundly, GoFundMe, WePay, RocketHub, Sponsume, StartSomeGood, Patreon, GiveFoward, and more. (More on choosing the right crowdfunding platform in the next tip, and ***see the appendix immediately following this chapter for tips on effective crowdfunding***.)

Content curation tools like Scoop.It, Storify, and Listly help you identify relevant content on the Web and make it easy to share it with your social networks.

Scheduling tools such as Hootsuite, TweetDeck, and Buffer that allow you to pre-schedule your posts and tweets and ensure a steady stream of content for your followers.

Analytics tools like Google Analytics, Facebook Insights, Sprout Social, RowFeeder, and Klout allow you to analyze the performance of posts and followers, plus measure things like audience engagement. (More information and links in the Resource Review below.)

(continued)

(continued)

And finally, good old-fashioned **spreadsheets** will help you track analytics and create things such as editorial calendars.

Non-traditional "tools" also include things like the people on your team supporting your efforts and promoting content, as well as giving days (a designated day like #GivingTuesday, where nonprofits promote an area- or industry-wide campaign and request gifts). Giving days are great for inspiring donors, because they hear about the campaign from multiple organizations, which drives increased giving.

2. Pick the Right Crowdfunding Platform

There are many platforms to consider, and every nonprofit has its unique set of needs and requirements. As you're reviewing the aforementioned platforms and more, keep in mind the associated costs (Is there a fee? What percentage of the donation do they take?), the platform's ability to integrate into your website or social outlet (you don't want people to feel like they are leaving to make a gift), whether it automatically makes your presence and donation page mobile responsiveness so people can easily view it on a mobile device, and user reviews (Are people who have used this platform happy with the results?). For more tips on effective crowdfunding, see the appendix immediately following this chapter.

Whatever tool you choose, it's critical that whenever people donate, either through your website or via a social media or crowdfunding platform, *your donation-processing engine must prompt donors to invite their social networks to follow their lead after they give*. This is as simple as adding a couple buttons to the thank you page where donors can click to share on Facebook or Twitter, after which a pre-populated message pops up saying something like, "I just gave to Save the Children and encourage you to join me in supporting their good work," followed by a link. Donors can choose to edit the text if they like, but either way this simple functionality typically *improves revenue by 20 to 200 percent;* plus it magnifies your campaign's audience.

Take the time to do your homework and make sure you're happy with the platform you choose, because once you start a crowdfunding campaign, you're pretty much stuck with it. Swapping out a donation-processing platform for social media or your website is a bit easier, but still entails a cumbersome transition that should be avoided if at all possible. A little work now saves you a lot of effort down the road!

3. Become a Content Curator

Social media should be leveraged as a platform for thought leadership, rather than as a megaphone to promote your work. To make it simple, I encourage nonprofits to follow the 50/50 rule: *at least half your posts should not be about you, your organization, or its needs and impact, but rather about the cause and issue you represent*. This includes relevant, insightful information and updates, such as research, articles, infographics, and industry events, including those of like-minded organizations. This also includes posts you share and retweet from relevant media and nonprofits. Your goal is to get people to think of you as the go-to resource for information on your cause, so when they decide to support the issue, they think of you. At the same time, this builds up social capital by strengthening relationships with industry experts and other organizations in your space and establishes your expertise. Pitch a big tent and the more people and groups you invite inside, the more you will become a pillar of the community.

4. Master Frequency and Timing

Again, it's key to have a steady stream of content to engage your users, but you also need to find a good balance. Social media is nothing but a digital cocktail party, and you never want to be the one sucking up all the air in the room. *On Facebook, post no more than twice a day* if possible, as engagement drops off after that point. To avoid hosting an empty store, post at least twice a week. *Post at least daily if you're on Twitter*, and ideally more, as there's really no limit to how often you can tweet—follow @GuyKawasaki if you don't believe me. But most importantly, as Ritu Sharma, executive director and co-founder of Social Media for Nonprofits, is fond of saying, find your drumbeat: consistency is key, and *never let your social media channels go silent*. Give your followers enough content so that they expect more, but not so much that you burden and overwhelm them.

Now, what time of day and what days of the week should you post? In general, it's best to reach people in their down time. I call this the "burrito principle," since during the week this tends to be during the morning commute, on their lunch break when they're checking their smartphones while eating a burrito, at the end of the work day, or even better, from 9:30 to 11 p.m. after the kids go to sleep. Weekends tend to perform even better.

This formula varies for different organizations and audiences, so you'll want to *test posts at different times of day and days of the week and analyze their performance, in terms shares, likes, comments, retweets, etc.* You should also use Facebook Insights to identify when your audience is online. (See the Facebook tips below for more information.)

5. Test and Learn

The only way to truly optimize your social media and crowdfunding presence is through testing and experimenting. Try posting and tweeting at different times of the day or days of the week, using different social media outlets, experiment with and without images and videos, try out surveys and questions versus statements, and so on. If you have a good analytics tool in place, you will quickly learn what produces the best results and engages the most people. You can also play with using different tones for your messages (serious, light-hearted, humorous) to see what works, but once you find your "voice," you'll want to stick with it for consistency's sake. Of course, remember that your social media posts are an extension of your overall messaging, so not all tones will be appropriate for experimentation.

Social Media Case Study: The ALS Ice Bucket Challenge

If you were alive and online in 2014, odds are you participated in what was one of the most viral nonprofit awareness and fundraising campaigns the world has ever seen: the ALS Ice Bucket Challenge. For a brief time, our newsfeeds were full of videos of friends, family members, and celebrities pouring ice-cold buckets of water over the heads, all to support the ALS Association and a relatively obscure cause. In only eight weeks, the $66 million organization saw over 440 million Facebook users upload videos with over 10 billion views, and raised over $115 million from donors across 200 countries, generating both tremendous financial support and awareness. To unearth the magic that made this incredible campaign possible, I spoke with Lance Slaughter, chief chapter relations and development officer of the ALS Association, who shared some tips that can benefit any nonprofit looking to embrace social media:

Be Open
The idea for the Ice Bucket Challenge didn't actually come from the ALS Association. Chris Kennedy, a professional golfer whose brother-in-law has ALS, posted a video and challenged his sister to raise awareness of the disease. That caught the attention of Pat Quinn

---

and Pete Frates, two young men living with ALS, who saw the video and realized the stunt was a great way to convey the tremendous shock of being diagnosed . . . and a viral phenomenon was born.

The concept bubbled up through the ALS Association's regional chapter, and headquarters saw a considerable spike in online donations, but more importantly, embraced it as a tremendous awareness opportunity. They jumped on board and put out the call to their local chapters to support the campaign by leveraging pre-existing communication channels, especially social media. Slaughter's big takeaway here? *Be open to ideas from both outside and within your organization, and embrace opportunities that come from your supporters.*

Be Prepared
Before the Ice Bucket Challenge was born, the ALS Association had already recognized and embraced social media's ability to deliver content and resources. For them, it was a key communication channel that enabled them to share information with those afflicted with the disease, many of whom suffer from limited mobility, but can still use a computer. Perhaps your nonprofit makes the same strategic decision to master social media for a different reason, such as wanting to reach youth, 24 percent of whom "live" online today, according to Pew Research. Either way, it is because of this commitment and capacity that ALS's 38 affiliates already had the infrastructure and expertise in place to leverage this transformative opportunity. By devoting resources to building your social media profiles and followers, and learning how to best engage them, you too will *be poised to seize opportunities as they arise.*

Be Adaptable
Using the kind of donor research and segmentation techniques outlined in Chapter 5, the ALS Association quickly realized the Ice Bucket Challenge was connecting them with an entirely new audience. Previously, they principally communicated with donors aged 45 to 64 and affected by the disease, either directly or through a loved one. But now, they were reaching younger donors, ages 18 to 34, the large majority of whom had no affinity to the disease. Once they realized this, they appreciated the need to adapt their communications and messaging to those new to the cause and with younger perspectives. They redesigned their website with new visuals and messaging, they cancelled a planned direct mailing campaign, and revised their tagline. Change can be hard, but by being willing to make strategic shifts in response to changes in the fundraising landscape, you will open up new opportunities.

(continued)

(continued)

Earn Ongoing Support
Every donor and participant in the campaign who provided their contact information was thanked, informed about the work of the ALS Association, and was told exactly what impact their contribution made possible. The ALS Association now faces a new, exciting challenge: how to continue to engage this enormous new group of supporters and sustain concern and loyalty to the cause, not just to the organization.

Given these new supporters' low affinity to the disease, and youth's overall predisposition to support causes versus organizations, they are finding success by focusing their communications on education, as well as sharing updates on progress toward a cure, instead of the success of their own work. By focusing on the impact, rather than the process to get there, you will have a better chance of creating an ongoing movement.

6. Survey the Landscape

Once you've established a solid social media presence, it's helpful to conduct Google, Facebook, and Twitter searches of key terms related to your issue, as well as to look up like-minded organizations. See what's out there and reflect on how you're different. Aside from programmatic considerations, look at what similar organizations are doing with their social and overall online presence. Try to get a sense of what these groups and people are saying and what their followers seem to be most responsive to.

Set up a free Google Alert at http://google.com/alerts to keep you abreast as new content is posted for key phrases and search terms, as well as news stories on your executive staff, board, allies, and similar organizations. Hashtagify.me is another great tool to help you stay on top of the most popular "hashtags" related to your cause. Hashtags are a way to group content into a stream, so that others searching or posting that keyword can find it. They're how "trending" happens in social media and are critical for helping people discover what other folks are talking about at the moment.

Conclusion

Social media has become an expected form of communication for many people. If your nonprofit isn't taking advantage of this huge opportunity, you are missing out on the biggest conversation happening in the world right now. Sure, there are lots of platforms out there, tips for the most important of which are outlined in the appendix immediately following this chapter. It may seem scary and overwhelming to jump in, but you can start quickly and easily with small steps and recruit others to help you. Ultimately, there is no such thing as a "social media expert"; the field is simply too new and evolving too quickly for that, so we're all learning by doing. Crowdfunding isn't quite as commonplace as social media, but it is quickly rising, and you don't want to be left in the dust as this becomes an even more powerful and popular fundraising tool. By following the tips we've outlined in this chapter and the appendix that follows, and learning from the success of organizations like the ALS Association, you will quickly be on your way to leveraging the power of the masses and catapulting your organization's impact and fundraising forward.

Do's and Don'ts

Do...

> . . . create a monthly editorial calendar to map out your social media and crowdfunding campaigns.

> . . . use a scheduling tool for social media posts to make sure there is no lapse in your content stream.

> . . . enable donors to easily invite their social networks to follow their lead after making a gift.

> . . . participate in giving days like #GivingTuesday and regional events typically supported by your local community foundation.

Don't...

> . . . launch a crowdfunding campaign without first preparing all of your marketing materials and securing at least 20 percent of your goal from your "inner circle" of supporters.

> . . . post content from your own organization more than 50 percent of the time.

> . . . rely only on scheduling tools like Hootsuite; make sure you are adding fresh and timely content.

About the Experts

Beth Kanter is the author of the best-selling books *The Networked Nonprofit* and *Measuring the Networked Nonprofit* and producer of *Beth's Blog: How Nonprofits Can Use Social Media*, one of the world's longest-running and most popular nonprofit technology blogs. Kanter has more than 30 years of experience in the nonprofit sector, with a focus on technology, training, capacity building, evaluation, fundraising, and marketing. Kanter is an internationally recognized trainer who was recently named as one of *Business Week's* "Voices of Innovation for Social Media."

John Haydon is one of the most sought-after digital marketing experts for nonprofits and charities. He is founder of the nonprofit consultancy, Inbound Zombie, and is a frequent keynote speaker on all aspects of nonprofit technology. Haydon is also an instructor for CharityHowTo and MarketingProfs University. He is the author of *Facebook Marketing for Dummies* and *Facebook Marketing All-In-One* and is a regular contributor to The Huffington Post, Social Media Examiner, npEngage, and the Razoo Foundation blog.

Resource Review

Beth Kanter's blog (www.bethkanter.org)
> This is a great resource for tips on crowdfunding, social media, and all aspects of nonprofit technology. Check out her posts on the "Five Best Practices in Nonprofit Crowdfunding," the "10 Best Practices for Planning Successful Crowd Funding or Giving Day Campaigns," which includes a detailed description of her P.O.S.T. framework, and the interesting case study about the Dalai Lama Foundation's use of crowdfunding.

> www.bethkanter.org/5-crowdfunding-tips
> www.bethkanter.org/10-best-practices
> www.bethkanter.org/dalai-lama-crowd

John Haydon's Blog (www.johnhaydon.com)
> This blog is full of helpful tips and tools regarding all aspects of social media. Download the guide to the "51 Best Social Media Tools for Any Nonprofit Marketer or Fundraiser," and sign up for John's weekly newsletter.

Socialnomics on YouTube (https://www.youtube.com/
watch?v=jottDMuLesU)
This is a series of well-produced videos with compelling social media
statistics that will help you make the case that social media should be a
priority for your organization. They're constantly posting new videos, so
be sure to search and see what's fresh.

Network for Good (www.networkforgood.org)
Find many great online fundraising and social media resources, including
an active, insightful blog, as well e-books on crowdfunding and online
fundraising.

GuideStar (www.guidestar.org)
Find helpful tips on fundraising, social media, and crowdfunding, and
be sure to subscribe to their newsletter and join their LinkedIn Group,
which is quite active.

NTEN (www.nten.org)
This website has great resources on all aspects of nonprofit technology; be
sure to check out their annual Nonprofit Technology Conference, NTC,
for a phenomenal networking and educational opportunity.

Association of Fundraising Professionals (www.afpnet.org)
Their site offers a wide range of fundraising resources, and their annual
international conference always features content on social media and
crowdfunding.

Social Media for Nonprofits (SM4NP.org)
This is the only conference series devoted to social media for social good,
with events throughout the U.S., Canada, and India. They also produce
a great blog and newsletter and offer a range of helpful tips on their
website.

Crowdfunding Platforms with Great Resources

- StayClassy.com—active, insightful blog.
- StartSomeGood.com—another active blog focused on social media
  and online fundraising.
- Indiegogo.com—check out their giving day playbook and field
  guide.
- Kimbia.com—great webinar series and useful online fundraising
  blog.

Analytics Tools

- Google Analytics (www.google.com/analytics) is a great free tool to assess your website traffic.
- Facebook Insights (find the tab at the top of your page when signed in as an administrator) helps you analyze your Facebook traffic and identify your most engaging posts and most valuable followers.
- SproutSocial (www.sproutsocial.com) is a paid analytics tool that also manages content and has scheduling capabilities.
- Klout (www.klout.com) is a tool that allows you to measure your online impact and influence.

Kanter, Beth. *The Networked Nonprofit: Connecting with Social Media to Drive Change.* Jossey-Bass, 2010.
This book shows nonprofits a new way of operating in our increasingly connected world: a networked approach enabled by social technologies, where connections are leveraged to increase impact in effective ways that drive change for the betterment of our society and planet.

Miller, Kivi. *Content Marketing for Nonprofits: A Communications Map for Engaging Your Community, Becoming a Favorite Cause, and Raising More Money.* Jossey-Bass, 2013.
This book explains how to design and implement a content marketing strategy, an essential component to any nonprofit's effort to raise money with social media.

Practical Tips for Key Social Media Platforms and Crowdfunding Case Study

Facebook

Ask questions. If your post ends in a question mark instead of a period, you can expect twice as many likes, comments, and shares; the currency in today's "attention economy."

Use photos and videos. Typically, you'll generate twice as many likes, comments, and shares if your post includes a photo, four times as many with a video. If you use a video on a crowdfunding campaign, according to crowdfunding platform Razoo, you're likely to receive eight times the amount of donations!

Use the right photos. Since people will likely only see the small thumbnail version of your photo, cut out the background and use cropping to zoom in on one subject. Ideally, use photos with pictures of people or animals, and focus on faces. As author Guy Kawasaki likes to say, "ABC: Always Be Cropping." Don't use boring photos—instead of people posing next to a house they just built, use an action photo of them carrying a ladder or building a roof. Use photos that capture your work in action and convey a sense of impact.

Promote the right posts. If you have a budget and choose to do promoted posts on Facebook, choose posts that have the best response rates, rather than promoting donation requests and other posts that fall flat. This may seem counter-intuitive, but your resources are best spent promoting posts that have proven to be most engaging.

Keep it short. Ideally, under 80 characters. Bufferapp.com found a 66 percent increase in engagement when you get to the point.

Learn about your donors. Upload your email or donor list and see how many of them are on Facebook. You can use Facebook Ads to gain invaluable donor segmentation information about them, including household income, home ownership, device use, how active they are on Facebook, how much they engage with your posts, etc. The more you know about your donors, the better equipped you are to effectively engage and solicit them!

Reply to comments. Again, think of social media as a digital cocktail party. If someone at a party says, "Hey, nice dress," you need to say "thank you" and reply back. If someone posts a comment or asks a question, reply in a polite and conversational manner.

Leverage Facebook Insights. To succeed at engaging people, you need to listen. Insights is a free analytics tool that allows you to analyze your posts and how they perform, that is, how many likes, comments, and shares or retweets they receive. It will also help you determine when the majority of your users are online, which can help you plan the timing of your posts. (Facebook Insights is accessed through a tab at the top of your page when you're signed in as an administrator.)

Twitter

Ask for retweets. Include the term "Please Retweet," often abbreviated as "Pls RT," to significantly increase the percentage of people who share your posts.

Use photos, videos, and links. Just as with Facebook, this will encourage people to spend a few more seconds with your content and increase the likelihood that they share it.

Recruit influencers. Twitter is a great place to make initial contact with donor prospects and key influencers like celebrities, leading academics, journalists, and bloggers. But before asking VIPs to support you, build up your social capital by retweeting them and writing comments on their posts.

Get your leadership active. Having your executive director and other leaders active on Twitter develops additional communication outlets for your organization and can establish them as thought leaders in your field.

Use keywords. Add keywords and hashtags to your profile so that people interested in your cause will find you when they search. Using these in your posts will also help people who aren't following you find your content and organization.

Create a hashtag. Come up with a short yet descriptive hashtag to include in many of your posts. Ideally, it's something that others in the field can adopt as well, promoting your thought leadership. For example, Social Media for Nonprofits launched #SM4NP, which is now widely adopted by others in the industry.

Use lists. Lists help you easily screen content and manage different categories of users. For example, if you are a breast cancer organization, lists can help you easily look at what's trending from breast cancer bloggers, pharmaceutical companies, academics, journalists, competitors, as well as things like campaign hashtags.

Use tools. Social media tools like Hootsuite will help you manage mentions, scheduling, and lists. Use tools like Klout (available as a Hootsuite plug-in) and BuzzSumo to identify key influencers in your field, so you know who to cultivate and prioritize.

Be active in the Twitter community. Twitter is a circular economy. Participate in Follow Fridays by sharing the handles of other leaders and organizations in your field on Fridays and including "#FF" in your posts to gain social capital. If someone mentions you with an @ sign, especially if it's an influencer, you should definitely take the time to retweet it and thank the person.

LinkedIn

Get your board and volunteers to link to you. When people include you in their profiles, it gives you additional exposure, and since this is a relatively new feature and not many nonprofits are using it, you will stand out.

Ask questions. People on LinkedIn tend to be very engaged, and you can receive well-thought-out answers to robust and complex questions. This will help you to build conversations and further engage people.

Start a Group. You can create a LinkedIn Group for free, which is a great way to mobilize and engage your community of interest. Invite people to join and make sure to post content, questions, or links to a blog post or article at least twice a month.

Ask for testimonials. Ask past employers, partners, and clients to write testimonials for your organization and on your personal profile. This provides credibility and reinforces your expertise.

YouTube

Create "Call to Action" overlays. YouTube offers nonprofits free access to this service, which increases subscriptions by 400 percent by creating a pop-up window inviting visitors to subscribe or even donate.

Keep it short. **Keep your videos on YouTube and crowdfunding sites short, ideally 90 to 120 seconds**. This will result in people watching the video when they first see it, instead of being daunted and saving it for later, which usually means they'll never watch it.

Instagram

Use hashtags. Just as on Twitter and Facebook, hashtags are a great way to create a conversation and create more avenues to your presence.

Focus on faces. The photos that typically receive the best response are close-ups of people's faces and animals. Remember Guy Kawasaki's ABC: Always Be Cropping.

Use action shots. As mentioned in the Facebook tips, instead of staged pictures, use images of people in action, delivering impact.

Pinterest

Girl power. Pinterest is a great place to reach women, as they're two-thirds of their audience, which recently surpassed 100 million users a month.

Get visual. This platform is best suited for visuals and infographics, both for finding and posting.

Crowdfunding Case Study: RE-volv

RE-volv provides solar technology for nonprofits and community centers by raising money through crowdfunding. They provide low-interest 20-year loans on the projects, which their beneficiaries pay out of energy savings, and then reinvest the funds into future projects. Over the past three years, the grassroots organization in San Francisco has conducted three crowdfunding campaigns on Indiegogo and raised over $120,000. They've managed to obtain over 1,000 contributions from donors in 38 states and 22 countries. To learn the secrets of their success, I sat down with their founder and executive director, Andreas Karelas, who shared some of the lessons he's learned along the way:

Prepare in Advance
Part of RE-volv's success has been due to the time and hard work they put in before they launch their campaigns. Establish partnerships, plan events, and create marketing materials in advance of any crowdfunding campaign, including a short video, email and social media messages, and website copy to enable you to focus on the campaign as it unfolds. You should also create an editorial calendar before your campaign, so you're clear about who is sending out which messages, where, and when, thereby ensuring a coordinated effort.

Events Drive Results
To drive awareness and garner initial support for their crowdfunding campaigns, RE-volv conducts what they call "small engagement tours." These are live events around the country that allow them to recruit campaign "champions" who agree to become volunteer marketers and promote the campaign on social media, similar to the "social media marketing committee" concept outlined in Chapter 4.

They also use these events to recruit initial donors to kick-start their efforts and seed the tip jar before launching the campaign to the public. In the beginning, before they implemented this tactic and launched campaigns with no donations secured, getting these efforts off the ground was much more challenging. And finally, in addition to engaging these champions online, they always bring marketing materials to hand out at their events, including posters, flyers, and stickers that people can easily use to evangelize the cause. Karelas says that nothing is better than an in-person experience to really share your passion and engage people in your cause.

(continued)

(*continued*)

Secure Marketing Trades

Trading marketing opportunities with like-minded partners is a great way to gain exposure with relevant audiences. RE-volv lists partner logos on their campaign page or mentions them in press releases in exchange for outreach support on social media and elsewhere, promoting the circular economy concept. It is important to *agree on specifics of any trade in advance, and document it in a simple agreement* so that both parties are accountable.

Engage Businesses

RE-volv reaches out to local businesses and national corporations to sponsor their engagement tour events and crowdfunding campaigns. They've recruited businesses like Whole Foods, Patagonia, and Aveda to donate supplies for events and even perks to offer donors to their crowdfunding campaigns. Having sponsor logos on your website and materials also helps lend credibility to your efforts.

Recruit Celebrities and Influencers

Karelas has successfully recruited key influencers to support RE-volv's campaigns by connecting them on Twitter and asking for retweets, especially when he offered to offer books they've written as perks in their crowdfunding campaigns. Although you may have much smaller reach than these movers and shakers, even celebrities respond to this gesture. Think about what you can do for a VIP passionate about your cause and amazing things become possible.

Experiment with Social Media

As outlined in this chapter, RE-volv experimented heavily on social media. In the process, they learned to *post screenshots of their campaign thermometer and post late at night to maximize results*. Both of these tactics have proven effective for a wide range of other nonprofits.

Simplify Your URL

RE-volv quickly learned that having a complicated link that isn't memorable hurts your campaign. *Create a simple URL that's easy to remember and have it redirect to your crowdfunding page*. This also helps you brand your campaign consistently.

Chapter 18

Mobile Fundraising

"The best way to predict the future is to create it."
—Abraham Lincoln

Introduction

Mobile is not the future; it's here and now. The people you are trying to reach, whatever their age, are on mobile devices. People are glued to their phones these days, keeping them within arms reach (even when sleeping), checking them obsessively, and increasingly using them to find and learn about nonprofits and to donate. PayPal alone processed over $800 million in mobile nonprofit payments in 2014, an increase of 60 percent from what U.S. and Canadian organizations earned in 2013. So we're talking about *real* money here, and the numbers are growing incredibly quickly. Because of this, it's critical that your organization is ready to meet people on their devices and able to take advantage of the immense opportunity mobile provides to send fundraising appeals and communicate key messages and updates.

Today, SocialNomics says that **over 40 percent of website traffic comes from mobile devices**, including those of nonprofits, so if your site isn't optimized for mobile, then you're already behind the times. This is particularly true for email communications, since, according to MarketingLand, about **two-thirds of people look at email on their mobile devices**, most of which will delete or ignore your email if it's not optimized for their device. Make no mistake, the party has already begun, and your presence is kindly requested.

Mobile and social media have changed the way people digest information; attention spans are growing shorter and shorter, and nonprofit communications need to accommodate this. Beyond email and fundraising, mobile also represents a tremendous opportunity for nonprofits to better serve their constituents. For example, I helped found a company called Sparrow: Mobile for Common Good, which partners with nonprofits serving the poor to power their mobile campaigns, helping the homeless find jobs and housing, supporting foster youth to reconnect with their birth parents, and more. Just like social media, mobile is a Swiss Army knife that can be employed in myriad powerful ways.

Too few nonprofits are investing in the crucial yet simple infrastructure needed to tap the potential of mobile, which means they're leaving money on the table. People need to be able to read your emails, look at your website, and easily donate through their mobile devices. If you aren't making this easy for them, you're missing out on critical opportunities to fundraise and engage your supporters. To get at the heart of mobile fundraising and identify the tips and tools needed for nonprofits to thrive, I sat down with Tanya Urschel, the nonprofit vertical manager for PayPal, and Heather Mansfield author and principal blogger at Nonprofit Tech For Good, who outlined seven great tips.

Critical Skills and Competencies

1. Optimize Your Website and Email

In order to reach people where they are these days—on mobile devices—*it is absolutely critical that your website and emails are mobile-compatible or "responsive."* That means basic technology, which is standard in many website content management systems and email marketing platforms, detects the size of the screen someone is using to view your content, and adjusts the layout accordingly. Technically, as Mansfield shared in *Mobile for Good*, dynamic websites "are built on a fluid, grid-based framework that allows for flexibility in page width and image sizes, thus enabling the website to automatically convert and reshape itself to fit the browser on which its being viewed—whether that's a two-inch smartphone screen or 17-inch laptop screen. For many nonprofits, it's simply easier and more cost-effective to launch a new responsively designed website than to try to retrofit or redesign their current website."

Your site and emails may already be responsive, especially if you're using a free template from a resource like WordPress.org or Constant Contact, respectively. Simply check this by logging onto your site or viewing one of your emails on a phone or tablet. Hopefully, what you see feels right, but if not you'll need to enlist a web developer or designer, which could require a financial investment, but one that is well worth it. Remember, on average about 40 percent of your website traffic and 60 percent of your emails are *currently* being viewed on smaller screens, and these numbers are going up daily. If you're looking for more concrete numbers specific to your organization, **use Google Analytics's free Mobile Performance Report to assess exactly how much of your traffic is derived from mobile devices, and which ones** (see Resource Review).

Another option is creating a dedicated mobile site, so when people log on from smaller screens they'll see a special version of your site optimized for that environment. Mansfield shared that, due to advances in responsive design, this is typically unnecessary for most nonprofits and generally produces little extra benefit.

Whether people are looking at a dedicated mobile site or a responsive version of your standard website, there are a few design best practices to keep in mind. It's best to **use minimal text and focus more on photos and videos, space out hyperlinks and leave ample white space, and minimize scrolling**, possibly through creating sections of your web pages that can expand. Perhaps most importantly, **focus on only one clear call to action—** likely encouraging donations—and include a big button (at least 200×60 pixels) promoting it at both top right and the bottom left of your page. And if you don't have the resources to re-create an entire website, you can tackle this one page at a time, starting with your home page and donate page, as these are the two pages that drive contributions.

For email, keep your content simple and use one- or two-sentence paragraphs and use a 13- or 14-point font. Nielsen found that 80 percent of readers only scan emails, so they'll miss anything more detailed anyway. Just like with your mobile website, links should be spaced apart and focus on one simple call to action. npENGAGE suggests keeping the header to under 100 pixels high, so readers can dive right into the content, and they also found that your email should be no wider than 500 pixels across. In today's attention economy, **you only have about two sentences to get people's attention with an email, or three on a website, so make them count**. And do whatever it takes to ensure your emails and website load quickly:

KISSMetrics found that 40 percent of people will abandon a site that takes more than three seconds to load, and 80 percent of them never come back!

If you don't have access to responsive email templates, at the very least use bigger fonts and switch out the links with buttons. Ideally, you should at least *invest in having a web designer create three mobile-responsive email templates: your newsletter, your fundraising appeals, and an event invitation*. This tends to cover a large majority of the emails most nonprofits send out and can be done inexpensively.

2. Optimize Your Donate Page

Every part of your online donation process must be mobile-optimized, from the first viewing of the donate page, to the filling in of the fields, to the thank you page and emailed acknowledgement. Make the process easy and quick so that you don't lose your donors before they complete the transaction. Minimize scrolling by separating the donation process onto more pages if needed, and *streamline the donation process as much as possible by asking only critical questions*. You can ask for additional information later, but if you lose the donor, you'll likely never see him or her again, nor receive that gift. Keep additional text to an absolute minimum, since the donor has already decided to support you when he or she clicked the donate button: a simple one-sentence impact statement at the top of your donation page is sufficient (for example, "Your donation will help us feed a hungry family").

3. Tell Your Story Effectively

Having your website, email, and donation page optimized for mobile won't help you if you don't have content that inspires people to give. Creating a content strategy—detailing how you tell your story—is the key to raising money. Your strategy needs clear goals that outline your target audiences and your tactics for reaching them. What kind of stories will you share, how often, and through which channels? What voice drives results and feels authentic to your cause? Will you use photos, videos, infographics, blogs, or annual reports? Who is in charge of creating and publishing these? As we discussed in Chapters 10, 16, and 17, *it is critical that communications are planned and included in your organization's editorial calendar* (the document where you schedule all outgoing fundraising and marketing communications, including mass email, direct mail, web, social media, etc.).

Planning for Success: The Mobile Matrix™

While working with our U.S. nonprofit customers and partners, the mobile startup I co-founded, Sparrow: Mobile for All, realized that many nonprofits were struggling with mobile because, just like social media, they didn't realize mobile is a tool: it's a means, not an end. As such, the key to success is asking yourself, "What do we want to use it for?"

To support this discovery process, we developed The Mobile Matrix™. It's a simple tool that helps nonprofits prioritize their goals and inform their mobile strategies. Simply look at the constituents up top and the objectives on the side, and then explore their intersection in each cell, using a group discussion to rate each cell 1 to 10 based on its priority. For example, is the primary reason we're embracing mobile to increase donations (i.e. "Revenue" from "Donors"), or are we hoping to engage our volunteers in fundraising, or to more efficiently communicate with our clients?

sparrow™
MOBILE FOR ALL.

Mobile Matrix™	Staff	Donors	Volunteers	Clients	The Public
Revenue					
Efficiency					
Communication					
Service					

Form follows function. Once you've clarified your mobile priorities, then you can begin to devise a strategy, identify relevant tools, and move forward in a thoughtful, planned way that maps to needed results, including fundraising targets. Whatever you're hoping to achieve with mobile, the key is to follow the great advice of T.E. Lawrence, who encouraged us all to "Dream your dreams with open eyes, and make them come true."

4. Mobilize Your Events

If your organization produces live events like runs or galas (see Chapters 12 and 13), you can benefit greatly by integrating mobile tactics for your staff, volunteers, and event participants. For staff and volunteers, they can use platforms like PayPal or Eventbrite to check people in using mobile devices, and then work the room and collect credit card payments on the spot for live and silent auctions or for donations and pledges. ***Giving supporters the ability to donate easily and securely on site means that you can capitalize on impulses to support you.*** For participants, they can use their mobile devices to check themselves in, as well as receive event updates and sign up for your email newsletter. If you are doing a walk, run, or ride and are using an event registration platform like Eventbrite, you can provide participants with a free app to download that gives them an event schedule and a route map, and some apps even track their progress while they run.

Text-to-Give

Text-to-give is a great way to make fundraising easy at large events. By using a variety of available platforms (such as Mobile Commons or Connect2Give), you can enable donors to text a preset number and give a donation of a set amount (usually $5 or $10). The donation is added to the person's phone bill, and a check is sent to your organization once the funds are collected. While text-to-give is easy and works well to acquire new donors in environments where people are impulsive (such as at events or after natural disasters), there are a few downsides to consider. The set donation amount (typically $5 or $10) and inability to sign up for recurring gifts can restrict the amount you might have raised with an alternative ask; it typically takes about 30 to 90 days to be paid, and these platforms typically do not integrate with your CRM or donor database. You should also carefully review the setup and transaction fees associated with these platforms, as that may lead you to realize it's not a feasible strategy. In general, text-to-give tends to be a great way to enlist new donors, but it's typically not a tool that delivers the big bucks.

---

5. Get Social

TechImpact and Unified found that fully 30 percent of the time people spend on their mobile devices is on social media and that *mobile users are nearly twice as likely to share content versus desktop users.* As noted above, images and videos are especially engaging, so one best practice is to make a viral thank you for donors, including a compelling photo and brief text outlining what kind of impact a certain size gift makes. These are designed to share on social media and are a great way to turn your donors into fundraisers (see Chapter 17 for more tips on using social media).

Optimize the size of viral thank you's to maximize impact: 500×500 pixels for Facebook and 500×250 pixels for Twitter.

6. Consider Building an App

Apps are a great way to engage your base, particularly if you're interacting with people on a recurring basis or if you have a lot of foot traffic, as at a museum or zoo. Apps are great because they are fast, can be accessed offline, and can integrate with phone functionalities like their GPS and cameras.

The downside to apps is that they can be expensive to develop, you need to develop separate apps for different mobile operating systems (Apple iOS, Windows, etc.), there is a lengthy approval process to bring them into the market, you need to heavily market them to attract users, and sometimes donations or payments through apps are blocked and force people to go through your mobile website. And, of course, just like a website or social media outlet, you need to commit to posting fresh content there; plus, you should plan on having to update the app as operating system upgrades occur. Start with the basics outlined above and, in nearly all cases, ***wait to develop an app until your website and email efforts are optimized for mobile***.

7. Stay Current

Being an early adopter gives you a leg up and helps your cause and message cut through the clutter, plus it reflects well on your organization when done right. Right now, mobile presents a great opportunity for you to do just that. Mobile technology, specifically mobile payment technology, is rapidly evolving, so if you do get on board, be sure to stay on top of it and keep an eye out for new platforms, developments, and resources.

For example, with the launch of the Apple Watch and Fitbit, wearables are now a hot trend, but what's coming next? Also, apps for donating, such as GiveApp.org and others like GreatNonprofits (think Yelp for nonprofits) or One Degree (Yelp for social services) are gaining ground, so use the resources outlined below to keep abreast of tools like these and assess how your nonprofit can take advantage of them as they arise. But just as with social media, ***don't spread your efforts too thin and focus on mastering the places where you already have a presence***. Less is more, but staying on top of the latest trends and tools is still crucial to maintaining a vibrant online presence and effectively engaging supporters.

Conclusion

Incorporating mobile tactics into your fundraising strategy will ensure that you are meeting people where they're at today—on their devices. The past two decades have brought a vast array of technological advances, and the pace of change and innovation isn't slowing. Technology is only going to continue to speed up and become the primary way in which we live, communicate, and fundraise. Focus on the big picture and view mobile as an opportunity to be innovative and successful. It's critical that your organization stay current on trends and technology, and that you strategically take advantage of new platforms and tools as they arise. But remember, no matter how many tools you have at your disposal, they won't make any difference unless you have creative, empowered people running your campaigns and telling your story effectively.

Do's and Don'ts

Do. . .

> . . . use at least a 13-point font for websites and email to optimize mobile viewing.

> . . . use clickable buttons, at least 200×60 pixels, for key calls to action.

> . . . test your donate page and preview emails on mobile devices before sending them out.

> . . . use Google Analytics's Mobile Performance Report to understand exactly how much of your traffic comes from mobile devices.

Don't. . .

> . . . launch a mobile strategy before taking the time to clarify your goals first.

> . . . complicate your message by trying to ask people to take more than one or two key actions.

> . . . build an app before optimizing your website, donation page, and emails.

About the Experts

Heather Mansfield is the principal blogger at Nonprofit Tech for Good and author of the best-selling books *Mobile for Good: A How-To Fundraising Guide for Nonprofits* and *Social Media for Social Good: A How-To Guide for Nonprofits*. Mansfield has twenty years of experience utilizing the Internet for fundraising, community building, and advocacy. To date, she has presented more than 100 social media and mobile media trainings worldwide. She was also named one of *TIME* magazine's Best Twitter Feeds of 2013.

Tanya Urschel has worked at PayPal for more than nine years and currently heads nonprofit marketing and oversees the growth of PayPal's nonprofit client base. Urschel combines a broad knowledge of PayPal's online and mobile payments offerings with deep fundraising industry experience, and most recently she was the lead content writer for *The PayPal Official Insider Guide to Online Fundraising*.

Resource Review

Sparrow: Mobile for All (www.SparrowMobile.com)
  In addition to providing discounted cell phone service to U.S. nonprofits and employees via TechSoup, Sparrow also partners with nonprofits serving the poor to power their mobile campaigns with devices, plans, and training on curated apps designed to connect people to jobs, housing, and social services.

Google Analytics' Mobile Performance Report (http://bit.ly/1kWVj34)
  This free report will help you figure out exactly how much of your traffic comes from mobile devices, and specifically which ones.

Nonprofit Tech for Good (www.nptechforgood.com)
  Heather Mansfield's blog is a wealth of information on all things social media and mobile. Also be sure to follow @NonprofitOrgs on Twitter.

Social Media for Nonprofits (www.SM4NP.org)
  This is the only conference series devoted to social media for social good, and they also produce a great blog that frequently covers mobile topics. Over time, they are more heavily integrating mobile into their conference agendas.

Eventbrite (www.eventbrite.com)
  This leading event registration platform integrates seamlessly with your mobile efforts and makes it easy for registrants to check in and receive updates on their phones.

PayPal (www.paypal.com/nonprofit)
PayPal produces regular mobile reports for nonprofits through this site; plus, they provide nonprofits a fast and safe way to accept donations online.

Mobile Marketing Watch (www.mobilemarketingwatch.com)
Find great articles on mobile marketing.

Mansfield, Heather. *Mobile for Good: A How-To Fundraising Guide for Nonprofits*. McGraw-Hill, 2014.
This is a practical, step-by-step guide to launching a new website and email newsletter that's compatible with mobile devices, as well as optimizing your efforts on Facebook, Twitter, Google+, LinkedIn, YouTube, and more.

Network for Good (www.networkforgood.org)
Find great resources about mobile and online fundraising on their website and blog, and you can also check out www.Fundraising123.org, their online and mobile fundraising website.

NTEN (www.nten.org)
Find great resources on their website, including Tim Arnold's article, "How to Make Your Website Mobile Friendly with Responsive Design." They also cover mobile topics at their annual nonprofit technology conference, NTC.

Pew Research Center (www.pewresearch.org/topics/mobile)
This is a great place to find data on mobile trends and usage statistics.

npENGAGE (www.npengage.com)
Blackbaud's online resource center for nonprofits has a lot of great information on mobile fundraising and other topics.

The Nonprofit Times (www.thenonprofittimes.com)
Find a wealth of information on fundraising topics, and check out their article on the "5 Fundraising Predictions for 2015." Hint: mobile is included.

Part

V

Foundations

Chapter 19

Research, Getting in the Door, and Securing an Invitation to Apply

"If we knew what it was we were doing, it wouldn't be called 'research,' would it?"

—Albert Einstein

Introduction

Foundations gave out over $55 billion to U.S. nonprofits in 2013, according to Foundation Center, and global giving is steadily increasing over time. When done right, foundation fundraising can deliver much-needed funding, support, and credibility to your cause, but the key to success is working smarter, not harder. Identifying the right prospects, securing a call or meeting to explore points of intersection, and making the most of those opportunities may not be intuitive or easy, but **with a few key pointers and best practices that we'll share in this chapter, you can turn your success rate from 5 percent to 50 percent**. And even better, you can do it in *less* time than you've been spending trying to secure grants.

Foundation Center tracks over 140,000 grantmakers globally, and if you don't take the time to figure out which funders are a fit for your organization and programs, you will waste precious resources pursuing grants that you'll never receive. You'll also leave the impression that you didn't do your homework, which might give you a bad reputation in the foundation community. Understanding how funders work and how to meet their standards and requirements will ensure you don't waste time pursuing dead ends. Directed research can also uncover personal connections your team has to foundation prospects who will help you get in the door. Ultimately, just like all aspects of fundraising, securing foundation grants is largely about relationships, so identifying or developing these bonds is critical to maximizing your chances for success.

To learn more about how to identify the best foundation prospects and secure those crucial calls and meetings, and ultimately invitations to apply for funding, I sat down with Tori O'Neal-McElrath, fundraising expert and author of *Winning Grants Step by Step*, and Leeanne G-Bowley, manager of capacity and leadership development at Foundation Center, who outlined a simple recipe for success.

Critical Skills and Competencies

1. Secure Informational Interviews

The best way to start your foundation research process is by asking peers at other organizations how they go about fundraising from foundations, and what they've learned along the way. We're all in this together, and nonprofits are pretty good about sharing resources and best practices. You will likely gain insights into particular funders that may be a fit for you and where your contacts know someone. In addition, look locally. Who funds your geographic location, and which of them care about the issues you're focused on? If you are new to foundation fundraising, try to *secure two to three informational interviews with local or regional foundations that support similar work*.

These interviews will help you gather facts, hone your meeting skills, and get a sense of how foundation funding works in your area. The goal of this initial process isn't fundraising per se, but is for you to learn about foundation fundraising *overall*. Often, though, even though you're not really going into your full pitch, you can still get practice summarizing your work to funders. In addition, you can also secure valuable input on potential targets and regarding that particular foundation's grantmaking process, and gain helpful insights on how to refine your efforts moving forward.

To secure these meetings, simply call or email with meeting requests. Make it clear you're just looking for an informational interview that you're new to foundation fundraising, keep your message short, and include who you are, and a short snippet of your work. Again, make it clear that you're not soliciting and that you just want to hear their input on foundation fundraising overall. This will help you develop relationships that can be used in the future.

The Different Kinds of Foundations

In order to raise money from foundations, it's helpful to first understand the difference between the various types of entities. Basic guidelines are below, admittedly more geared toward U.S. regulations, but remember that *every foundation is unique, so thorough research is the key to knowing whether any particular funder is a fit* for your organization and its programs.

Private Foundations
"Private foundation" is an IRS term and, technically, it includes family foundations. However, when we talk about these foundations, we're really talking about professional foundations with a paid staff. As a result, they tend to have a more systematic, strategic approach to giving, with established priorities and areas of giving or "programs." They're mission-driven and typically have clearly articulated goals and processes.

Usually, a "program officer" oversees grantmaking for each program area. But the chain of command usually goes higher, with grants formally approved by the board or investment committee. The size of the foundation, as well as the grants they disburse and how they do so, vary greatly, and there is usually a competitive grantmaking process. Private foundations are known for innovative solutions to big problems and are open to funding things that are unproven but have high potential if your organization is well established. Typically, you'll need a two-year track record before you can apply for funding, and I like to call these players "domino tippers," since they're a *great source of money to launch new initiatives, but they want to know you have a plan for reaching sustainability once their funding runs out*.

Family Foundations
These are typically smaller, family-led groups where family members' personal passions drive grantmaking. As such, they often behave like major donors, and many of them do not accept unsolicited proposals. So *you need to develop a personal relationship*

(continued)

(continued)

with someone in the family or on the foundation's board to secure support. Family foundations are best suited for nonprofits that are also engaged in major donor fundraising and understand what motivates donors, know how to read people, and take the time to understand relevant family dynamics. Given that their funding is personality-led, the types of issues and causes these foundations support can vary widely and change from one year to the next. When researching family foundations, look into whether or not they regularly add new grantees, in which case they may be a good prospect, or whether they give to the same institutions every year, which means they're not a likely supporter.

Community Foundations and Donor-Advised Funds
Instead of establishing a family foundation, some high net worth individuals choose to set up a donor-advised fund (DAF) at their local community foundation. Although the law states that once the money is contributed, the foundation decides exactly how to allocate it given the donor's priorities, in practice the donor directs its grants. As such, DAFs behave like family foundations, but community foundations typically also have discretionary grant budgets at their disposal. Those grants are issued in ways similar to private foundations, but the chief executive often has a personal "president's fund" he or she can grant from. There are generally multiple ways to approach community foundations, and **talking with the person who oversees major donors can result in them sharing your information and needs with potential supporters**.

If you're a newer organization, community foundations can be a good starting point for foundation funding, because they often work with a smaller set of applicants and grantees, given their geographic focus. Also, **after you secure one grant, others will be easier to obtain**; some funders look to see whether a nonprofit has a community foundation grant as a stamp of approval. Finally, many community foundations offer support beyond grant programs, including technical support, professional development, networking opportunities, and even in-kind space and services.

Corporate Foundations
Although corporate foundations are separate entities from their parent companies, ultimately the funds they grant out were originally the company's money. Because of this, they are almost always driven by similar values and tend to focus on program areas that relate to the parent. Like with family foundations, you have to read between the lines and understand their motivations. **Having a lot of donors or volunteers from a company**

is very helpful in securing corporate grants, because it demonstrates a strong connection. Corporate foundations like to support the geographic areas where they have employees to build morale, and getting in-kind support or matching gifts from companies are great ways to begin to establish a relationship.

Government Grants
Government grants can be complicated, so we've dedicated all of Chapter 20 to this topic. Generally speaking, since these grants are made with taxpayer dollars, they require a high level of accountability, and there is a lot of infrastructure required to apply and fulfill onerous reporting requirements. To pursue government grants, you need to be a well-established and well-resourced organization, fit the criteria closely, and have the capacity and track record to demonstrate you can accomplish the work. As you'll read in Chapter 20, even in this arena, building relationships with decision-makers is key.

2. Get Your House in Order

Are your organization's mission, strategy, and programs well-established and clearly articulated? Do you have a strategic or operating plan in place to provide confidence that your strategy is well-established and feasible? Do you have financial systems in place so you can track and monitor impact, especially as it relates to grants? Things such as program evaluations, quarterly reports, and impact reports will help foundations feel confident that you have the staff and systems in place to deliver on what you want to do and adequately report on your progress and impact. Aggregate these key documents so they're easy to access and share, and make sure you familiarize yourself with them before talking with potential funders.

3. Prepare Your Pitch

Now that you have your strategy in place, take the time to identify exactly what you want to fund and how much capital is required. This starts with your overall organizational needs, but also includes each of your programs, plus the initiatives you'd like to launch if and when they're funded. These "fundables," as I like to call them, are like arrows in a quiver, and being crystal clear about each of them will help you seize opportunities that arise with potential funders and donors.

Simply identifying your needs, with clear budgets for each, is not sufficient; *prepare a one-page overview for each of your fundables, along with a compelling 30- to 45-second elevator pitch* that succinctly conveys the need, your solution, and the impact it will have. It's crucial that you be able to articulate your organization's mission and goals in an inspirational yet concise way, as well as each of your programs and initiatives. Knowing these elevator pitches really well is absolutely critical to succeeding in fundraising, including securing and maximizing foundation calls and meetings. Practice these short pitches in advance as much as possible and ask for input to fine-tune them on an ongoing basis. This will prepare you to present whatever fits best with the priorities of funders and donors.

Types of Grants

Restricted grants from foundations can only be spent on specific programs or expenses, as dictated by a funder. Similarly, restricted gifts from donors must be used as directed. You are legally and ethically bound to adhere to these requests, but if plans change you can absolutely circle back and make the case for redirecting funds. To ensure you fulfill your obligations, your accountant needs to track all restricted funds immediately after they're received, and also as they're spent down.

Most restricted grants are directed to things like supporting your soup kitchen program, your capital campaign to buy a building for low-income housing, or for buying art supplies to serve more at-risk youth. Beyond these, you should also look for "capacity building" grants, which are usually provided by a foundation that is already supporting you to increase your ability to advance your work. These grants can be used for things like staff development, strategic plans, or technology upgrades.

Unrestricted grants—also known as general operating support—are less common, but ideal. These funds can be spent on anything to advance your mission, and certain funders exclusively provide this kind of flexible support. Many gifts from individuals are unrestricted, but major donors may want to direct their giving to specific needs and initiatives (see Chapters 8 and 9 for more on this).

---

4. Narrow Your Sights

Once you've completed the above steps, you're ready to conduct the research needed to identify your most likely funders. *The best resource for finding potential funders is Foundation Center's Foundation Directory Online*, which is available online through paid subscriptions and can also be used for free through Foundation Center offices in five U.S. cities, as well as through its network of more than 450 libraries and community centers worldwide.

More importantly, when you access their robust database through these venues, an experienced guide can help direct your efforts and show you the in's and out's of their system. If you're not as concerned with having an expert support your search, another unpaid option is their Foundation Directory Online Free, which provides grantseekers with essential information about nearly 90,000 foundations and enables keyword searches for more than 250,000 IRS Forms 990-PF.

The Grant Professionals Association is another great resource that offers free access to its prospect research database through regional partners and a paid online subscription. And of course, there's the Internet. Use the Web to research specific foundation prospects once you identify them through other tools, and also to identify the funders of other organizations in your field and region. Once you have a list of prospects, dive deeper and determine what drives their giving and, ultimately, whether they're truly a fit for your needs. Prioritize your leads based on connection and capacity—just as with individual and major donors—and *whittle your list down to the top 20 or 30 prospects, so you can focus your efforts where you're most likely to gain traction and funding*.

5. Get in the Door

I promised to share the secret to increasing your grantwriting success rate from 5 percent to 50 percent when we started this chapter. It starts with what I *personally* consider **the cardinal rule of foundation fundraising: _never_ apply for a grant unless you're invited**. You wouldn't show up to a party you weren't invited to, and the same is true in foundation fundraising. But this isn't as easy as it may sound; program officers and other grantmaking decision-makers are very busy, so you'll need to be both persistent and strategic in your outreach to get that crucial call or meeting.

The best way in the door is through leveraging a personal connection to the foundation. If you or someone on your board or staff knows someone at the foundation, even if it's the office manager, have him or her make a personal introduction. LinkedIn is a helpful tool to uncover these connections, and you can also obtain the foundation's board and staff list from their website or Foundation Center's database. Email that to your team and ask whether anyone knows any of the people there, but do this with one prospect at a time, so you don't overwhelm your board and staff with requests. If you're lucky enough to find a connection and get an introduction, follow up immediately and, if you don't hear back, continue to follow up every 10 or 20 days until you do. The key to success here is walking the fine line between being persistent and being annoying.

Your initial message should be brief: *keep it to no more than one-to-two short paragraphs and focus on getting the call or meeting* or a referral to a decision-maker. Thank your colleague for the introduction and quickly summarize why you think you're a fit with the foundation's priorities. Use the language of the organization, if possible, for example: "Given your work eradicating poverty in San Francisco, I'd love to talk with you about our innovative microlending program." Anything that lends an authentic connection also helps; perhaps you went to the same university, you have a friend in common, or you're partnering with one of their other grantees. Most importantly, *propose one or two specific days and times a week or two away for the call or a meeting*. Again, if you do not hear back, follow up every other week or so. You may also have luck by reaching out to the decision-maker's assistant or the relevant program associate to see whether that person can get you on the program officer's calendar or refer you up the chain of command.

Finally, be sure to leverage social media. You can glean a lot of important information through Facebook, Twitter, and LinkedIn. Facebook and LinkedIn are great for identifying shared connections, and Twitter is a useful forum to gain a better understanding of both the foundation and the program officer's interests and to build social capital by retweeting and following them. Google Alerts (http://google.com/alerts) is another useful tool, especially if you're having a hard time securing a call or meeting. Set an alert for the program officer's name and you'll receive an email whenever a new web page is posted that references him or her, including speaking engagements. Then you can prioritize attending those events and meeting your prospect in person.

6. Maximize Your Meeting

Once you've secured your call or meeting, your primary goal is to secure an invitation to apply for funding, which will double the 5 percent success rate of going in "cold." Just as being invited to a party is useless without the date, address, and time, success with foundation fundraising requires a bit more effort. Spend the first five or ten minutes of your conversation building the relationship, asking the program officer to share a bit about his or her background and connection to the work, and then ask open-ended questions to ascertain what drives the foundation's and program's funding decisions. This is essentially the same as the "appreciative inquiry" process outlined in Chapter 9.

It's critical that you *do your homework before your call or meeting; nothing turns off program offices more than fielding questions that can be answered through their website*. Instead, focus on "level two" questions that both demonstrate your familiarity with their efforts and provide useful insights as you prepare to contextualize your pitch in a way that's most compelling given their goals. For example, why did the foundation choose to focus on combating climate change, specifically by reducing carbon emissions? What specific impact are they hoping to generate from the grants they make? Ultimately, you are trying to figure out how you can help them do their job and fulfill their mandate. If they indicate that they are not interested in this level of conversation and relationship building, don't force it and move immediately to your pitch.

Now comes what I call the "pasta test," where you *quickly share your various elevator pitches and see what sticks*. As outlined above, 30 to 45 seconds is all you should need to give them a top line of each of your fundables, and be sure to only share the pitches that are most likely to resonate. Make sure to pause between pitches in case the program officer has any questions, but often he or she will wait until you're finished with the aggregate 3- or 4-minute pitch before asking questions and sharing which of your initiatives are most interesting. It helps to say in advance that you'd like to share a bit about your organization and X particular initiatives that you believe may be of interest.

Typically, he or she will let you know if anything resonates and feels like a fit, and why. Take copious notes and be sure to capture which initiatives are of interest and the exact language the program officer uses to explain why it's compelling. For example, "I think your vocational training program could be a potential fit for our economic security program, given our commitment to offering those in need a hand up, not a hand out." Many times this language is used internally and guides decision making, but cannot be found on their website or public documents, and you'll want to include it in your proposal.

If the program officer doesn't indicate that any of your pitches are a clear fit, you will need to ask outright by saying something like: "I see you're taking applications for your environment program, and I think our climate change initiative might be a good fit. What do you think?" or "I know you don't accept unsolicited proposals. Do you think we're a fit? Can we receive an invitation to apply?" Either way, if you proposed something in alignment with their goals, they may well ask questions and want to know more about the initiative. Go as far down the rabbit hole as your audience wants, but always remember to focus on the need and the impact.

At this point, you've received an offer to apply for grants for specific fundables, and hopefully secured a bit of context in terms of why they're a fit, but your success rate is still only 25 percent or so. Your work isn't quite done yet!

Your next step is to *ask what size grant you should write for each of the fundables the person expressed interest in*. Your research will likely give you a sense of an appropriate ask amount, which should be on the high end of their range, since they'll tell you if you're overreaching. But if you're operating in a vacuum, I suggest giving a range of 50 to 100 percent of a program's budget, or 12.5 to 25 percent of your total budget for a general operating support grant, since funders never want to underwrite your entire organization.

This sounds something like: "Thanks so much for your interest in our art therapy program! The overall program budget for next year is $100,000. Would it be realistic to apply for the full amount, or as a first-time grantee, might $50,000 be more reasonable?" or "We're ecstatic to hear that you'd consider making an unrestricted grant to support Save the Whales! Our operational budget next year is $1 million. Do you think a quarter-million-dollar grant request is reasonable, or would $125,000 be more appropriate?" *After each ask, be silent and let the person think and respond*. It's critical that the program officer be the next person to speak.

Providing the foundation with two options often leads to a response that also includes a range, for example: "Well, honestly, even $50,000 is well beyond our grantmaking range. We typically keep first-time grants to $10,000, but perhaps we could consider something as large as $25,000." The next thing you're writing down after that statement is the ask amount for your proposal: $25,000. In your proposal, *always* ask for as much funding as possible within the range they've shared.

About one-third of the grants written at this point will hit home, but there's one final piece of the puzzle that can take you to 50 percent, which I call my "Jedi mind trick." After you have all the other information outlined above, *ask the program officer if he or she would be willing to review a draft of your proposal before it's formally submitted.* If he or she agrees, make sure to ask when you need to send the draft to leave enough time for the review. Realistically, though, I've used this trick many times and program officers almost always say "yes," but almost never deliver. That's OK: what you're after isn't edits and fine-tunes, although that'd be even better, but more importantly, your goal is to get the program officer to "adopt" your proposal and actively champion it as it's reviewed internally.

Now that you have the 50 percent secret, there's only one final question to ask, which is who else you might approach for funding. Program officers tend to be knowledgeable and well connected in the areas they fund, so they are a great resource for identifying additional prospects. As any seasoned fundraiser or salesperson will tell you, you should ***never miss a chance to ask a prospect or supporter for referrals to other leads***, ideally including a personal intro via a short email or at least someone's contact information.

7. Stay in Touch

After your call or meeting, be sure to follow up, ideally with a hand-written card or at least an email expressing your gratitude for the time and insight. Reiterate any action items and timelines, possibly including a bullet point list of next steps. Be sure to promptly deliver any information, documents, introductions, or anything else promised in your meeting.

If you were lucky enough to receive an invitation to apply for funding, it's important that you are in contact before submitting the proposal, as well as afterward, even if you don't get the grant. Keep in touch and send occasional updates on your work as it relates to their funding goals. Two to four updates a year should suffice. Add them to a list in your address book that you can use to share big news, such as a front-page article or an exciting new hire. Stewarding these decision-makers as you would a major donor will help you build valuable relationships, increasing your chances for funding from that foundation and others over time (see Chapter 9 for more on stewardship).

Conclusion

The lion's share of work that goes into securing foundation grants happens before you even submit a proposal. If you want to succeed in institutional fundraising, you'll need to invest time, money, and people into properly researching and cultivating foundations. But remember to go deeper versus wider, since your efforts are best spent on a small list of top prospects whose philanthropic goals closely align with your work. Once you have identified these targets, you'll need to be persistent and creative to get in the door and receive an invitation to apply, along with other crucial information that will help your proposal rise to the top. This is not an easy process, but you are infinitely better off spending time investing in building these relationships, instead of applying for grants that you have not been asked to submit. After all, foundation fundraising, like all fundraising, is about building relationships, and in this case it is with foundation staff, especially program officers. Now that you have your recipe to achieve a 50 percent success rate, it's time to start cooking!

Do's and Don'ts

Do. . .

>   . . . meet with peer fundraisers to hear their insights on foundations before you start.

>   . . . take advantage of Foundation Center and identify your 20 to 30 top foundation prospects.

>   . . . craft a series of compelling yet concise elevator pitches for your organization as a whole, and for each of your programs and proposed initiatives.

>   . . . go beyond securing an invitation to apply for funding by asking which "fundables" are a fit, why, how much to request for each, and ask the program officer to review a draft of your proposal.

Don't. . .

>   . . . waste precious resources and time by applying for grants you haven't been invited to submit.

>   . . . overwhelm your staff and board by asking them whether they have a connection to too many foundation prospects at once.

>   . . . assume that foundations are alike just because they're focused on similar issues or regions or have similar structures.

About the Experts

Tori O'Neal-McElrath is the director of institutional advancement at the Center for Community Change and has more than 25 years of experience in the philanthropic and nonprofit arenas. She previously ran her own consulting practice (O'Neal Consulting), served as executive director for The Price Scholarship Program and director of special programs at The San Diego Foundation, vice president of development at Planned Parenthood Los Angeles, and associate development director at The College Fund/UNCF in Los Angeles. She is also author of the third and fourth editions of *Winning Grants Step by Step*.

Leeanne G-Bowley is manager of capacity and leadership development at Foundation Center and the artistic and executive director at In-Sight Dance Company. G-Bowley is the lead instructor for Foundation Center's national capacity and leadership development program, and through facilitation, coaching, and the creation of curriculum, she develops social sector leaders who have strong nonprofit acumen, confidence, and renewed dedication to the social sector.

Resource Review

Foundation Center (foundationcenter.org)
> Foundation Center maintains the most comprehensive database on grantmakers and provides resources through its website and webinar series, and free education opportunities through local chapters.

Grant Professionals Association (www.grantprofessionals.org)
> A national member organization, the GPA hosts an annual conference on effective grantwriting, offers a valuable newsletter, and has regional chapters across the United States that meet regularly for networking and educational events.

GrantSpace (www.grantspace.org)
> A service of Foundation Center, GrantSpace provides easy-to-use, self-service tools and resources to help nonprofits worldwide become more viable grant applicants and build strong, sustainable organizations. Foundation Center resources will give you valuable insight into the grantmaker's perspective:

GrantCraft (www.grantcraft.org)
> GrantCraft combines the practical wisdom of funders worldwide with the expertise of Foundation Center to improve the practice of philanthropy.

Glasspockets (www.glasspockets.org)
  Glasspockets provides the data, resources, examples, and action steps
  foundations need to understand the value of transparency, be more
  open in their own communications, and help shed light on how private
  organizations serve the public good.

IssueLab (www.issuelab.org)
  Identify important reports and studies in your field, as produced by a
  wide range of nonprofits, practitioners, and researchers.

Nonprofit with Balls (www.nonprofitwithballs.com)
  Vu Le's blog offers practical tips for foundation fundraisers and gives
  readers a good reality check on cultural competency.

You can identify unique opportunities by staying connected to the rest
of the world by reading *The New York Times*, *Crain's Business*, *Forbes*, the
Corporate Social Responsibility Newswire, and the like.

Staying connected to your field is an important way to ensure relevancy,
while raising your organization's profile. Identify and connect with
your relevant service organizations, regularly read industry blogs and
publications, and identify and attend the top conferences in your field.

20

Chapter

Government Grants

"The care of human life and happiness, and not their destruction, is the first and only object of good government."
—Thomas Jefferson

Introduction

According to the Urban Institute's *Nonprofit Sector in Brief*, **the U.S. government awarded nonprofits over $198 billion in grants in 2014**. Government grants are available for a large variety of issues and programs, and are often sizeable. However, they also come with intense demands around implementation and reporting. *Unless you have at least one staff person dedicated full-time to managing government grants, think carefully about your organization's capacity before moving into this territory.*

There is a saying among nonprofit professionals: "If you've seen a thousand foundations, you've seen a thousand foundations." Basically, every foundation—government, private, or family—operates differently and has different requirements and expectations. So while there are best practices for how to research, request, and report to foundations, each situation will differ and require a customized approach, particularly among government entities.

To learn more about securing, managing, and surviving government grants, I sat down with Joshua Sheridan Fouts, government grant veteran and executive director of Bioneers, and he outlined top five tips to maximize your results.

Critical Skills and Competencies

1. Get Help

If this is your first experience applying for a government grant, Fouts highly recommends hiring a consultant. There are people who specialize in helping nonprofits secure government grants and who know exactly what it takes to apply for, and report on, them. A professional consultant can help you effectively communicate how your project will meet the goals of the grant program, and he or she will know the jargon and language that increase your chances. Most importantly, the consultant will likely have relationships with key decision-makers. In foundation fundraising, as in *all* fundraising, *the key to success is building relationships*. A grantmaker is much more likely to give you serious consideration if he or she recognizes your name on the application and already knows something about your work.

Where to Find Government Grants

Grants.gov is the best place for finding U.S. government grants. You can register on the site and choose which grant opportunities are of interest. They will send you email notifications of grant opportunities (often a lot, Fouts says), and you can research and choose which to pursue. If you're based outside the United States, use Google to find an equivalent resource in your country, ideally provided by the government at no cost to you.

---

2. Don't Apply Cold

Following up on the previous point and chapter, the most significant determinant of your success in securing government grants is making contact with a decision-maker before applying and, ideally, securing an invitation to apply. In government, the decision-maker's title can change from department to department, but grants, program, or desk officer are the most common. Once you figure out who calls the shots, reach out to ask for an informational interview (see Chapter 19 for tips on how to maximize your first meeting). At this meeting, focus on developing a relationship and obtaining pointers on how to optimally position your application. This will help you stand out from the others who fail to make contact in advance and submit more cookie-cutter proposals.

3. Plan for Long Nights

Every government grant application is unique, and most of them are quite onerous to complete. They are often detailed and elaborate and require you to use specific computer programs to submit the grant. There is little consistency, and you may even get stuck with an interface that is so outdated that your computer isn't compatible. This is where having a consultant comes in handy, because they're aware of these issues and have solutions for overcoming them. Hopefully, these challenges will decrease as the government invests in updating their systems, but don't hold your breath.

4. Be Patient and Prepared

Receiving a response to your grant application can take months, or even longer. Government officials, like grant officers, often change positions, so **keeping in touch is key**. Don't bother with email; a phone call every couple months is much more effective and creates a much stronger relationship with your contact and your cause. And once you're approved, receiving the funds can often take longer than you expect. You need to be ready to start working on your project right away regardless, so be prepared to use cash reserves until the grant funds are dispersed. If that's not an option, there are groups like the Northern California Community Loan Fund (www.ncclf.org) that can loan you the funds temporarily. Either way, prepare yourself in advance: *it is critical that you are prepared to begin both work and reporting immediately after being approved*.

5. Stay in the Loop

Once you've received a government grant, the likelihood of receiving additional funding goes up by an order of magnitude. This may affect the return on investment calculations and justify hiring a consultant or research service. Either way, keep in touch with the people you've developed relationships with, especially grantmaking decision-makers, and continuously keep an eye open for additional opportunities. Resources like grants.gov can also be helpful, as you can sign up for notifications of relevant grants.

Conclusion

Government grants represent your tax dollars at work. They can enable very rewarding opportunities for your organization, while benefitting society in needed ways. While they may seem difficult and overwhelming to secure, don't be discouraged. If you have the capacity and wherewithal, you can raise large amounts of money to do critical work. There are hundreds of billions of dollars in government grants available to nonprofits in the United States alone, plus much more abroad since many global cultures support heavy government funding of nonprofits, so this is not an area to quickly dismiss as "too difficult." Take a look at grants.gov and other resources to see whether there are any opportunities that fit the work you do. Think carefully about how you can build capacity and dedicate the staff needed to secure and administer these grants. With help from consultants who specialize in this area, your chances of success increase significantly, as they do when you take the time to build and nurture relationships with the individuals who decide which organizations receive funding. And once you receive a government grant, you're in the game, and your chances of receiving additional grants increase tremendously. Onward and upward!

Do's and Don'ts

Do. . .

> . . . dedicate at least one staff person to managing your government grant full-time.

> . . . register your nonprofit with grants.gov if you're based in the United States, or with similar government services abroad.

> . . . be prepared to implement your proposed program immediately after receiving a decision.

Don't. . .

> . . . sign up for paid services that promise to give you access to government grant opportunities; this information is free to the public in the United States and most countries.

> . . . apply for a grant without first making contact with key decision-makers, ideally including them inviting you to apply.

. . . expect the process to be simple and straightforward; in fact it's
lengthy and cumbersome.

About the Expert

Joshua Sheridan Fouts is a globally recognized media innovator and
social entrepreneur, known for his visionary work paving new inroads for
meaningful understanding between cultures. Fouts is an anthropologist,
thirty-year fundraising veteran, and former U.S. State Department
employee responsible for grants management. He currently serves as
executive director for Bioneers, a nonprofit think tank that produces
conferences and media that bring together social and scientific innovators
to solve the world's most pressing environmental and social challenges.

Resource Review

Grants.gov (www.grants.gov)
   This is the best place to find and apply for U.S. government grants.
   Register online and sign up to receive customized notifications of grant
   opportunities.
GovFresh (govfresh.com)
   This is a great blog that features public servant innovators, civic
   entrepreneurs, and ideas and technology that are changing the way the
   government works.
Browning, Beverly A. *Grant Writing for Dummies* (5th ed.). John Wiley &
   Sons, 2014.
   This book will help you navigate federal grant databases and apply online
   for grants, find current public and private sector grant opportunities,
   create strong statements of need, and submit applications that meet
   funders' expectations.
Richardson, Kimberly. *The Official Federal Grants Prep Guide: 10 Tips to
   Position Your Organization for Success*. Kimberly Richardson Consulting,
   LLC, 2013.
   This book is for anyone who wants to participate in the U.S. federal grant
   writing process. At the end of each chapter in this incredibly useful guide,
   Richardson lists some questions to ask yourself, which help you reflect
   and prepare; plus it offers many useful tools and examples.

eCivis (www.ecivis.com)
Provides a cloud-based grants management system to assist with researching, tracking, and reporting, and that serves as a knowledge base for nonprofits, municipal governments, and educational institutions. They also provide nationwide grant writing services and webinars.

Find Consultants Specializing in Government Grants

- *The Chronicle of Philanthropy* (https://philanthropy.com)
- Idealist.org (www.idealist.org)

Urban Institute (www.urban.org)
Find a variety of research on the nonprofit sector in general, as well as government contracts and grants.

Research portal: www.urban.org/research-area/nonprofits-and-philanthropy

Nonprofit Sector in Brief 2014: www.urban.org/sites/default/files/alfresco/publication-pdfs/413277-The-Nonprofit-Sector-in-Brief.PDF

Chapter 21

Writing a Winning LOI and Proposal

"If you've seen one foundation . . . you've seen one foundation."
—Anonymous

Introduction

In Chapter 19, we discussed how important foundation funding is to a successful fundraising strategy. It accounts for 16 percent of the over $300 billion given to U.S. nonprofits in 2013, according to Giving USA. Foundations can be more accessible than major donors, since you don't need to have a personal relationship with a high net worth individual; you just need to get in the door and prove that you are doing relevant work that meets their goals, using the tips we provided in that chapter. However, the vast majority of foundation grant requests are denied. In addition to putting those tips to work to get you to that 50 percent success rate, it's still critical that you write letters of inquiry and proposals that break through the clutter and clearly articulate your work and impact, inspiring the reader to fund you. You need to *get their attention, explain clearly what you're seeking funding for and how it maps to their goals, and get them engaged as partners in your work* so they're excited about the impact they can help make possible.

When you write a letter of inquiry, also known as a letter of interest (LOI), the better the impression you make, the more likely you'll be funded. An LOI is traditionally the first step in being invited to submit a full proposal—although this is changing and the LOI seems to be falling out of favor with some funders, who prefer a one-step application process—but can sometimes directly result in a grant. With few exceptions, I *personally* believe **you should only apply for grants you've been invited to submit**.

That said, the experts I interviewed for this chapter agree it's ideal to be invited, but also suggest applying "cold" if your research tells you you're a solid fit and the foundation's guidelines prohibit you making contact. Either way, whether you've already done the hard work to get in the door and secure an invitation to apply, plus secured a few key additional pieces of information outlined in Chapter 19), or decided to apply anyway, then your next step is implementing the best practices outlined in this chapter for proposal writing to maximize your chances for success.

It's not rocket science, and by implementing these tips, you can unlock huge sums of funding and build important relationships and credibility. In short, whether you're writing an LOI or a full grant proposal, your primary objective is to eliminate any reasons they may have for saying no, and to give them compelling reasons to say yes. Ultimately, **it's not about you or your organization; it's about how you can help advance their goals**.

To learn more about the secrets to writing killer LOIs and proposals, I interviewed Susan Fox, veteran fundraising consultant and co-author of *Grant Proposal Makeover: Transform Your Request from No to Yes,* and Jane Geever, fundraising expert and author of *The Foundation Center's Guide to Proposal Writing*. They outlined the following simple tips to improve your success rate and help you secure more funding, both from U.S. and global foundations.

Critical Skills and Competencies

1. Communicate Clearly and Follow Directions

An LOI is usually a one- to three-page letter introducing your organization and concisely laying out what you want funding for, how much, and most importantly, how your request maps to the funder's goals. In order to write a successful LOI or grant proposal, you don't need to be a great writer. You simply need to be able to succinctly articulate and clearly communicate key points to outsiders, ideally grantmakers who already expressed an interest in your work and invited your proposal.

Based on the funder's priorities and insights gained in the call or meeting where you received the invitation to apply, focus your proposal on what you're doing that will help meet *their* goals and clarify why you're in a unique position to fulfill this need. Lead with your organization's strengths, and ***include the dollar amount requested and use of funds in the first paragraph.***

You also need to be detail oriented and ***follow the grantmaker's directions and guidelines precisely***—from the deadline, to the length, format, and things like font size and spacing if those are specified. And make sure you answer all the questions asked. Even if you are a perfect fit, you may be denied if you fail to follow the application directions.

2. Do Your Homework

Nothing annoys a funder more than having to read a proposal that is clearly out of sync with their priorities. Most foundations provide plenty of information on their websites about what they fund and why, and hopefully you gained valuable insights into why specific initiatives and programs are a fit in the call or meeting where you were invited to apply.

Either way, if you don't educate yourself and align your application with their stated priorities, you are wasting everyone's time, including your own. You need to succinctly articulate why you fit within the foundation's scope of work; especially how the impact your work will have is aligned with the goals of the foundation. As outlined in Chapter 19, ***any language the program officer uses to explain why they may be interested in funding you should absolutely find its way into your proposal.***

3. Show Vision

When applying for a grant, it's very likely that there are lots of other great organizations competing for the same funding. You must convince the foundation that they should fund your organization rather than another because you have a vision and long-term plan in place. The foundation is looking to further a specific set of objectives so, as mentioned, you have to articulate how your work is in sync with that, but they also want to understand how the proposed program or initiative fits within the context of your overall organizational goals. Concisely explaining your long-term strategic goals and quickly articulating how the specific, proposed program advances those helps strengthen your case.

Programs should connect your vision to action, and this should be summarized in a simple sentence like: "Your support of $100,000 will help enable us to hire two field officers, enabling us to serve 250 additional homeless next year and advancing our vision of a Minneapolis where no one goes without housing, food, and medical care." Even if you don't volunteer this information, many grantmakers find the context helpful, and as such they sometimes ask for strategic plans as attachments to your proposal.

4. Verify Facts and Math

Nothing spells disaster for your proposal more than numbers that don't add up or false citations. Before submitting your materials, make sure to review these one last time. Remember that your audience is likely an expert in your field, so verify your sources for all data and statistics used. And, of course, *double-check the math on all your budgets and any numbers mentioned within the proposal to ensure they add up*. Funders pay attention to these details and will notice if something is off, creating an embarrassing situation that undermines your credibility and potentially resulting in you not receiving the grant.

5. Establish Credibility

It is important that you demonstrate the competency of both the organization and the people undertaking the actual work you're requesting funding for. By including short professional biographies outlining the relevant expertise of key personnel, in addition to a short overview of the organization and its accomplishments and accolades, you will bolster the funder's confidence. You can also provide past examples of similar work, clearly articulating their impact, or compare your approach to similar methodologies successfully used elsewhere, showing that you are using proven best practices. Anything you can do to establish credibility will go a long way toward making your case for support.

6. Make It Easy to Read

When in doubt, cover your butt. On one hand, as mentioned above, you should assume the grantmaker reading your proposal is an industry expert who can spot faulty citations. At the same time, when it comes to jargon and acronyms, assume you're talking with a novice. Spell things out and define industry terms when first used.

Re-read your application before you submit it with fresh eyes and ask yourself: What questions might someone possibly have when reading this? How can I proactively answer these so they don't need to be asked in the first place? If possible, have someone else in your organization, or even one of your friends or family, read the proposal and see whether it makes sense to them and feels compelling. This is also a fun and useful way to get your mom to stop asking you what you do at work all day!

It's also helpful to ensure your proposal is easy on the eye and not challenging to read. *Use a minimum 11-point font and avoid using something smaller to meet a page number requirement.* Put headers in bold and underline them to highlight key points, or put them in all CAPS if it's an online form. You can also use things like colons and numbered or bulleted lists to underscore important ideas and break up your proposal so your concepts are easier to digest.

7. Be Persistent

As outlined in Chapter 19, it's important that you take the time to develop and nurture relationships with foundation staff. This is critical not only for getting a meeting or securing an invitation to apply, but also when one of your proposals is denied. Take the time to follow up and ask why it was determined that you were not a fit, ideally in a phone call.

Just like with individuals and major donors, this can provide important insights on your ongoing fundraising efforts and sometimes open a window for subsequent appeals. Geever likes to say, and Fox readily agrees, "A rejection is the first step in the process." Perhaps it wasn't the right timing for the foundation, or you didn't clearly articulate your program. Odds are you won't be able to convince them to change their mind, but you may receive feedback that can refine your efforts with other funders and help you prepare a more compelling ask for that funder on your next try.

You must be persistent and be willing to go back to foundations over and over again and, as you develop strong relationships, your chances of securing funding in the future increase. At all costs, *avoid behaving rudely, being disrespectful, or talking badly of foundations if you are rejected*; foundation fundraising is a smaller world than it seems, and developing a bad reputation is easier than you might think.

Conclusion

Just as nonprofits help people with resources achieve the change they want to see in the world, so, too, are they an integral partner for advancing foundation goals. In short, we are partners to foundations, and they're in the business of serving the community by working with us. A program officer's job is selecting the right partners to collaborate with, and if you can develop a relationship and submit a clear, concise proposal that makes a strong case for why your organization is in a unique position to advance their work, amazing things become possible. More than you think, foundations understand your needs and want to be your partner in creating impact and making a difference. They are very knowledgeable and passionate about the areas they fund, which creates a wonderful opportunity for connection. Take the time to gracefully and intelligently approach foundations and program officers, view them as partners, and nurture relationships with them. And when you're writing LOIs and proposals, remember that there's a human being out there who will read it. Make sure that you present something that is clearly and succinctly articulated, easy to read, engages your audience, and inspires them to fund your work.

Do's and Don'ts

Do. . .

> . . . respond to inquiries from program officers in a timely manner, putting your best foot forward.

> . . . tailor your proposal to the foundation's goals and objectives.

> . . . verify all statistics and data you quote, and double-check your math.

> . . . have a long-term plan and be able to articulate how your proposal fits into it.

Don't. . .

> . . . preach to a program officer when he or she likely knows as much as you do about the subject.

> . . . send out a cookie-cutter proposal.

> . . . provide extraneous information and attachments that are not requested.

> . . . exaggerate in your application.

About the Experts

Susan Fox has worked as an independent fundraising consultant to nonprofit organizations since 1980 and is co-author of *Grant Proposal Makeover: Transform Your Request from No to Yes*. Fox has held the designation of Certified Fund Raising Executive since 1995 and provides services in strategic fundraising.

Jane C. Geever is the founder of J.C. Geever, Inc. (est. 1975), the first woman-led fundraising company admitted into membership in the Giving Institute, formerly American Association of Fund Raising Counsel (AAFRC). Geever has written widely on topics related to fundraising, and is author of *The Foundation Center's Guide to Proposal Writing*, now in its sixth edition.

Resource Review

Geever, Jane C. *The Foundation Center's Guide to Proposal Writing* (6th ed.). Foundation Center, 2012.
　This book provides numerous samples of successful grant proposals and gives you insight into the mind of foundation grant readers and what they're looking for in a proposal.
Foundation Center (www.foundationcenter.org)
　Foundation Center maintains the most comprehensive database on grantmakers and provides resources through their website and local chapters.
Association of Fundraising Professionals/AFP (www.afpnet.org)
　Their international conference and regional fundraising days offers tracks on foundation fundraising. They also have regional chapters that do local events throughout the year.
Resource Alliance (www.resource-alliance.org)
　This is a wonderful resource for fundraisers around the globe. Find great resources on their website, learn about educational opportunities, and check out their International Fundraising Congress conference.
Alliance for Nonprofit Management (www.allianceonline.org)
　Find a great resource library on their site, and connect to state nonprofit associations, management support organizations, and universities.

Grant Professionals Association/GPA (www.grantprofessionals.org)
  GPA has a robust website with many online grantwriting resources and
  articles, as well as an annual conference and regional chapters.

Clarke, Cheryl. *Storytelling for Grantseekers: The Guide to Creative Nonprofit
  Fundraising*. Jossey-Bass, 2001.
  This is an introduction to the ins and outs of foundation proposal writing
  and grantmaking, which gives concrete examples of pitfalls to avoid and
  best practices for proposal writing.

Chapter 22

Tracking Progress and Reporting Back

"The right thing to do and the hard thing to do are usually the same."

—Steve Maraboli

Introduction

Securing a grant is wonderful, but unless you also set up systems to track and report on the progress of your work to that funder, it will likely be the only grant you receive from them. *When you sign a grant agreement, you are legally and ethically bound to use the grant funds as dictated in the agreement.* Moreover, by being accountable and transparently reporting your efforts to the funder—and especially what impact their support enabled— you strengthen your relationship and increase your chances of securing additional support.

Evaluation and reporting aren't something people typically are trained in because, let's face it, the pressure to bring money in the door is all-consuming. However, it's critical that you recognize the connection between foundation reporting and revenue opportunities and invest resources in it. Just as you steward individual donors to increase and renew their gifts, ***to maximize foundation funding it's crucial you steward***

235

relationships with funders by letting them know exactly how you've spent their money and what difference it made.

Investing time into training employees, creating systems to track grant progress, and reporting back to funders is key. But this organizational capacity can also help you secure new backers, since it enables you to include evaluation metrics in your proposal, demonstrating your expertise and ensuring the funder and you are on the same page regarding measuring success. This gives funders confidence that you know what you're trying to accomplish, and how you'll get there.

To learn more about tracking progress toward grant objectives and successfully reporting back to funders, I sat down with Dr. Beverly Browning, author of *Grant Writing for Dummies* and 40 other publications, and VP of Grant Writing Services at eCivis, who shared five simple tips for success.

Critical Skills and Competencies

1. Get SMART

As we discussed in the introduction, tracking progress starts with your proposal. That's where you share information on how you plan to evaluate the proposed work, including key metrics and benchmarks. To do this, Browning recommends utilizing what she calls "accountability language." This means including—and subsequently tracking—SMART (Specific, Measurable, Attainable, Realistic, and Time-Bound) objectives into your proposal and reporting against each of them in a detailed way. This helps ensure a concrete strategy and goals, and will ultimately facilitate you proving the program was successful and that the funder's money was well spent.

SMART goals are clear and specific, instead of vague and undefined. So instead of saying something like, "We aim to help low-income students of color graduate and pursue higher education," a SMART goal would be increasing the number of students from Mission High School who enroll in college by 30 percent, as demonstrated by the number of students enrolled in our university mentorship program by the end of the year. Especially when a program like this has a history of directly contributing to the goal—college enrollment in this case—this framework allows you to build off your work and garner additional support.

Just as your SMART goals are detailed and specific, so, too, must you be when tracking progress against them. If you received a restricted grant (see Chapter 19), you'll also need to keep accurate reporting of all expenses incurred against the program supported by the grant. To facilitate this, most foundations provide their own budget proposal and financial reporting templates, and some also request a budget narrative or a written description of any significant discrepancies from your plan.

2. Have an Evaluation Plan

Once a grant is received, you need a plan in place to start monitoring and tracking both impact and expenses. It is critical that you sit down with all the team members involved to review the scope of work proposed and the SMART goals you agreed to with the funder. Of course, this should have already been discussed during the grant-writing process, but once you actually receive the funds, things inevitably change. Either way, *host a grant kick-off meeting to ensure the entire team is in alignment regarding your evaluation plan and understands what's expected of them.*

At this meeting, take the time to reiterate program and grant objectives, assign responsibility to key staff for the various components of the work—including collecting and reporting back on the metrics you've identified—and create timelines for each objective. Discuss the methods by which each objective will be measured (spreadsheets, surveys, or other means), and exactly how the data and stories will be collected. (See Chapter 7 for more tips on this.)

Make sure you include both quantitative and qualitative inputs, such as number of clients served, as well as individual testimonies from clients regarding how the program has impacted their lives. *Establishing an evaluation plan from the start will allow you to regularly check in and assess whether the work is progressing as intended and implement corrective actions when necessary.* Some organizations also work with experienced evaluation consultants who help them monitor progress and develop data collection tools like data logs, oral interviews, and case management files to define and capture these outputs.

3. Be Diligent

As soon as you're awarded a grant, the clock starts ticking. In addition to developing your evaluation plan, *schedule a SWOT analysis quarterly*, if not even more frequently. SWOT stands for Strengths, Weaknesses,

Opportunities, and Threats, and this is a great framework for taking stock in your program, identifying potential breakdowns and corrective actions, and soliciting input regarding how to fine-tune and expand your efforts. Your SWOT analysis should involve all of your stakeholders: program staff, clients served, volunteers, partners, board members, and anyone else who plays an active role or will be affected by the program. Regular SWOT analyses help you stay proactive and ensure everyone is in active communication, minimizing the chance that you'll face a crisis you didn't see coming.

Logic Models

Developing a logic model is the process of creating a roadmap for implementing and evaluating your program. There are different approaches for creating these, but in Browning's world, *a logic model is an easy-to-read, one-page graphic with four sections*, presented in landscape mode so the paper is wider versus taller. In the first section she lists *resources* or *inputs*. What do you need to make this program work and succeed?

The second section is for *strategies* or *goals*. What are the goals you intend to accomplish with this program to advance your mission? Then there are *outputs*. What are you going to count to gauge progress? These are the key metrics discussed above and in detail in Chapter 7. Browning reserves the fourth section for *outcomes*, split into two columns: short-term and long-term. Refer back to the SMART objectives from your proposal and identify the ultimate impact you seek.

Use the short-term column to evaluate programs for interim grant reports, usually presented halfway through the grant, and the long-term column is focused on impact for the final report. If your grant term is longer than 12 months, consider adding an intermediate-term outcomes column and define the timeline for collecting the measurement in months. For example: short-term (6 months), intermediate-term (12 months) and long-term (24 months).

At the bottom of Browning's logic model, she includes an impact statement to underscore why this model is important, and what the program is designed to achieve. This is where you share your vision of success, or how the world will be different once this project is complete. It's a way to convey the big picture, and envisioning your long-term impact can be exciting and inspiring for both you and the funder, instead of focusing only on the immediate accomplishments of the program and impact of the grant.

4. Recruit Expertise

While you should always evaluate your own impact, having an objective third party also review and assess your metrics and methodologies is always helpful and adds crucial credibility with funders. Ideally, engage this expert or firm from the beginning, when you craft your proposal and evaluation framework (the formative phase), but definitely enlist support with implementation and reporting once the project is complete and you're compiling a final report for a funder (summative phase). ***If you don't have the resources to hire a professional consultant, engage a volunteer or student with experience in statistics or program effectiveness and evaluation.*** This resource will help you answer these questions:

During the Formative Phase

- What needs attention immediately?
- What should the project try to accomplish?
- What are the goals and objectives of the project?
- Is there agreement on the goals from all involved parties?
- What do stakeholders perceive they need?
- What problems are they experiencing?
- What do project staff and/or volunteers perceive they need?
- What problems are they experiencing?
- How will we gauge the effectiveness of the project in addressing problems perceived by the stakeholders?
- How will we identify where and why the project is failing to achieve goals, and how often will this be assessed?

During the Summative Phase

- What were the goals and objectives of the project?
- Did the planned project occur?
- Were the intended goals and objectives achieved?
- How effective was the program?
- What conclusions can be drawn about the impact and effectiveness of the project?
- What programs are available as alternatives to our project moving forward?

- How effective is our project in comparison to these alternatives?
- Is our program differentially effective with particular types of participants and/or in particular locations or communities?
- How costly was the project, and how did these expenses align with what was projected?

5. Share Bad News Quickly

Even if you have SMART objectives and conduct regular SWOT analyses, there is still room for the unexpected and problems can still arise; programs can still fail. If this occurs, be honest and communicate with your funder as soon as possible, ideally conveying not only obstacles and problems, but also how you intend to address and correct them. *Transparency engenders trust.*

Your funders are your partners, so engage them in solutions, keep them abreast of progress, and let them know as problems arise so you don't surprise them later. ***Funders appreciate transparency and communication; they're invested into your vision and share the same goal as you.*** Also, if you delay delivering bad news, well-connected funders may hear about it from another source, and you may lose your funding and the opportunity to turn the situation around.

Conclusion

When you receive a grant and sign the award letter, you enter into a legal agreement. You are obligated to spend this money on the work proposed and agreed on, and to do this you must carefully track your expenditures and impact. Foundations are investing in you and your approach when they give you a grant, and they want to know that they made a good investment. Did their investment pay off and generate the outcome you both envisioned? Can you *prove* that? To do so, you need a system to evaluate and report on the work accomplished. By setting up a plan for evaluation as you write your proposal, you give yourself a roadmap to follow and a basis for accountability. Be honest and transparent with your funders, and build your relationship into a partnership. Work together with your funder to innovate and create solutions that advance both your goals. Remember that it's not just about this one grant; the work you do will lead to future funding opportunities and benefit your reputation with other funders.

Do's and Don'ts

Do. . .

> . . . use a third-party evaluator or firm to help you evaluate progress.

> . . . track expenses using the same line items that you incorporated into your proposed budget.

> . . . share your findings with all stakeholders, including clients, staff, board members, community partners, funders, and the public.

> . . . ensure the objectives outlined in the grant agreement align with the objectives you evaluate.

Don't. . .

> . . . evaluate your own programs, because you can't be objective, so include someone outside of the organization in the process.

> . . . pretend that your program was successful if it wasn't or hide failures or problems.

> . . . wait until the end of your grant to follow up with your funder; keep in touch throughout the grant period to share successes and obstacles.

About the Expert

Dr. Beverly Browning (Dr. Bev) is an award-winning grant writer, and author of more than 40 publications, including *Grant Writing for Dummies*. Browning is VP of Grant Writing Services for eCivis, founder and director of the Grant Writing Training Foundation, and an online instructor for Ed2Go, A.K.A. Cengage Learning. She is also a visionary, capacity-building coach, mentor, researcher, curriculum developer, professional facilitator, and keynote speaker.

Resource Review

Browning, Beverly A. *Grant Writing for Dummies* (5th ed.). John Wiley & Sons, 2014.
   This book will help you navigate federal grant databases and apply online for grants, find current public and private sector grant opportunities,

create strong statements of need, and submit applications that meet funders' expectations.

Richardson, Kimberly. *The Official Federal Grants Prep Guide: 10 Tips to Position Your Organization for Success.* Kimberly Richardson Consulting, LLC, 2013.
This book is for anyone who wants to participate in the U.S. federal grant-writing process. At the end of each chapter in this incredibly useful book, Richardson lists some questions to ask yourself, which help you reflect and prepare. The book also offers many useful tools and examples.

Grants Northwest (www.grantsnorthwest.com/resources)
Michael Wells' site has great publications on grant writing and reporting. Check out his article, "Basic Grant Tracking for the Small Nonprofit."

eCivis (www.ecivis.com)
Provides a cloud-based grants management system to assist with researching, tracking, and reporting, and that serves as a knowledge base for nonprofits, municipal governments, and educational institutions. They also provide nationwide grant-writing services and webinars.

Foundation Center (www.foundationcenter.org)
Foundation Center provides resources on evaluation and reporting through their website and in print, and educational opportunities through local chapters.

Browning, Beverly A. *Perfect Phrases for Writing Grant Proposals: Hundreds of Ready-to-Use Phrases to Present Your Organization, Explain Your Cause, and Get the Funding You Need.* McGraw-Hill, 2008.
With this comprehensive, user-friendly approach to grant writing, you'll be able to tackle various proposal formats, create a professional purpose statement, and back up your plan with solid data and evaluation.

Grant Professionals Association/GPA (www.grantprofessionals.org)
GPA has a robust website with many online resources, as well as an annual conference and regional chapters.

Foundation Group (www.501c3.org)
Check out their article, "Are You Misappropriating Your Nonprofit's Funds?"

The Grant Helpers (www.thegranthelpers.com)
Find good articles on their blog, including "Grant Tip #5: Tips for a Strong Grant Evaluation Plan."

Corporate Support

23

Sponsorships

"The best partnerships aren't dependent on a mere common goal, but on a shared path of equality, desire, and no small amount of passion."

—Sarah MacLean

Introduction

Corporations are all around us, every day. We buy their products and services, and increasingly, they're interested in partnering with nonprofits to reach more customers, increase employee loyalty, and improve their image. Billions of dollars a year flow from companies to good causes globally, and when pursued strategically, corporate sponsorships can yield significant revenues and bolster awareness of your organization.

Personally, when I was helping to produce and spearhead sponsorships for both Craigslist Foundation's Nonprofit Boot Camp and Social Media for Nonprofits, I witnessed the transformative impact of these partnerships first-hand. We raised well over a million sponsorship dollars between the two programs during my tenure, providing much needed resources; plus the sponsors we engaged provided valuable resources to our audience and helped promote our events.

Corporate sponsorships are also a great way to align your organization with a brand that people respect and recognize. This can give you legitimacy with people unfamiliar with your cause and bring attention to your nonprofit, specifically to fundraising events. And while getting corporate sponsorships revolves around the same basic principle of all fundraising—building relationships—it does require a slightly different and unique approach.

Unlike foundations, corporations are not in the business of making social impact. Their focus is on driving profits, which in part comes from generating goodwill and loyalty among their consumer base. Take advantage of this: know your audience and what kind of products and companies they use. Consider also the kinds of companies you want your organization and reputation linked with; the intersections you find will lead to valuable fundraising opportunities. In short, if your nonprofit produces an event that gathers decision-makers of any kind, ideally in large numbers, odds are sponsorships are a promising fundraising vehicle for your cause.

To dive deeper into the secrets to successfully securing corporate sponsorships, I sat down with Maureen Carlson, president of Good Scout, a social good consultancy focused on corporate alliances. Carlson shared seven great tips in a straightforward, step-by-step formula.

Critical Skills and Competencies

1. Dedicate Personnel

In order to secure corporate sponsorships, you need to identify a champion in your organization dedicated to the task. This can't be the same person coordinating an event, whether it's a gala, luncheon, conference, or run/walk/ride, as that person will have his or her hands full overseeing logistics. Identify someone who can focus on securing meetings and calls and who's able to speak passionately and articulately about your cause and event.

The person you charge with spearheading corporate sponsorship should have a fundraising or sales background, be able to discuss audience size and demographics with sponsor prospects, identify his or her goals, and frame your event in the context of those. In the corporate world, return on investment rules. That means you'll need a good listener who can clearly identify sponsors' interests and priorities, and then speak in a language that's most compelling to them. He or she should excel at stewardship and will need to ensure you fulfill any promises made to sponsors. Above all, your champion needs to be persistent and willing to follow up with people consistently, even if that means being told "no" often.

2. Price Yourself Right

Once you have a point person spearheading your efforts, the next step is carefully determining sponsor benefits and pricing levels. Think through the demographics of your audience, and ***consider what kind of decision-makers you're mobilizing at your event, and how you can offer sponsors valuable access to them***. Your marathon doesn't attract youth; it attracts emerging *leaders*. Understand the kind of assets your event has in paid, earned, owned, and shared media and how you leverage those assets in your sponsorship packages. Go beyond simply throwing up a logo or sign and offer key sponsors the ability to address your audience and receive recognition in a relevant and customized way. Identify how many people sponsors will reach through each benefit and how valuable each of them is; ultimately, ***the combination of reach, audience, and engagement drives corporate decision making***.

What companies want more than anything is access to their consumers and potential customers. Offer things like logos and short descriptions or ads in event materials, and through all your marketing channels, including the World Wide Web, press releases, email, and social media. If you've enlisted media sponsors (see Chapter 25), offer corporate sponsors inclusion in those bartered ads, which can have tremendous reach. Let sponsors give out product samples and have a physical presence at your event, like a booth or table, or a branded, customized area.

Offer top sponsors things like experiential access to participants, free tickets, recognition from the main stage, and public, post-event recognition. If you have a VIP event or speaker dinner, invite top sponsors and perhaps let them say a word or two. Offer things beyond exposure; benefits that garner goodwill for the sponsor, such as underwriting scholarships.

Some say it's difficult, if not impossible, to share a rule of thumb for pricing sponsorships. Carlson says it's as simple as doing a valuation of your event to understand the overall combined assets around paid, earned, owned, and shared media, combined with the value of aligning with your cause and providing access to your constituents. Her agency, Good Scout, created a tool called CauseRATE that uses your data and metrics to clearly value and define what your packages should be priced at and what benefits are in each package as a baseline framework.

Most nonprofits *offer event sponsor packages (like bronze, silver, and gold), plus a la carte opportunities.* To share a couple simple examples of what this might look like, a basic sponsorship package typically includes little more than a couple tickets, a logo and description in the program and on the event page, and perhaps a table. The silver level includes more benefits, like signage, more tickets, an ad in the program, verbal recognition, a VIP ticket, and the ability to distribute samples or products. Finally, top sponsors receive all the other benefits, plus a chance to speak from the main stage, a scholarship fund in their name, and inclusion in media sponsor ads promoting the event, customized owned areas, etc.

A la carte options can include underwriting scholarships, sponsoring specific tracks or portions of the event, such as a VIP reception, the finish line, or simply the ability to include a promotional item in the event goody bag. The key here is *scale*, meaning making sure you provide your most valuable assets to your highest-level sponsors.

3. Create a Killer Deck

Once you've identified your sponsor levels and benefits and thought about how you present your audience, it's time to create your sponsor deck. Due to lack of resources, most organizations rely heavily on a PDF that you can email to people, but you may also get a lot of use out of a print version for meetings; either way, *creating a professional, well-designed sponsorship packet is your key to success*.

If resources are available, Carlson recommends creating your materials using a digital application that allows you to customize it easily and create related follow-up materials. It's also ideal, she adds, to ensure your deck can be accessed online so it can be sent as a link, and for it to have impactful, embedded video and infographics. No matter what format and platform you use, your deck should be a smart, stylish representation of your event and your "brand." Your packet should contain a sign-up form if sponsors want to be involved, and the electronic version should be easy to fill out, save, and return, ideally without requiring them to print it.

Sponsorship Proposal Template

After fifteen years courting and securing corporate sponsors for nonprofit events, I've developed a simple formula for crafting an effective sponsorship proposal. The key elements I recommend include:

- **Cover Page**: Include a large, compelling image, your logo, the name, date, and location of the event, and "Corporate Sponsorship Packet" written in large font.
- **Overview**: *Briefly* talk about the organization's history and impact, as well as the event itself and the impact it will have on your cause. More important than talking about your nonprofit and the event, which you're really just doing to establish credibility, this is where you want to share information on why sponsoring your event might be attractive to companies. Talk about your audience demographics and the types of decision-makers you're mobilizing.
- **Sponsor Benefits**: The next few pages of your proposal will include the various sponsorship packages and a la carte options, with a price associated with each, and a bullet point list of associated benefits. If possible, share the reach of various benefits, and arrange them with the most compelling/valuable benefits up top. It's also great to share the kind of impact different levels of support make possible for your cause, but if you do this, be very brief and focus on the benefits.
- **Contact Info**: End your proposal, or at least the main part of it, with a bolded line simply saying something like, "For more information, or to join us as a sponsor, please contact Impact Investing Global Summit at the UN Co-Chair Darian Rodriguez Heyman at (415) 123-4567 or darian@example.org."
- **Appendices**: If appropriate, especially as it relates to making sponsorship of your event more appealing to prospects, include additional information in appendices, including detailed audience demographics, testimonials, and so forth.

4. Fill the Pipeline

Chapter 5 of this book is dedicated to prospecting, and there are many practical tips there that will help you with finding sponsor prospects, as well as some thoughts on corporations in particular in Chapter 24. As you'll see in both chapters, *your first step is uncovering the prospects already in your network*. Gather your board, staff, and key volunteers, and have everyone bring their connections and ideas to the table.

Evaluate which prospects are the best fit, especially those you're already connected to. Then look outside your inner circle and find prospects by looking at who sponsors similar events, who the big companies are in your area, and who's already associated with your cause. And remember, it's important to look at *every* corporate contact you have in your organization, even if he or she is not a traditional "sponsor" of an event yet. Connections are what matter most, and if your relationships are strong enough, you can often layer on this kind of partnership, to the benefit of both your organization and the corporation.

5. Be Flexible

Listen to your sponsors and help them meet *their* needs by creating customized sponsor packages and benefits whenever possible. For example, if a sponsor is more interested in getting product samples into the hands of consumers rather than logo exposure through media, ***be prepared to mix and match benefits and price***. Being flexible will help you secure more sponsors and unlock additional revenue opportunities, but be sure to document any of these one-off custom arrangements to ensure proper fulfillment. If you work with many sponsors and have a small staff, be prepared to leave some money on the table in order to avoid driving your staff crazy.

6. Have a Conversation

When you pitch a corporate sponsor, don't deliver a cookie-cutter presentation. Your pitch should be a conversation and your deck, a framework. Deals are really closed through dialogue, where you listen to sponsors and present a dynamic opportunity based on the needs and priorities they share. Emphasize the benefits you can offer based on what the sponsor is most interested in. Is it online exposure, association with your cause, or access to live audiences? And don't forget that you are likely not the only organization coming to them with sponsorship requests. Be memorable and make your pitch meaningful. Convey your passion for the cause and your personal connection so that you can begin to build a relationship with the decision-maker.

7. Keep Your Sponsors Happy

Securing corporate sponsorships can be difficult and time-consuming. All the more reason why you want to invest heavily and steward your sponsors, increasing the likelihood they'll sign up again. Make sure you deliver, if not over-deliver, on every detail in the agreement, and that the sponsor is satisfied with the result. Thank your sponsors privately and publicly, and thank participants on the sponsors' behalf.

When the event is complete and you've collected all your data (ideally, within 30 days), ***create an impact summary for all sponsors***. In this report, tell them specifically what impact their sponsorship had, both in terms of the benefits directly to them (how many times and where you gave them marketing exposure, how many people they reached, etc.), as well as the benefits to your cause and the impact the overall event made possible. Don't ever make them guess at what they got out of their sponsorship. Stay in touch with your sponsors throughout the year with brief emails, handwritten notes, or updates on your work so that you aren't only communicating with them when you need money.

Conclusion

Going after corporate sponsors may seem daunting, but if you dedicate resources and follow the right steps and best practices, they can deliver substantial revenue, exposure, and other helpful support. Your sponsors can become long-term partners if properly stewarded, not only helping you get new events off the ground, but providing stable sustenance for your cause over many years to come. Take the time and invest the resources needed to build and nurture these key relationships. Always listen for *their* goals and ensure you offer sponsors value that's in line with their objectives. Take these simple steps and you will create fulfilling and mutually beneficial partners for life.

Do's and Don'ts

Do. . .

> . . . begin soliciting sponsorships at least six months in advance of the event.

> . . . aim to raise at least 25 percent of your event revenue from corporate sponsorships.

> . . . dedicate staff resources to corporate sponsorship.

> . . . send an event summary and impact report to all sponsors after your event.

. . . include questions about sponsors in attendee event surveys to find out whether participants gained a more favorable impression of them, and if so, use that information to steward and pitch.

Don't. . .

. . . make your event coordinator responsible for securing and fulfilling sponsorships.

. . . only communicate with sponsors when asking them for money.

. . . set sponsors up for disappointment with unrealistic projections of audience size.

. . . undervalue your assets and "give away" valuable benefits to lower-level sponsors.

. . . fail to customize a sponsorship package when valuable to, and feasible for, your event or organization.

About the Expert

Maureen Carlson is the president of GoodScout, a social good consultancy focused on corporate alliances. Carlson has extensive experience and a successful track record in corporate alignment and cause marketing strategy, corporate sponsorship development, and consumer marketing. She is a sought-after speaker and facilitator on the topic of corporate alliances and sponsorship, frequently presenting at events for the Cause Marketing Forum, Peer to Peer Professional Forum, American Marketing Association, and Association of Fundraising Professionals, among others.

Resource Review

IEG (www.sponsorship.com)
    IEG is the leading resource for corporate sponsors and sponsorship seekers. They have an annual conference and great resources on their site. Check out their "Nonprofit Sponsorship Survey."

Wild Woman Fundraising (www.wildwomanfundraising.com)
    This is an e-learning company focused on helping nonprofits professionals succeed. Check out their blog on corporate sponsorships and access other free resources on their site.

National Council of Nonprofits (www.councilofnonprofits.org)
 Find a helpful overview of corporate sponsorships, including tax
 implications, tools, and a list of resources. (www.councilofnonprofits.org/
 tools-resources/corporate-sponsorship)

Selfish Giving (www.selfishgiving.com)
 Joe Waters' blog is a leading resource for cause marketing partnerships
 and provides valuable insight on what companies desire out of
 partnerships with nonprofits.

Nonprofit Hub (www.nonprofithub.org)
 Find helpful resources on a variety of fundraising topics, including
 corporate sponsorships. Check out their article "The Five Things
 Corporate Sponsors Want from Nonprofits."

Cause Marketing Forum (www.causemarketingforum.com)
 Find helpful resources tailored for nonprofits. Check out their online
 resource center, e-class series, and annual conference.

Waters, Joe. *Fundraising with Businesses: 40 New and Improved Strategies for
 Nonprofits*. John Wiley & Sons, 2013.
 This book offers forty practical fundraising strategies to help small- to
 medium-sized nonprofits raise more money from businesses.

For Momentum (www.formomentum.com)
 This Atlanta-based consulting firm offers custom services for nonprofits
 and provides great resources on corporate sponsorship on their site and
 blog.

The Chronicle of Philanthropy (www.philanthropy.com)
 This is the leading publication on all things nonprofit, and they frequently
 feature information on corporate sponsorships.

Peer-to-Peer Professional Forum (www.peertopeerforum.com)
 They hold an annual conference and have a useful website with a lot of
 resources and insights tailored for nonprofits.

On Twitter, follow corporate hashtags of the companies you're targeting
in order to gain insights into their marketing efforts, and follow general
hashtags like #corpgiving, #sponsorship, and #causemarketing to keep your
finger on the pulse of current sponsorship news.

Chapter 24

Cause Marketing Partnerships

"The problem with many cause marketing programs is that there's too much cause and not enough marketing."

—Billy Shore

Introduction

Cause marketing partnerships are corporate initiatives designed to do well by doing good, meaning that a company does well by driving sales or enhancing its image, while a nonprofit benefits through additional income and awareness of its cause. We see frequent examples in today's world: buy a yogurt, return the lid, and the company will donate 10 cents to fight breast cancer; donate to a cause when checking out at the grocery store and get a coupon for a future discount; tweet a picture using a branded hashtag and the company donates a dollar to charity; etc.

Cause marketing allows companies to align with good causes, create and deepen relationships with target audiences, and give themselves a competitive edge with today's increasingly conscious consumers. Research firm Nielsen discovered that, as of 2014, more than half of Americans want to align their spending and values, and this important trend creates huge opportunities for nonprofits willing and able to partner with corporations.

In most cases, the amount of money that companies spend on marketing dwarfs their philanthropic contributions. By going beyond traditional corporate grants and sponsorships (see Chapters 19 and 23, respectively), your nonprofit can tap into much larger pools of money, while generating huge awareness with people who may not already be familiar with your work. If you have the financial stability and resources to sustain your efforts long-term, cause marketing can greatly benefit your organization.

Successful cause marketing is based on understanding the business' objectives and values, and then articulating how your work aligns with those. Typically, that means leveraging their support of a good cause to build goodwill among consumers, adding to their bottom line. But these partnerships aren't a fit for every organization or cause. Non-divisive causes that appeal to a broad base of people—like feeding the hungry or educating children—are best suited for *cause marketing. And cause marketing should never be your primary source of funding.* These partnerships take a long time to develop, and you have to be prepared to invest significant resources into sustaining them.

To learn more about the ins and outs of cause marketing, I interviewed two subject matter experts. David Hessekiel is the president of Cause Marketing Forum and co-author of *Good Works*, and Joe Waters is a published author, blogger, and founder of Selfish Giving. Hessekiel and Waters outlined six simple steps and tips to help you succeed in securing and sustaining fruitful cause marketing partnerships.

Critical Skills and Competencies

1. Think It Through

Before you devote any resources to cause marketing, take the time to decide whether it's the right fit for your organization. Do you have the staffing and resources to sustain this long-term, and how comfortable will your organization be aligning itself with corporations? Are there certain companies or industries that would not make appropriate allies? Address these questions with your organization's leadership before moving forward, since otherwise you can waste a tremendous amount of time prospecting and securing a partner, only to have your board veto it. Plus, it's crucial these alliances never undermine your work; if you're an environmental organization fighting climate change, perhaps a partnership with a gas and oil company sends the wrong message.

Once you've established what is and isn't appropriate, sometimes embodied in a "gift acceptance policy," ensure you have the fundraising and marketing resources needed to identify prospects, craft compelling materials, make calls, attend abundant meetings, and deliver on the partnership. You'll also want to ensure access to the appropriate leadership and program staff, so that as these conversations unfold, you can strategize internally and propose compelling benefits that also advance your work. Setting boundaries and ensuring you're able to meet both your own goals and your partner's objectives *before* embarking in cause marketing will lead to more successful partnerships.

2. Do Your Homework

What makes you an attractive cause marketing partner, and who are you targeting? Figure out which companies to focus your efforts on and consider how you can best appeal to them. ***Think deeply on the companies that have a demonstrated interest in your cause or that have a strong presence in the communities where you work***. This prospecting effort is similar to the individual and foundation processes outlined in Chapters 5 and 19, although it's a bit more challenging and requires creative thinking, since there's no third-party database like Foundation Center that can easily tell you which companies are most appropriate. As such, talking with peers and looking at the philanthropy or "CSR" (corporate social responsibility) page of corporate websites is likely your best bet.

In addition to researching prospects, it's also crucial to do some internal work. Take inventory of your assets. Do you have organized volunteer opportunities where you can engage the company employees, like Habitat for Humanity constructing homes, or KaBOOM! building children's playgrounds? Do you have an engaged social media audience that the company may want exposure to, or can you mobilize thousands of decision-makers who align with your partner's target market? Does your cause have a logical and obvious connection to their product? Take the time to ***contemplate how your work intersects with the goals of potential partners and what you have to offer them that may be of interest***.

3. Get in the Door

Once you've identified your top prospects and are prepared to present relevant, compelling opportunities and ideas, your next step is getting in front of a decision-maker. Ideally, you should ***pitch cause marketing partnerships to the head of the marketing, community affairs, or*** *corporate social responsibility department*, since otherwise, even if you're convincing, you'll likely have to make the same pitch again to someone more senior. That's not to say that securing allies inside the company isn't a huge help, but ultimately—as in all institutional fundraising—you want to *talk with the person who oversees the actual budget*.

Securing a call or meeting is not always easy, but it's absolutely crucial. Everything discussed in Chapter 19 regarding getting in the door at foundations applies perfectly here, so put those detailed tips to use to secure some face time. Be persistent but respectful, and *look for existing connections that can facilitate personal introductions*. Ask your board and search your LinkedIn connections to identify these, use Twitter to create social capital, and develop relationships with others in the relevant departments of the company.

Cause Marketing Proposal Tips

Once you're in the door, most prospects will want some type of proposal on your cause marketing program. But consider yourself warned: *Proposals are often a crutch for both nonprofits and prospects*. Many fundraisers use proposals to avoid selling to a prospect, hoping to let the document do it for them. This is bad form, since ultimately *proposals don't close deals, people do*. Moreover, your proposal will be infinitely more effective if it's customized to the needs and goals of the prospects, just as we advise with your pitch in the next tip.

But not bringing a proposal to a meeting may disappoint or even insult your audience. So bring a proposal, but use it strategically:

> *Save it for later*. Proposals are not for first meetings; for those, just bring a pen and notebook or a laptop. When you first talk, it's time to listen and explore. Save your proposal for later, after you have a better idea of their objectives.

> *Customization is key*. A proposal is about converting a prospect into a partner. So make sure to include the examples, metrics, and benefits a partner needs to make an educated decision about working with you. See tip 4 below for more on this.

Be clear. Everyone wants to know just how much time, effort, and resources executing a cause marketing program will involve. Make sure that your partner has a short checklist to work from. Be sure he or she sees yours.

Money matters. This is critical. How will the campaign raise money? *Put it in the proposal.* Have you agreed on a financial goal, and a per-action contribution? *Put it in the proposal.* What if the company doesn't reach the agreed upon goal, or exceeds it? *Put it in the proposal.* How long after the promotion ends will you have to wait to receive the money? *Put it…*you get the point, right?

Ask for legal input. If you have a legal department, have them review the proposal before sharing it with the prospect. If you don't, have a lawyer on your board read it over, or hire one for just this purpose. It may seem like overkill, but it's worth it, especially when you're new to cause marketing.

Remember: You are the closer. Too often, fundraisers mistakenly think that if they send out enough proposals, they'll eventually land a partner. This *never* works. *Your physical presence and role in outreach is the most important part of closing a deal.* The proposal is just a nail. You're the hammer that will cobble the deal together and drive it home.

4. Listen Up and Speak *Their* Language

Once you secure a call or meeting, your goal is to gather facts and establish rapport. You'll rarely close a deal in the first conversation, so building a relationship will be key. While you've already done your homework, it's important to hear directly from the company regarding more specifics on their target markets, the values their brand represents, and their social impact priorities, especially as they relate to their CSR and philanthropy strategy.

Find out what success means to the company and how you can help them accomplish that; *the formula for success is identifying the company's objectives and priorities, and then positioning your organization— and the partnership—as a promising strategy for achieving them.* Ask intelligent questions, use what you learned from your research, and strive to integrate business language and terminology they relate to. Just as with individual donors and foundations, it's not about you or your organization; it's about how you can help advance their interests and goals. Finally, if they ask questions that you don't have the answers to, don't make something up. Instead, let them know you will get back to them with the information.

5. Close the Deal

Securing a cause marketing partnership will almost always require long-term cultivation of the prospect. Stay in touch and develop a relationship with the decision-maker. Address any questions or doubts with thoughtful and articulate answers, but be brief and respect his or her time. Once you come to an agreement on the parameters of the partnership, including details around marketing and fundraising campaigns, *create a written agreement that outlines each party's commitments to ensure accountability*. This can be a full-blown legal contract or a simpler Memorandum of Understanding (MOU), but either way you'll want to *have your legal counsel review it before signing*. Include details like budgets, timelines, deliverables, and so forth. When making these commitments, remember that it's always better to *under-promise and over-deliver*.

6. Keep Them Happy

Just like any long-term relationship, cause marketing partnerships take work and require stewardship and attention over time. As problems and issues inevitably arise, be honest and transparent, and address concerns proactively and immediately. Keep your partner updated on the impact the campaign has on your cause and organization, and ideally *create an automated dashboard that regularly shares key performance indicators with key personnel* (see Chapter 7).

Share positive feedback and touching stories you hear from your supporters about the company, its products, and the partnership. Recognize your partners often, and use marketing vehicles like social media and email to express gratitude for their support. *When a campaign or partnership is finalized, have a debrief meeting with the company and send a final wrap-up or impact report*. And keep in touch to maintain the relationship and keep the door open for future opportunities.

Conclusion

Cause marketing partnerships represent a huge opportunity for nonprofits to secure both funding and exposure, and the potential for corporate alliances will only rise as more and more consumers seek to support companies whose values they admire. However, these partnerships are resource- and time-consuming, so before diving in, think carefully to ensure it's the right decision for your organization. Identify the companies you're most excited to partner with and do the homework needed to find and take advantage of intersections between your work and their goals. Appeal to companies by speaking their language and letting them know how you can help them achieve *their* goals. Make sure that you can fulfill your end of any partnership before entering into a commitment and that the company is accountable for contributions as well. When this recipe for success is followed and nonprofits remember to stay true to their mission, but are flexible enough to entertain mutually beneficial corporate partnerships, amazing things become possible.

Do's and Don'ts

Do. . .

. . . have frank conversations with your leadership before investing energy into securing a cause marketing partnership.

. . . review the websites of prospects to familiarize yourself with their corporate social responsibility and philanthropy goals.

. . . recognize the financial value of marketing benefits potential partners bring to the table.

. . . understand your base of supporters online and off, especially how their demographics intersect with the target audience of a corporate prospect.

Don't. . .

. . . create lengthy materials that over-describe your mission and work.

. . . pursue corporate partners whose brand you wouldn't support yourself.

. . . try to close a deal on the first meeting.

. . . promise deliverables you aren't prepared to fulfill.

About the Experts

David Hessekiel is founder and president of Cause Marketing Forum, the world's leading resource on building mutually beneficial business/nonprofit alliances, and of the Peer to Peer Professional Forum, which produces conferences and online resources for nonprofits and companies wanting to produce more successful run/walk/ride programs. Hessekiel is also co-author of *Good Works: Corporate Social Initiatives That Build a Better World and the Bottom Line.* His comments on doing well by doing good are frequently featured in leading media outlets, from National Public Radio to *The Wall Street Journal.*

Joe Waters is the founder and author of Selfish Giving, the Web's leading cause marketing blog. Waters is the author of three books, including *Cause Marketing for Dummies* and *Fundraising with Businesses*. He has raised millions of dollars from local, regional, and national corporate partners and is a frequent public speaker and writer for publications such as *Forbes, Nonprofit Quarterly*, and *The Chronicle of Philanthropy.*

Resource Review

Cause Marketing Forum (www.causemarketingforum.com)
> Hessekiel's site provides practical information for both nonprofits and companies, including best practices, articles, case studies, and more. Check out the article "Ten Commandments of Cause Related Marketing" by Kurt Aschermann.

Waters, Joe, and Joanna MacDonald. *Cause Marketing for Dummies.* John Wiley & Sons, 2011.
> This guide shows both businesses and nonprofits how to build and sustain cause marketing partnerships using social media, identify potential partners, engage supporters, and model a campaign on proven successes.

Selfish Giving
> Waters' blog is one of the leading cause marketing blogs on the web and has hundreds of posts on cause marketing, fundraising with businesses,

nonprofit branding, mobile technology, content marketing, and corporate sponsorship.

Cause Update (www.causeupdate.com)
Find a wealth of information on current cause marketing campaigns and valuable insights from Cause Marketing Forum's insightful blog.

Kotler, Philip, Nancy Lee, and David Hessekiel. *Good Works Marketing and Corporate Initiatives That Build a Better World—and the Bottom Line.* John Wiley & Sons, 2012.
Marketing guru Philip Kotler, cause marketing authority David Hessekiel, and social marketing expert Nancy Lee teamed up to create a guide rich with actionable advice on integrating marketing and corporate social initiatives into broader business goals. This book offers nonprofits insight into corporate thinking and language, preparing you for more effective partner solicitation.

Good Scout Group (www.goodscoutgroup.com)
This cause marketing agency provides excellent content for nonprofits.

IEG (www.sponsorship.com)
IEG is the leading resource for corporate partnerships and sponsorships. Find great insights and resources on cause marketing partnerships.

The Chronicle of Philanthropy (www.philanthropy.com)
This is the leading publication on all things nonprofit, and they frequently feature information on partnering with corporations.

Cone Communications (www.conecomm.com/case-studies)
Access a great repository of cause marketing case studies.

In-Kind Fundraising and Media Sponsorship

"Help thy brother's boat across, and lo! thine own has reached the shore."

—Hindu Proverb

Introduction

Whether it's having a venue or food donated for your upcoming gala, receiving a free billboard or full-page ad in the local newspaper, or securing tablets to distribute to low-income youth to help them do homework, in-kind fundraising and media sponsorships are a great opportunity to build key relationships and gain valuable support from local and national businesses. These alternative forms of support are just as valuable to your organization as cash donations, since *spending less money on your operations and events is the same as raising more revenue*. In Economics 101, instructors share one of the basics of finance: profit (or net income for nonprofits) equals revenue minus expenses. So as much as this book is focused on raising your top line, let us not forget that minimizing bottom-line costs drives your mission and impact just as much.

Moreover, in-kind fundraising and media sponsorships provide an easier way to engage companies because they don't require them to open their checkbooks. *Businesses are often much more willing to donate products, services, and ad space instead of money.* These partnerships work well for everyone: businesses gain an opportunity to align their brand with a cause and organization, creating goodwill among existing customers, and potentially reaching new consumers, while your nonprofit obtains something it needs or at least can benefit from without having to tap your budget. Ultimately, any money you save will have a huge impact on your organization.

Media sponsorships are usually done for large-scale events, like conferences, high-profit events like runs/walks/rides, or galas that benefit from public advertising, but also provide a great opportunity to offer benefits in exchange to the sponsor. Advertising is extremely expensive, but it can also be incredibly effective in spreading awareness of your cause or event.

It's also possible to secure media support for your organization overall, although in these cases the benefits you'll offer in exchange typically revolve around an event or offering recognition at your physical location. Media organizations often have lots of unused inventory, and sponsorships can take your marketing and credibility to the next level. Similarly, in-kind supporters also typically want recognition for their donations, but if you can offer this, you can save money on operational expenses, expand the impact of your programs, and enhance the quality of your events, all while spending less money on them.

To learn more about how nonprofits of all sizes, both in the United States and around the globe, can successfully secure in-kind and media donations, I talked with Gayle Samuelson Carpentier, in-kind fundraising veteran and chief business development officer at TechSoup Global, which has secured billions of dollars worth of resources from corporate partners. She outlined six great tips to ensure your success.

Critical Skills and Competencies

1. Clarify Your Needs

In-kind and media partnerships are unique for every organization and event. Your first step when identifying opportunities is to look at your nonprofit's or event's budget (see Chapter 12 for tips on creating an event budget). *Conduct a detailed review of all your expenses and identify the things that can potentially be donated or provided at a discount.* Even if you don't get something for free, many businesses will give nonprofits special discounts, and you will never know unless you ask!

Some obvious things can be identified for in-kind donations, like food and wine for events, items for your auction, and your top operational expenses, but also look for the non-obvious things that may not already be in your budget. Do you need new computer equipment or software? Do you have small offices and need somewhere more professional to hold your board meetings? Are you building a new website and need someone to develop it? Could your program serve more homeless if more food was donated? Could your event or cause benefit from an ad in the local paper or on a popular website?

Host a brainstorming session with your development, events, program, marketing, and finance or operations staff and create a list of all your needs, prioritizing those that'd have the biggest potential effect and provide the largest savings for your organization. Invite key volunteers and board members, especially those with relevant experience, to participate if possible; the more input you secure when considering the possibilities, the better. Don't be afraid to dream and think big at this meeting. Ask those present: "What would we do if our marketing budget were doubled or tripled?" and "What kind of product and service donations would enable our programs to serve more people in need?"

2. Identify Your Prospects

Once you identify and prioritize your in-kind and media sponsorship opportunities, think about which businesses, corporations, and professionals are viable prospects. Start with businesses you already have a personal connection to. *Ask everyone at the brainstorming session which partners would be best suited to meet the needs you've outlined, see whether they have any relationships that can be useful and whether they're willing to make an introduction or ask.*

From a marketing perspective, discuss who you want to reach for your event, awareness campaign or, in general where you can best reach them. Is it online, in print, on billboards, or somewhere else? Think through the top media vehicles that communicate with your targeted audience. Who reaches the most people?

To identify additional prospects, look at similar organizations and events. Who is sponsoring or donating to them? Most organizations and events list their supporters on their websites, so this information is fairly easy to come by. Look at companies that regularly support your cause, as well as those that are particularly philanthropic in your geographic location.

Put all this information in a simple spreadsheet, outlining both your prioritized needs and the prospects you've identified thus far, plus comments regarding any personal connections that can facilitate outreach. *Share your list of needs, prospects, and contacts with the rest of your board, staff, and volunteers, and see whether they have any personal connections to the prospects listed or to others they believe might be interested*. And, as you did during the brainstorming, ask whether they're willing to make an introduction or ask. Remember, it's OK if you don't know where to turn to secure pro bono legal support, donated laptops, or free printing; share these needs via your spreadsheet and ask for input on people and businesses they know that might offer donations or discounts.

Solidifying your prioritized list of needs and prospects are your first two steps, and don't despair if you don't have a personal "in" with a lead. Just as with any type of fundraising, *going in cold is never ideal, but when securing in-kind and media donations, your odds of success are much higher than trying this approach with foundations, donors, and paid sponsors*.

3. Prepare Your Pitches and Materials

Before asking for an in-kind or media donation or sponsorship, be prepared to articulate exactly what you need and what benefits you can offer in exchange. It's also helpful to have a sense of the approximate retail value of each benefit. Take the time before making a call or going to a meeting to research your prospects. What have they supported in the past, and at what level? What are their philanthropic priorities?

Begin soliciting three to six months out from your event or deadline. While in-kind and media sponsorship decisions typically happen much quicker than paid sponsorships (see Chapter 23), be prepared to wait a month or two as they decide. If you are holding a large-scale event such as a gala, conference, or sporting event, *prepare a sponsorship proposal for prospective media sponsors and in-kind donors that outlines the specific benefits they will receive at each level of sponsorship*.

Personally, I've secured millions of dollars of in-kind and media support simply by taking the corporate sponsor proposal template I outlined in Chapter 23, doubling the prices at each level, adjusting a select few benefits as needed, and changing the title on the cover page to "Media and In-Kind Sponsor Proposal." Finally, I make it clear the "prices" aren't for cash support as with traditional sponsors, but represent the retail value of donations.

4. Make Your Pitch

Leverage the personal connections you've already identified to get in the door, or simply cold call your prospects and ask who you can speak with regarding them donating products or services to support your nonprofit or event. Some large corporations have processes and policies for making in-kind donations, and that's the only way to secure their support. But even then, finding an internal champion is always helpful.

One way or another, you need to **connect with a decision-maker at the business, share your story and need, relay potential benefits, and explore a potential partnership**. Spend time listening and find out about their goals before making your pitch and, of course, integrate any research findings you discovered in advance. Be sure to **contextualize your pitch around what _they_ care about** to the full extent possible (see Chapter 23 for more on this, as related to corporate sponsorship). And remember, even when the answer is no, be gracious. Take an opportunity to respectfully inquire why and try to overcome any objections, but don't push too hard, as some folks just can't be convinced. Most importantly you want to maintain a good relationship for future opportunities and not chance undermining your reputation.

5. Treat Them Like Royalty

Just as with other key supporters, recognize your media sponsors and in-kind donors as much as possible, including leading up to and at your event, if appropriate. Make sure you **fulfill all of the benefits agreed on, and go beyond that and thank sponsors publicly in ways they didn't expect**.

Acknowledge a company representative at the event and have him or her stand up while you encourage the audience to applaud the person for supporting such a worthy cause. Give them free tickets, put them at good tables, and personally introduce them to VIPs at your event. Think through the things you can do to keep your sponsors not only satisfied, but delighted with the outcome of their involvement. Odds are, you'll circle back to them for additional support later, and anything you can do to deliver a great experience will make future requests infinitely easier.

6. Invest in the Relationship

All successful fundraising is based on relationships, so it's critical that you follow up and properly steward your sponsors and donors. Immediately after the donation or event, ***send personalized, handwritten thank you notes emphasizing the impact their contributions made possible***. Make sure you also send any necessary acknowledgements for tax purposes, although in my experience few in-kind or media sponsors ever request or use these.

If a sponsor clearly had a good experience, ask him or her to share a one- or two-sentence testimonial for future sponsorship proposals, and provide a draft quote to make this as easy as possible. If the person was a major sponsor, offer to do an in-person or phone debriefing to obtain feedback on what worked and what you can improve upon next year. If possible, send a summary of the impact the contribution and the overall event had, along with the value of the benefits, about one month after the event (see Chapter 23 for more on impact summaries). Send brief updates about your organization's impact and future plans to lay the groundwork for future sponsorships and maintain the relationship. ***Avoid making another ask until you have sent at least two to three communications thanking and updating any sponsor.***

Conclusion

Securing in-kind donations and media sponsorships is a wonderful opportunity to engage professionals, businesses, and corporations and obtain valuable donations that reduce your expenses and add to your impact and events. ***Donated products and services are almost always easier for businesses to provide than cash***, and if you get the right people around a table and review your budgets and plans, you can identify many compelling opportunities to collaborate with these kinds of partners. Think out of the box when it comes to listing not only the needs you've already budgeted for, but also the contributions that can take your efforts to the next level. Capitalize on any personal connections you have, do your homework on top prospects, and don't be afraid to make a few cold calls if needed. You'll find it surprisingly easy to get your foot in the door, and businesses will often jump to support your cause and promote themselves in the process. Remember that these relationships are true partnerships, so remain flexible and always bear in mind the goals of your sponsors, nurture the relationships over time, and if things go wrong at any point, be honest and transparent, and fix problems immediately. Keep these supporters satisfied and excited to continue supporting you in the future, and you'll unlock the full potential of in-kind donations and media sponsorships.

Do's and Don'ts

Do. . .

> . . . think through what would delight (rather than just satisfy) your in-kind and media sponsors.

> . . . start your solicitations three to six months before your event or deadline.

> . . . create a package for large events that outlines the benefits you can offer to media sponsors and in-kind donors.

Don't. . .

> . . . forget that securing in-kind donations and media sponsorships can be just as powerful as obtaining cash support.

> . . . neglect giving your in-kind supporter at least three benefits they'll get from supporting your organization or event—ones that will really make an impact.

> . . . have a meeting or call with a prospect without first doing your homework and preparing key talking points.

> . . . accept "no" for an answer without inquiring as to why and trying to overcome any objections.

> . . . produce an event without insurance to protect both you and your in-kind donors and sponsors.

> . . . ever say the words: "You should give us this/do this for me because we are doing good things." If you can't be specific, you shouldn't waste your time or theirs.

About the Expert

Gayle Samuelson Carpentier is the chief business development officer at TechSoup Global and a member of the Nonprofit Technology Network's (NTEN) board of directors. Carpentier joined TechSoup Global in 2001 as their founding business development lead and developed the strategic structure of their product donation service, which has grown into the largest provider of IT to nonprofits in the world by leveraging in-kind donations from corporate partners.

Resource Review

TechSoup (www.techsoup.org)
> Provides a variety of resources to help nonprofits make smart technology decisions, as well as access to deeply discounted software and IT products. Check out their active online community, wealth of articles and tutorials, and their free webinar series.

Foundation Directory Online (https://fconline.foundationcenter.org)
> Foundation Center's online directory of companies and grantmakers is a great way to search for prospects. When searching, choose "In-kind gifts" in the "Types of Support" field. You can narrow your search by a variety of categories, including geography, fields of interest, total giving, etc.

The Nonprofit Times (www.thenonprofittimes.com)
> This print and electronic publication covers all areas of nonprofit operations and management. Check out their article, "11 Online and Mobile Sponsorship Ideas."

Good360 (www.good360.org)
> This is a company whose sole purpose is connecting nonprofits with in-kind donations from companies, all of which are outlined in their online catalog.

Google Grants (www.google.com/grants)
> Google offers $10,000/month AdWords grants to nonprofits around the world and approves these grants for almost all nonprofit applicants. This is a great in-kind media donation opportunity and will enable your cause or event to pop up on the top of relevant search results pages.

Nonprofit Accounting Basics (www.nonprofitaccountingbasics.org)
> This is a great site for questions related to nonprofit financial issues, including the tax deductibility of in-kind donations. Find a great explanation online in their article, "Donated Goods and Services" in the Federal Tax Issues topic area.

Taproot Foundation (www.taprootfoundation.org)
> Taproot provides grants of professional consulting services for nonprofits. Check out their offerings, as well as their whitepaper, "Beyond Cash: A Guide on How Nonprofit Boards Can Tap Pro-Bono and In-Kind Services."

Strengthening Nonprofits (www.strenghteningnonprofits.org)
> This site offers a wide array of e-lessons on various nonprofit topics, including working with businesses and corporations. Check out their e-learning lesson, "Planning for, Securing, and Documenting In-Kind Donations."

Part VII

Unlocking Social Enterprise

26

Earned Income Strategies

Guest Contributor: Rick Aubry

"Social entrepreneurs are not content just to give a fish or teach how to fish. They will not rest until they have revolutionized the fishing industry."

—Bill Drayton

Introduction

The word "entrepreneur" is French and literally means "to take into hand." It's about owning your own destiny, which is appealing to any organization that's suffered when economies take a downturn or after a long-term supporter disappears or decreases funding you were counting on.

Moreover, many nonprofits are innovative and entrepreneurial in their approach toward tackling social issues. Combined, these notions can sometimes lead to the idea that generating revenue from earned income via a "social enterprise" is a natural extension that will strengthen financial independence and create a more sustainable organization.

If only it were that straightforward.

This chapter, contributed by guest author Rick Aubry, longtime director of Rubicon Programs, professor of social enterprise at Stanford and Tulane Universities, and earned income veteran, is designed to introduce you to the basic tenants of earned income/social enterprise strategies and help you assess whether it's appropriate for your organization. We'll also share a framework for success and provide guidelines on how to make the decisions in a social enterprise environment. Let's get started.

Critical Skills and Competencies

1. Define the Terms

Our working definition for "earned income" is an activity or business venture within a nonprofit organization that generates income from selling goods and services to customers "at a profit" to supplement philanthropic and grant support. A "social enterprise" or "social venture" is an entity that generates revenues—and hopefully profits—while advancing a social mission. Hence, this term applies to all earned income strategies, but also more widely, including describing mission-led for-profit companies.

There are two basic forms of earned income strategies. One entails earning revenues not directly related to your mission or core activities. For example, a restaurant located in an art museum or the sale of candy bars, holiday cards, or other third-party items. While these may generate income, the activity does not directly advance the mission or purpose of the organization.

The second form of earned income is a revenue-generating activity that inherently furthers the mission. Think of a homeless shelter that creates jobs for clients by starting a business or a group that's developed a new system to help at-risk students graduate, which then creates and sells software based on their method to scale its efforts and generate funding. Given the limited resources of almost all nonprofits, *when an earned income strategy does not __directly__ advance your mission, it's often a distraction and should not be pursued*.

2. Ensure Support

Social enterprises are usually a departure from business as usual in a nonprofit, and doing whatever it takes to get buy-in and support before you start is crucial; you need a supportive environment within your organization for your venture to flourish. Part of this is clarifying, in advance, that running a successful social enterprise is more complicated than operating a traditional nonprofit or business and that it may not succeed.

It's also about securing the *full* commitment of senior management and your board, ensuring they see this venture as a core asset of the organization. Most nonprofits are resource-constrained with numerous competing needs for limited resources, plus charitable organizations exist to advance a social mission, not run a business. During the inevitable downturns and headaches, your venture will require resources to succeed, and during the first few years, it will require a lot more investment than it returns.

Part of what's required to ensure this success initially and moving forward is a focus on asking, and answering, what success looks like. We discussed key performance indicators for nonprofits in Chapter 7, and ***social ventures require a robust set of metrics to evaluate both social impact and financial success***, often referred to as a "double bottom line." These KPIs are especially important for earned income strategies, since you'll need to benchmark your impact against traditional approaches to assess success. For example, if your goal is creating jobs for those with barriers to employment and your venture invests $500,000 annually and only creates three jobs, you're likely better off expanding your nonprofit programs or pursuing other approaches.

Another critical tip: go in with your eyes open. As with any new business, success with a startup is extremely difficult. Most studies indicate over *60 percent of small businesses fail within the first four years.* ***If your goal is simply to increase income for your organization, most nonprofits are best served focusing on traditional fundraising***. Funding, launching, and managing a social enterprise requires lots of work, and many don't make it. That said, if you decide the potential mission and revenue benefits are worth the risk, this chapter will offer some tips and strategies to maximize your probability for success; we'll also help you decide whether starting a social venture is the right decision for your nonprofit.

So *plan for the best and prepare for the worst;* ***talk with your board about a "realistic time horizon" for the venture to reach breakeven, and clarify the exact limits to the organization's patience and support in advance***—in terms of both money and time—should things take longer to get there and require more resources, as they inevitably do. Putting your programs at risk for a venture that might not succeed will prove unacceptable to your board at some point, and it's best you identify that ahead of time versus in the moment.

When preparing for "plan B," take into consideration that tight times in a business environment are different from those at a nonprofit. If a grant is cut, you can reduce staff or programs to stay on budget, but if it costs more to make a biscuit than your budget projected, you can't just cut out the butter. Take the time to learn about business-focused cost accounting, production management, and sales forecasting if that's not part of your background.

All these key elements, along with conservative financial projections, a market survey to support those estimates, a list of strong leaders, including executives and advisors, a detailed strategy and timeline, a detailed competitive analysis, and a really strong but concise executive summary must find their way into a compelling business plan, approved by your board. Given the vast amount of free online resources for creating a plan, including a few specific to social enterprises outlined in the Resource Review, we won't go into detail here, but suffice it to say this is critical in your effort to secure the necessary support and approval to move forward.

3. Solidify Leadership

Before you can think any further about diving into earned income, it's critical that you have a zealous, empowered entrepreneur who is committed to the venture as an all-encompassing job for at least the first several years. Savvy start-up investors will tell you that the credibility and dedication of the management team is even more important than the business model, and *having a champion to spearhead your efforts—ideally with ample, relevant industry experience—will be one of the biggest factors determining your success*.

To find the right leader, look for what social enterprise pioneer Jed Emerson calls "the mutant manager." Look first and foremost for a deep experience base in the specific business or industry you've chosen, a clear commitment to the social mission of the organization, and the ability to work well with the leadership team of both your nonprofit and the business.

Under almost all circumstances, *do not promote the best nonprofit manager at your organization to run a venture if he or she lacks relevant business experience*. The requirements for success in a business environment are fundamentally different. Instead, *find leaders from the industry who are ready to devote the next phase of their professional lives to advancing your social mission through the business*. Often, mid-career executives are eager to apply their skills and industry knowledge to a business that offers both purpose and profit, and this is the typical profile of your CEO.

To recruit someone like this, you may be able to secure a small discount off corporate salary potential, but don't plan on this. Instead, ensure you *budget for a competitive compensation package that's in line with salaries at comparable for-profit businesses*. You'll also want to allocate time and resources into successfully integrating someone from the for-profit sector into a nonprofit environment, with its unique culture, focus, and pace.

Rob Waldron, a successful for-profit CEO who became CEO of the nonprofit Jumpstart, once shared in a presentation to a Stanford Social Entrepreneurship class: "I feel like I have moved from being a general in the army to a member of the Senate. In for-profits I gave a direction and people jumped to it. In the nonprofit I have stakeholders, various interest groups, a whole different culture, and I have to *lead through persuasion rather than through authority*."

4. Understand Your Competitive Advantage

For your social enterprise to succeed, you must find and take advantage of the inherent competitive advantage of your nonprofit. What are the abilities and competencies that make you best positioned to solve the social problem your organization was created to address?

Does your nonprofit have a strong relationship with the community you serve compared to traditional businesses in your space, and how can these benefit the venture? Do you have a way of providing services more effectively or efficiently? Can you leverage your physical locations in some unique way? Have you developed a unique way of addressing a problem that would be hard for others to copy without significant time and resources? Do you have team members with talents or expertise others don't? Would your nonprofit's reputation translate well into a social venture? Gather as a team and organization to discuss these questions and any others you can think of to unearth your unique advantages, and be sure to also ask clients and potential customers how they perceive your organization.

This process may bring to light advantages so significant that they provide one of the few exceptions to the rule that you should *only* pursue social enterprises that directly advance your mission. For example, a museum with a great location can realistically generate significant revenue from a restaurant. If your nonprofit is lucky enough to have a unique geographic advantage, there may be an earned income strategy worth undertaking.

Ultimately, your competitive advantage will translate into your actual delivery of products and services. That's when it's crucial to remember that simply offering "a worthy cause" in the marketplace is not necessarily a competitive advantage. Typically, customers don't buy to support a cause, but to get the best value.

In study after study of customer behavior, any *social benefits associated with a product or service are a tertiary consideration, after quality, and then value and dependability*. All other things being equal, many will choose the conscious option, but, as Carrie Portis, a former general manager of Rubicon Bakery, once said to me, "Our Rubicon Cakes have to be the best cake in the dessert case, not the best nonprofit cake." There are some rare circumstances where the social purpose of your venture will prove instrumental, such as government "set aside" contracts. For example, the Javits Wagner O'Day law carved out U.S. federal contracts for organizations that hire disabled workers. Keep an eye out for such opportunities and, if appropriate, lobby to advance policies that create additional ones.

5. Secure Capital

Even with the right leadership, business idea and plan, and internal support in place, finding and securing sufficient capital is both critical and difficult. Social ventures often suffer from undercapitalizing the business at the beginning. No matter how conservative your business plan, more financial and other resources will be needed than you originally anticipate.

Typically, *it will take more than twice as long to achieve the most conservative revenue goals projected in your financial model*, so plan for that when setting your fundraising goal, or ensure your ability to deficit spend if needed. Expenses also almost always run high, so *budget for unexpected "miscellaneous" costs of 25 percent in your budget*. Better safe than sorry.

When it comes to identifying investors for your social enterprise, there's good news and bad news. The good news is that, although traditional sources of startup capital will likely be unavailable, there's a movement around "impact investing," where people and institutions are actively looking to support social ventures. The bad news is that it's still relatively small, so you'll need to budget a lot of time for securing funds from this community.

"Social capital market" is a term widely used to describe grants, loans, program- or mission-related investments, equity, and other financing tools to support nonprofit and for-profit social ventures. Here, funds are made available by foundations, government agencies, corporations, and individuals, known as "impact investors" or "social investors," seeking both financial returns *and* social impact, typically with a focus on the latter.

This so called market, however, is not well coordinated, but it's typically your only option since typically you cannot issue equity or ownership in your nonprofit's business. As such, if you're going to start a social enterprise, be prepared to spend an inordinate amount of time raising money. By most estimates, traditional businesses invest 3 to 5 percent of leadership time raising funds for the venture, with the rest devoted to making the business work. ***Your nonprofit should expect to spend 20 to 50 percent of its leadership time raising money***, a significant distraction from the actual work of the organization.

6. Find Your Angel

It may sound like one in a million—and in fact maybe it is but after spending decades analyzing the formula of success for the most prosperous social enterprises, most of them had an "angel" customer or investor who made all the difference and got them off the ground. Greyston Bakery in New York scored a crucial partnership with Ben Cohen of Ben & Jerry's Ice Cream, who agreed to use their brownies and other products.

As you can imagine, for a small startup this was transformative, yielding a huge, steady customer in the early years that even made a long-term commitment to purchase from Greyston at sustainable prices. Although it's a long shot for your scrappy start-up to score this kind of partnership, it's worth investing the resources needed to identify and cultivate a select few prospects—similar to what's outlined for major donors in Chapter 9—and see whether your lottery ticket comes due.

More common than the magical appearance of an angel is one of the biggest pitfalls your start-up social enterprise needs to avoid: the investor who pushes you too far, too fast. A 20-year-old, successful social venture nearly went bankrupt when the overly ambitious growth plan it developed in partnership with a foundation led it to the brink of financial collapse.

They lost over $2 million of foundation funding and bank debt trying to implement a business plan that wasn't adequately tested, and when the business crashed and burned, the parent nonprofit shrunk overnight from a budget of $8 million and 150 employees (mostly hard-to-employ workers) to a budget of $2 million and 30 staff. Remember to know your limits since businesses come and go, and in the for-profit world, it's primarily the capital that's lost. In the nonprofit world, if you're not careful the entire social benefit organization is at stake.

Social Enterprise Case Study: Grow Dat

Grow Dat is a nonprofit social venture "operating at the intersection of food justice and youth development." The group was incubated in 2010 when it set up a farm in New Orleans, and in 2015, in order to clarify and grow their impact, they articulated their mission: *to nurture a diverse group of young leaders through the meaningful work of growing food.*

Grow Dat initially was primarily supported by foundations and individual donors. Internally and among its funders, there was a hope that they could reach self-sufficiency if they could just grow their farm big enough, unlocking economies of scale. As they examined an earned income strategy, they realized primarily relying on selling produce was *not* going to deliver this goal, and so they needed to diversify to advance their social mission. By diligently talking with their supporters, participants, and the community, they developed a comprehensive revenue strategy that leverages a variety of assets and identifies some unique sources of competitive advantage, which they built their business model around.

Strategic Focus to Grow Revenue and Impact
Launching earned revenue activities gave Grow Dat a chance to hire program "alumni" into part- or full-time positions as educators, creating much-needed opportunities for employment. Educators teach the general public about sustainable agriculture and its link to the environment, the economy, and personal and community health. In addition to creating jobs, Grow Dat identified a series of income-generating programs that also directly advance its mission:

1. **Field Trips**. Grow Dat designed experiential, standards-aligned field trips for young students, ranging from Kindergarten to eighth grade. These trips provide a great forum to teach the next generation about sustainable farming, food justice, and environmental issues. Alumni lead the field trips, providing not only relevant information, but also sharing their own experience as farmers.

2. **Farm Tours**. In addition to the learning tours Grow Dat already provides to groups, they added tours for individuals. Led by

youth and alumni, these tours provide a revenue generation opportunity and chance to introduce new people to sustainable agriculture and the importance of localizing food systems.

3. **Farm Dinners**. Grow Dat realized they could tap into the interest many outside groups have in utilizing their space by partnering to host dinners on the farm, showcasing their produce and providing a valuable educational and revenue opportunity.

4. **Volunteer Groups**. Corporations, foundations, and other large entities frequent the New Orleans landscape for various retreats, conferences, and other events. Grow Dat offers them the opportunity to build a tailored, unique experience shaped to their interests, engaging individuals and groups in their service model.

5. **Community Classes**. The group launched "Learn Dat" classes run by staff, guest educators, and external partners. These classes provide educational opportunities for residents of New Orleans to come to the farm and learn about the merits of sustainable agriculture.

Conclusion

Many nonprofits look for additional revenue sources to supplement their income. A social enterprise that accomplishes this looks enticing, but it's something that must only be undertaken with the proper consideration and commitment. That includes a realistic analysis of the risks, rewards, true costs, impact on the parent nonprofit's culture, and core competitive advantage. It's hard to make any blanket statements in the world of business, but one thing is for certain: go into it with your eyes open. On the plus side, a successful social enterprise not only supports your work financially, but it also can advance your mission and create a "halo" effect with funders and the broader community. *Balancing your mission with the business goals is the critical element in any social business success.*

Do's and Don'ts

Do. . .

. . . take the time to develop a robust business plan before seriously considering launching a social enterprise.

. . . focus on a venture that directly advances the mission of your organization.

. . . identify the limits of the time and money your nonprofit can provide to support your start-up enterprise if it falters or fails.

. . . ensure access to cash or lines of credit for the long periods between when you buy ingredients and produce your wares and when you collect payment.

Don't. . .

. . . hire one of your best nonprofit employees to run a business he or she knows little to nothing about.

. . . assume that being a nonprofit will get you regular steady customers if you don't have a great product or service.

. . . kid yourself with a self-serving business projection; everything can be made to work on an Excel spreadsheet.

About the Guest Contributor

Rick Aubry served as president of Rubicon Programs for 23 years, starting numerous successful (and unsuccessful) social ventures and cutting-edge programs that created jobs and transformed lives for thousands of worker/program participants in Richmond, California. He founded and launched New Foundry Ventures, "the laboratory for scaling social enterprise," and has been a professor and assistant provost for social entrepreneurship at Stanford and Tulane Universities.

Resource Review

Elkington, John E., and Pamela Hartigan, *The Power of Unreasonable People*. Harvard Business Press, 2008.
  A definitive book about social entrepreneurs around the world and the work they're doing to change the world.
Bornstein, David. *How to Change the World*. Oxford University Press, 2007.
  A *New York Times* journalist takes an in-depth look at some of the world's leading change-makers.
Sharon M. Oster, Cynthia W. Massarsky, and Samantha L. Beinhacker. *Generating and Sustaining Nonprofit Earned Income: A Guide to Successful Enterprise Strategies*. Jossey-Bass, 2004.

A comprehensive review of all the issues involved in developing a social enterprise, including detailed tips, tools, and templates for creating a business plan for your earned income strategy.

Stanford Social Innovation Review (www.ssireview.org)

The quarterly publication of the Stanford Center for Social Innovation is currently the best place to find the leading thinking on social impact.

REDF (www.redf.org)

A valuable website to learn about the lessons learned from one of the funders of social enterprise.

Social Enterprise Alliance (www.SE-alliance.org)

The leading U.S. membership organization for nonprofits starting or running social enterprises. Beware, however, the glut of "consultants" in the field who will often tell you to start a venture, even if it's not your proper course.

Impact Investment Conferences

A wide range of conferences bring together impact investors and leaders in the social capital market, including:

- SOCAP (www.socapmarkets.net) in San Francisco and Europe
- Opportunity Collaboration (www.opportunitycollaboration.net) in Ixtapa, Mexico
- ANDE (www.aspeninstitute.org/policy-work/aspen-network-development-entrepreneurs) gathers impact investor and social impact thought leaders at their annual conference and through webinars, local working groups, and regional chapters around the globe
- SRI (www.sriconference.com/) mobilizes advisors and funds annually in Colorado
- The Skoll World Forum in Oxford, England

New Foundry Venture (www.newfoundryventures.org)

A website providing information and links about building scalable social enterprises.

Yunus, Muhammad. *Building Social Business: The New Kind of Capitalism That Serves Humanity's Most Pressing Needs*. Public Affairs, 2009.

A Nobel Peace Prize winner lays out his vision for what a "social business" is, and how it can change the world. Yunus asserts a financially viable business, which reinvests all its profits back into the business of helping people, is the highest form of social enterprise.

Dees, J. Gregory, Jed Emerson, and Peter Economy. *Enterprising Nonprofits: A Toolkit for Social Entrepreneurs.* John Wiley & Sons, 2001
  The late Greg Dees, recently professor of social entrepreneurship at Duke University, and Emerson, recently of Uhuru Capital, are two of the most savvy hands in the field of social enterprise, "blended value theory," and understanding social impact as the real goal of all social enterprise.

The Calvert Foundation (www.Calvertfoundation.org)
  One of the early and still-engaged providers of capital in the "social impact" world. They "connect individual investors with organizations working around the globe, developing affordable housing, creating jobs, protecting the environment, and working in numerous other ways for the social good."

Afterword

Finding Your Path

Premal Shah

"Don't ask yourself what the world needs; ask yourself what makes you come alive, and then go do it. Because what the world needs is people who have come alive."

—Harold Thurman

My path to nonprofits, fundraising, and building Kiva.org began at a pretty young age, when my eyes were opened to the injustice and poverty facing humanity. My parents are from India, and when I was five I went back to my father's small village in the state of Gujarat. In the middle of this village is a market, which I walked through with my mother.

To keep me occupied, she allowed me to hold onto a one-rupee coin. It was the rainy season, and there was mud and sewage streaming through the streets. As we were dodging vendors, cows, and other shoppers, I dropped my precious coin into the dirty water. As I started to reach for it, my mother slapped my hand and pulled me away, telling me to leave it. It was *gunda*; it was dirty. As we walked away, I turned my head and looked back to see an old woman in a ragged *sari* walk over and pick up the coin. She held it up to the sky, and thanked G-d for the blessing.

My life hasn't been the same since. As it's said, "one man's trash is another man's treasure," or more accurately, one auntie's blessing.

What my mother made me throw away was something that literally answered someone else's prayers. As I returned to my comfortable life in the suburbs of Minnesota, I couldn't get rid of the uncomfortable feeling that I needed to *do something*. I later realized this feeling was a sign to follow my calling—to help the world's poor by listening to, and acting on, what is in my heart.

287

I've come to realize that *fundraising is the key to accomplishing change and doing good in the world*. To me, fundraising is a holy expression of one's highest self, a way to fulfill one's calling in the world. It's not about begging; it's about inviting people to direct their resources to affect the change they want to see in the world. It's about helping to close the gap between those people's dreams, and transformation in the world.

Fundraising is a profound responsibility that, in order to do well, needs to be done with not only humility, but also tenacity and integrity. I don't think of myself as a natural fundraiser, but I believe in what we're doing at Kiva.org, and most importantly, in our dream of helping people all over the planet gain access to capital from others who believe in them.

It is my belief in, and focus on, this mission that drives me and continues to fuel our efforts. I encourage you to stop often and reconnect with your mission, with your calling. *As a fundraiser, focus first and foremost on establishing your personal connection to the cause, and then on sharing that vision with others, along with a realistic plan for achieving it*. Then people will *want* to join you and support both your vision and your plan. I believe that we all want to be in community with one another, and that we are naturally drawn to be a part of something greater than ourselves.

Remember to take the time to recharge as you heed your call, because ultimately, impact is multi-dimensional. It has depth, breadth, and duration. *In order to sustain your work, you have to tend to your own garden*. Without balancing your work—however important it may be— with your personal life, you won't be able to maximize impact. Many of the issues we focus on will not be solved in our lifetime, so sustaining yourself is critical. We must all *find grace in the struggle*.

Ask yourself: Can you add more life to your work? Think about what you can do *less* of, in order to focus on what's truly important. Take the time to rest and to reflect on the good you do. Too often, we let ourselves be taken away from the "why" of our work by meetings, tasks, and the demands of the office. As you move forward, never forget what Lynne Twist shared in the Foreword: that *your work is an act of love and an expression of your purpose on this planet*.

Remember that every life has value, right here and right now. We can all share more with each other, especially within the nonprofit sector. *As you advance in your career, don't forget to lend a hand to peers and emerging leaders.* As I introduce my newborn daughter to others when she starts school, sharing is one of the first and most valuable lessons I will teach her. *Our best hope is to make the world a better and more fair place for the next generation born into it.*

Many of the issues we seek to address are thorny and complicated. At Kiva. org, we raise funds by finding allies and connecting with partners and supporters who share our vision and who believe in our strategy. Ultimately, it's not about us. We are all links in a chain, and none of us is the beginning or the end. As Darian likes to say, *the rope is stronger than the thread,* and **when we work together across issues, organizations, and even sectors, great things become possible**.

We need to work together to achieve the social change we all dream about. Many nonprofits are unwilling to collaborate due to a scarcity mentality, but when we partner with one another, we get more leverage and accomplish greater things. Alone you may feel small, but together we thrive.

The beautiful thing about helping others in life is that, when you die, your work lives on. We all have only a brief time on this planet, so ask: What is the legacy I want to leave? Think about the Statue of Liberty. France gave the United States the statue without a base, so the newspaper mogul Joseph Pulitzer ran a crowdfunding campaign to raise the money needed to buy one. The average donation was just 83 cents, and donors didn't get t-shirts or their names on a plaque. They donated because they *believed* in the statue as a symbol of liberty and wanted it to stand tall and reflect their belief in the greatness of American society.

Thanks to Pulitzer's fundraising, and the donors who contributed, the Statue of Liberty continues to inspire millions of people a year. If you think about many of the enduring institutions on our planet, including churches, universities, and well renown organizations like the Red Cross, they are nonprofits that provide an anchor point for humanity in a world that can sometimes lose sight of what really matters.

Fundraising is difficult, and there will be setbacks along the way that are often beyond your control. Many times there are no easy answers. Seek solace in your mission and in the eyes of those you help. *Look inside yourself and find your own personal calling and purpose, and answer it in your work.*

That is ultimately what we exist to do in this sector, and in this world, in my opinion. Remember that we're all in this together—as a sector, as a movement, and as a planet—and our goal is nothing short of unleashing the full potential of the human race. And at the end of the day, none of our work is possible without the funding that makes it move forward. Thank you for the important work that you do each and every day to make this world a better place.

About Premal Shah

Premal Shah is president and co-founder of Kiva.org, a website that's engaged thousands in lending over $1 million to low-income entrepreneurs from 75 countries, in increments as low as $25. Shah's inspiration for Kiva.org came in 2004, after taking a sabbatical from PayPal to volunteer in India. Working there to help low-income women sell handcrafts online strengthened his belief that the right combination of technology, business, and love can dramatically accelerate opportunity for those who need it most.

Closing Thoughts

Darian Rodriguez Heyman

"I am of the opinion that my life belongs to the whole community, and as long as I live it is my privilege to do for it what I can.

I want to be thoroughly used up when I die, for the harder I work, the more I live.

I rejoice in life for its own sake.

Life is no 'brief candle' to me.

It is a sort of splendid torch which I have gotten hold of for a moment, and I want to make it burn as brightly as possible before passing it on to future generations."

—George Bernard Shaw

One of my best friends, Chris Portella, once shared something that will always stay with me: "When you're in the zone, you never stop." We may have been talking about snowboarding at the time, but I've found the insight equally relevant professionally.

We all wonder why we're here at times and question our calling in this world. My hope for you is that you discover that intention and purpose, and that it involves fundraising for causes worthy of your support. And once you discover this, may you unlock even more passion for your work and follow the lead of many of our contributors, devoting your career to connecting donors and funders to nonprofits that stir your passions.

Che Guevara once shared: "A true revolutionary is guided by great feelings of love." As professionals and leaders focused on social change, we are all revolutionaries. But as you read in the Foreword and Afterword, ***the most effective fundraisers are those whose actions and work come from a*** *place of love.* As you connect with your love for a cause, or of fundraising in general, I hope you discover a lifelong passion. After all, *the world needs you.* Every cause, every organization, and every movement needs funding to achieve its goals. That means they all need *you,* so finding work as a fundraiser won't be difficult. So pick wisely and choose the causes and nonprofits you're most committed to, and support them with your best work.

Love is one thing, arguably even a prerequisite for success in this work, but I'd add another key variable in the recipe for success: persistence. In my experience, *in order to thrive as a nonprofit fundraiser, above all, you must be persistent*. Fundraising can be tough, and for every "yes" you receive, odds are you will hear "no" even more. That means not being afraid to be turned down and, more importantly, keeping your head high and continuing on your path after every rejection. This is where the connection to that love, to your passion, comes into play. It's the fuel that drives you to continue working, because you know the cause is worth it.

There are myriad problems in the world today, but personally, I believe that nonprofits aren't meant to focus on those. We exist to provide *solutions.* This book contains a huge array of proven solutions, best practices, resources, and ideas. Put them to work as you look to unlock your full potential as a fundraiser. And remember, when you're pursuing solutions, it's not enough to dream; we have to act, and act *strategically*.

I love asking nonprofits what they think the difference is between a dreamer and a visionary. To me, it's about the "B to the Y." You see, I believe *a dreamer can see A to Z.* A is the world as it exists today, with all its flaws and imperfections. And Z is the utopian vision of tomorrow—the world where every child is fed, clothed, and educated; where we live in a thriving local green economy; or whatever it means to you. And that, in my mind, is a dream. It's inspiring, powerful, and stirs us emotionally.

But dreaming is not enough. *The visionary sees this dream, but also sees the B to the Y.* These letters represent the steps involved in getting from here . . . to there. They are the plans, partners, metrics, tactics, and every other consideration needed to achieve the change you seek.

I trust this book will fill in a couple of letters in the alphabet for you, enabling you to move past the dream and into the *reality* of impact. And as you move along your path, remember to help others in their pursuit of a better world.

There's a story I once heard about a young nonprofit fundraiser. She was walking along a country road when she fell into a pit. It was dark and the walls were sheer. She tried to pull herself out but couldn't, and started calling out to anyone in earshot, to no avail. Despondent, she sat down in the pit and pondered her fate, when suddenly a policeman walked by. She could make out his hat over the brim of the pit, and she yelled out, begging for help. Sadly, he just kept walking by, ignoring her cries.

After fruitlessly continuing to yell for a while, she sat back down and started to cry. After another half hour or so, a fireman walked by. Once again, she called for help: "Mr. fireman, help me! I'm a nonprofit fundraiser, and I've fallen into a pit and can't get out!" Unfortunately, the fireman ignored her cries and simply carried on his way.

This is where she lost it. If a fireman and a policeman wouldn't help her, who would? She sat in that dark pit for what seemed like an eternity, when an old man walked by. She didn't even bother calling to him, since if a policeman and a fireman ignored her, how could she possibly expect this elderly fellow to hoist her out? To her amazement, the man peeked over the edge of the hole and, seeing her below, jumped down without hesitation.

He greeted her briefly, saying, "Hi there. I see you're stuck down here." She picked her jaw up off the ground, and replied, "Yes, I'm a nonprofit fundraiser, and I've been stuck down in this pit for hours! Thanks for jumping down here, but why on earth would you do that?"

"Well," he responded, "I'm a nonprofit fundraiser, too. Many years ago I fell down into this same pit. A fellow fundraiser was kind enough to jump down and show me that, back here through the darkness," he pointed, "there's a stairway up to the surface."

He slowly guided her up the passage, sharing: "She led me to safety and told me that sometimes, we *all* fall into a pit. And as passionate, persistent fundraisers we owe it to our profession, and to the many worthy causes in the world, to help each other out when we can. So next time you walk by this pit, or any others you've fallen into, take a peek inside. If there's a poor fundraiser trapped down there, jump in and help him or her out."

The point of this story is that together we thrive, and alone, we struggle in the darkness. ***It is the responsibility of every fundraiser to support and*** *help your peers*. I hope the chapters and resources in this book shed light on any pitfalls you face in the coming years and that they guide you to success and impact. Remember that *we're all in this together*, and it's only in unity and solidarity that the Z—the just world we all dream of—can become real.

Book Partners

"When a thousand spiders unite, they can tie down a lion."
—Ethiopian Proverb

In all, 77 amazing partners supported this book project. Collectively, they represent some of the most important resources for nonprofits and fundraisers globally, and I encourage you to learn more about them and take advantage of everything they have to offer.

Book Sponsors

CommitChange

Founded in 2012, CommitChange is one of America's fastest-growing nonprofit software companies. They're committed to building technologies that change lives and help nonprofits raise money, more sustainably. www.commitchange.com

Eventbrite

Eventbrite is a global event marketplace empowering people to easily discover and create events. Over 75,000 nonprofit events have been ticketed through the Eventbrite platform to date. From mobile ticketing and check-in at charity concerts to seating plans for fundraising galas, Eventbrite offers features for all types of events. www.eventbrite.com

Sparrow is a mobile company on a mission: Digital Inclusion for All. They are bridging the digital divide with the Mobile for All buy-one-give-one mobile service, as well as a platform that connects economically disadvantaged people—and the organizations who serve them—with the mobile economy. www.SparrowMobile.com

Publication Partner

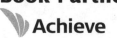

Since 1960, The Association of Fundraising Professionals (AFP) has inspired global change and supported efforts that generated over $1 trillion. AFP's members raise over $100 billion annually, equivalent to one-third of all charitable giving in North America and millions more around the world. AFP members throughout the world work to advance philanthropy through advocacy, research, education, and certification programs. The association fosters professional development and growth and promotes high ethical standards in the fundraising profession. www.afpnet.org

Book Partners
Achieve

Achieve is a research, design, and technology services company that helps companies and nonprofits inspire action and change the world. Achieve combines globally recognized research with thoughtful strategy, powerful messaging, and stunning design to understand and activate audiences, donors, and employees. www.achieveguidance.com

Ashoka's Youth Venture develops and facilitates changemaker workshops for youth by enabling parents, schools, businesses, and nonprofits to

support them. This enables them to launch their own youth-led ventures to solve social issues and to develop 21st century skills to prepare them for today's work environment. They offer competitions, feedback, and fiscal sponsorship for their Youth Venturers. www.youthventure.org

The Aspen Leadership Group is a national network of fundraising leaders. Through executive search and consulting services, and with a focus on careers rather than on isolated jobs, ALG builds productive and enduring relationships with individuals pursuing careers in philanthropy and with leaders of organizations engaged in philanthropy. www.aspenleadershipgroup.com

Attentive.ly

Attentive.ly is a social media engagement platform that turns your audience into advocates. They provide organizations with rich social media data on their supporters and donors, and then help them use that data to better target and personalize outreach for dramatically improved response rates. They enable customers to send highly targeted, triggered communications to contacts and donors based on digital body language on the social web. www.Attentive.ly

bigduck

Big Duck develops smart communications for nonprofits. They work primarily in three areas—brandraising, campaigns, and consulting—to help nonprofits of all shapes and sizes reach supporters, build awareness, and raise money. Learn how they can help you inspire audiences and help people connect with, and invest in, your nonprofit's mission. www.BigDuckNYC.com.

BIONEERS

Since 1990, Bioneers has acted as a nexus for game-changing social and scientific visions, knowledge, and best practices, advancing the great

global transformation toward a human civilization that honors nature's genius, human ingenuity, and future generations. Through their annual National Bioneers Conference, award-winning media, local conferences and initiatives, and leadership training programs, they support individuals, communities, organizations, and funders to connect, collaborate, and co-create a shared future. www.bioneers.org

Blackbaud is the leading technology provider to all types of nonprofits because they offer innovative software and services and the largest philanthropic network in the world. Their mission is to empower and connect nonprofits to take their missions as far as possible, so that good can take over the world. www.blackbaud.com

Care2 is a highly engaged social network of 30 million citizen activists standing together for good and making extraordinary impact—locally, nationally, and internationally—by starting petitions and supporting each other's campaigns. Care2 has been a pioneer of online advocacy since its inception. They provided the first central platform for online petitions and were the first to help nonprofit organizations tap into this passion to grow their organizations. www.Care2.com

CAUSE MARKETING FORUM

Since 2002, the Cause Marketing Forum has been the go-to source for nonprofit professionals seeking education, training, and connections in their corporate alliance efforts. From monthly best practice webinars to their annual conference, online resources, and industry benchmark reports, CMF is the place to go for tips, trends, and tactics that help further the efforts of those doing well by doing good. www. causemarketingforum.com

© CAUSECAST

Causecast is the leading employee cause engagement platform, providing a modern employee engagement solution to companies of all sizes. Their robust system allows nonprofits to submit giving and volunteer opportunities at no cost. In turn, corporate employees adopt or build their own philanthropic campaigns, including offering their professional skills to nonprofits and sharing their experiences using the Causecast Story Capture feature. www.causecast.org

CEN
Center for Excellence in Nonprofits

The Center for Excellence in Nonprofits (CEN) fosters highly effective leaders and vibrant nonprofit organizations that transform the quality of life in our communities. They are committed to building a strong community of nonprofit leaders, fully understanding the challenges of our sector, providing access to exceptional resources, and connecting nonprofit and community leaders in ways that strengthen all of us. CEN puts on a variety of leadership development programs, and has a strong focus on the importance of fundraising to attain organizational sustainability. www.cen.org

Center ●
FOR NON-PROFITS
Helping organizations build a better New Jersey

The Center for Non-Profits is New Jersey's statewide umbrella organization for the charitable community. Its mission is to build the power of New Jersey's nonprofit community to improve the quality of life for the people of the state. For more than 30 years, the Center has served as the leading champion and first-stop resource for and about New Jersey's nonprofits, providing advocacy, tools and resources, strategic convenings, training, phone and email consultation, cost-saving programs, and member services to strengthen organizations and help them thrive. www.njnonprofits.org

change.org

As the world's largest petition platform, Change.org empowers people everywhere to create the change they want to see. Over 100 million people in every country come to Change.org to start campaigns, mobilize supporters, and work with decision-makers to drive solutions. Thousands of nonprofits use Change.org to advance their causes and connect with new supporters and donors. www.Change.org

Commongood Careers is a mission-driven search firm that is committed to supporting the hiring needs of nonprofits tackling today's most pressing social problems. Because of their clients' ambitious goals, they work hard to ensure they're able to secure the talent needed to create even greater social impact. Commongood Careers supports the hiring needs of high-performing nonprofits at every stage of organizational growth—in all functional areas and at all levels of seniority. www.commongoodcareers.org

CONNECTICUT ASSOCIATION of NONPROFITS | ...to serve, strengthen and support Connecticut's nonprofit community.

Connecticut Association of Nonprofits (CT Nonprofits). There are thousands of nonprofits in Connecticut—each striving to make a difference on their own. Connecticut Association of Nonprofits (CT Nonprofits) brings them together, so that each organization may benefit from collective strength and a unified voice. As a capacity-building organization, they focus on the tools and knowledge nonprofit professionals need to diversify funding streams for their organization. www.ctnonprofits.org

Connecting Up

Connecting Up is a not-for-profit organization that works to unleash the power of not-for-profits by providing a variety of information, products, resources, and programs. As the local partner of the U.S.-based TechSoup Global network, Connecting Up manages technology donation programs of companies such as Microsoft, Cisco, Adobe, Symantec, and many more to qualified not-for-profit organizations in Australia, New Zealand (under the TechSoup New Zealand banner), and South East Asia (under TechSoup Asia). www.connectingup.org

Constant Contact introduced the first email marketing tool for small businesses, nonprofits, and associations in 1998. Today, the company helps more than 650,000 customers worldwide find marketing success through the only all-in-one online marketing platform for small organizations. Anchored by their world-class email marketing tool, Constant Contact helps nonprofits drive donor engagement and find new supporters. www.constantcontact.com

For 50 years Development Executives Roundtable has provided exceptional fundraising education to professionals in the San Francisco Bay Area in an inclusive, supportive atmosphere. DER offers accessible, affordable education and support to fundraising professionals. www.DERSF.org

eBay for Charity helps nonprofits and causes of all sizes raise funds on eBay, the world's most vibrant marketplace for discovering great value and unique selection. Established in 2003, eBay for Charity has enabled the eBay Community to raise over $600 million globally. It also gives eBay users a secure and efficient way of donating to a charity of their choice when they buy or sell on the site. http://charity.ebay.com

ECHOING GREEN

Echoing Green's mission is to unleash next-generation talent to solve the world's biggest problems. Through Fellowships and innovative leadership initiatives, they unleash potential by tracking down the best and brightest leaders, bringing them together, and launching them on a path to success. Echoing Green continues to build a global community of emerging leaders—almost 700 and growing—who launched Teach For America, City Year, One Acre Fund, and more. www.echoinggreen.org

eCIVIS

eCivis is the leading cloud-based grants management system in the United States for local governments, educational institutions, and nonprofits. Their innovative solutions address both programmatic and fiscal grant funding requirements, helping clients easily overcome the challenges and heavy workload that come with finding and managing grants. Entities rely on eCivis to identify appropriate grants, submit strong applications, and efficiently manage awarded grants, while dramatically reducing administrative costs. www.ecivis.com

For Momentum is a nationally recognized cause marketing agency. Focused exclusively on cause alliance strategy and support, For Momentum represents leading nonprofit organizations, corporations, and agencies to form and strengthen strategic corporate partnerships. Founded in 2003 by advertising and nonprofit executive Mollye Rhea, For Momentum has been recognized by *Corporate Responsibility Magazine* as one of the top five cause marketing firms in the United States. www.formomentum.com

FOUNDATION
CENTER
Knowledge to build on.

Foundation Center is the leading source of information about philanthropy worldwide. Through data, analysis, and training, it connects people who want to change the world to the resources they need to succeed. It maintains the most comprehensive database on grantmakers and their grants, and operates research and capacity-building programs that advance knowledge of philanthropy at every level. Its website, five regional centers, and more than

450 Funding Information Network locations offer free access to resources. www.foundationcenter.org

⁞FUNDINGP⬤RTAL
Get Funded!

Improve your access to government funding, private investors, and foundations by using The Funding Portal's comprehensive funding services. Search more than 14,000 sources of U.S. and Canadian funding aggregated on the Portal, order their unique data and analytics products, and access their partners and services that greatly improve funding outcomes. More than 17,000 organizations use The Funding Portal to find funding each month. TheFundingPortal.com

FUNDRAISING
INSTITUTE OF
NEW ZEALAND
MATATIKA MĀTAURANGA KAITAUTOKO

The Fundraising Institute of New Zealand (FINZ) is the professional body for charities and those employed in, or involved with, fundraising, sponsorship, and events in the not-for-profit sector. They lead the growing professionalism of the sector in New Zealand with education courses, advocacy support, mentoring, and maintenance of high ethical standards. www.finz.org.nz

#GI♥INGTUESDAY

#GivingTuesday is a global day of giving that unites organizations around the world for one common purpose: to give back. Launched in 2012, the movement has created a community of philanthropists dedicated to giving and sharing how they are making a difference. www.givingtuesday.org

building people-to-people ties

For over 25 years, Global Exchange has been an incubator and hub for movements and grassroots campaigns. They helped found the first Fair Trade certification body in the United States, 50 Years Is Enough, United for Peace and Justice, Code Pink, Green Festivals, and more. Today, Global Exchange sponsors and supports nearly 20 small grassroots programs, providing start-up projects and grassroots leaders the opportunity to connect with others in their network and access nonprofit resources. www.globalexchange.org

GOOD SCOUT

Good Scout is a social good consultancy that helps brands take smart, impactful, and sustainable leaps in how they contribute to the greater good. Using their proprietary data tools and decades of corporate alliance experience as a foundation, Good Scout helps their nonprofit clients maximize opportunity with corporate partners across a spectrum of tactics, igniting consumer and donor activation and resulting in millions in incremental fundraising. www.goodscoutgroup.com

The Grant Professionals Association (GPA) is an international membership association for everyone in the grants industry. GPA and its affiliates work to advance the profession, certify professionals, and fund professionalism. GPA offers continuing professional development through local chapter meetings, regular webinars, the *GPA Journal*, and an annual conference. www.GrantProfessionals.org

Grassroots.org serves as a catalyst for positive social change by offering nonprofits free and deeply discounted technology tools, resources, and best practices to save them money and serve their stakeholders more effectively. www.grassroots.org

GuideStar is the world's largest source of information on nonprofit organizations. They collect, organize, and distribute crucial data about nonprofit results, financials, operations, and more. Over 144,000

foundation staff and board members use GuideStar to evaluate grantees and direct more resources to organizations. This information is spread by a network of more than 120 organizations, including AmazonSmile and VolunteerMatch. www.guidestar.org

HUM∧NITY IN ∧CTION

Humanity in Action is an international organization that educates, inspires, and connects a network of emerging leaders committed to protecting minorities and promoting human rights—in their own communities and around the world. Since 1997, Humanity in Action has educated more then 1,500 emerging leaders via their offices in Amsterdam, Berlin, Copenhagen, Warsaw, Paris, New York, and Sarajevo. www.humanityinaction.org

Nonprofits can drive strategic partnerships, establish key foundation and corporate relationships, cultivate existing donors, and leverage board connections with LinkedIn for fundraising. https://nonprofits.linkedin.com

Mal Warwick Donordigital
Integrated fundraising, advocacy and marketing

Mal Warwick | Donordigital is a full-service, integrated fundraising consulting agency that has worked with exceptional nonprofit organizations and progressive political candidates and causes since 1979. Their senior-level professionals provide strategic insight, in-depth analysis, award-winning creative, and comprehensive management services. Their focus is integrated direct mail, online, and telephone fundraising and advocacy. www.malwarwick.com

Media Cause is a digital marketing agency specializing in nonprofits and social enterprises. They help the world's most impactful organizations navigate the digital world as they change the real world. Media Cause

creates, shapes, and refines digital strategies to drive growth—whether it's developing a brand, raising awareness, building online communities, creating engagement, or prompting action—and generate unparalleled results. www.mediacause.org

The Minnesota Council of Nonprofits supports nonprofits and their fundraising efforts through an annual conference focused on fundraising strategies, trends, and techniques; a frequently offered Grantwriting Clinic; Minnesota Grants Alert, an e-newsletter featuring grant deadlines and foundation news and personnel updates; an annual publication, *Minnesota Grants Directory*, profiling the largest public, community, and private foundations in the state; the popular Minnesota Foundations briefing, an annual review of recent changes in foundation priorities and processes; and periodic Philanthropy Leaders events, where heads of prominent foundations share their viewpoints with MCN members. www.minnesotanonprofits.org

Mission Capital, formerly Greenlights for Nonprofit Success, provides tools and guidance, including consulting, training, research, and more, to help mission-driven people and organizations tackle complex community problems in Central Texas. They promote the convergence of mission-driven human, financial, intellectual, social, and political capital; the kind of capital required to change the world. www.MissionCapital.org

⁄mission minded

Strong brands raise more money. Mission Minded is a branding firm that works exclusively with nonprofits to help them determine the brand—or reputation—for which they want to be known. Then they help them bring that brand to life with compelling key messages, inspiring campaign collateral, powerful visual identity design, innovative website design, and more. www.mission-minded.com

The Mobile Giving Foundation was founded in 2007 to create a "mobile giving channel" that empowers nonprofits and donors, and that provides mobile solutions for social good. Working with North America's top mobile carriers, the Foundation pioneered the use of "carrier-billed" donations and owns the billing, reporting, and remittance infrastructure that makes impulse giving on your phone possible. They partner with the BBB Wise Giving Alliance to grow the mobile-giving channel, strengthen mobile-giving industry standards and accountability, assure donor confidence, and reinforce nonprofit acceptance of the mobile-giving medium. www.mobilegiving.org

NEO Law Group provides nonprofit corporate and tax counsel to hundreds of organizations on matters regarding charitable trust requirements, solicitations, registration, sponsorships, gift acceptance policies, restricted gifts, pledges, deductions, commercial fundraisers, and social media. The firm's lawyers are popular speakers and writers on nonprofit legal issues and contributors to the popular Nonprofit Law Blog and Tony Martignetti Nonprofit Radio. www.neolawgroup.com

NET IMPACT 🌀

Net Impact is a leading nonprofit that empowers aspiring impact makers to use their skills and careers to change the world. At the heart of their community are over 60,000 emerging leaders from more than 250 volunteer-led chapters across the globe, all working for a more just and sustainable future. They provide the network and resources to help students and professionals make a net impact that transforms the world. www.netimpact.org

Network for Good helps nonprofits grow individual giving through online fundraising software and expert-backed training and resources, such as the free Nonprofit 911 webinar series and The Nonprofit Marketing Blog. Since 2001, they have distributed more than $1 billion to over 100,000 charities through their secure online giving platform. www.networkforgood.com

NetSuite.org is the Corporate Citizenship arm of NetSuite, a leading ERP/CRM cloud platform. They support nonprofits and social enterprises to create greater impact around the world in part by offering them five free licenses to support donor relationships and financials. www.NetSuite.org

The Nonprofit Association of the Midlands (NAM) is the state association for nonprofits of all sizes and missions in Nebraska and southwest Iowa. They strengthen the collective voice, leadership, and capacity of nonprofits in the region by providing resources to make running nonprofit businesses easier. www.nonprofitam.org

THE NONPROFIT ASSOCIATION OF OREGON

The Nonprofit Association of Oregon (NAO) is a statewide membership organization that provides a unique vehicle for nonprofit sector expression and support. They believe the nonprofit sector strengthens the fabric of our democracy and our communities. By representing and supporting charitable nonprofits of all sizes and geographic locations across Oregon, NAO strives to convene, build capacity, promote best practices, and be a thought leader to help nonprofits build a thriving and vital Oregon. www.nonprofitoregon.org

The Nonprofits Insurance Alliance Group is dedicated to exclusively serving the insurance needs of nonprofits and currently provides specialty liability

coverage for more than 15,000 501(c)(3) nonprofits. The Nonprofits Insurance Alliance of California (NIAC) provides coverage in California. The Alliance of Nonprofits for Insurance, Risk Retention Group (ANI) provides coverage in 32 states, plus D.C. www.insurancefornonprofits.org

Nonprofit Leadership Alliance

Certified to Change the World

Since 1948, the Nonprofit Leadership Alliance has worked to strengthen the social sector with a talented, prepared workforce. Its Certified Nonprofit Professional (CNP) credential is the only national nonprofit management certification in the United States. The Alliance system, which includes 50 colleges, universities, and national nonprofit partners and more than 9,000 CNPs, is the largest network in the country working to build a talent pipeline for the social sector. www.NonprofitLeadershipAlliance.org

Nonprofit Marketing Guide.com

Nonprofit Marketing Guide offers free and affordable online training and downloads, as well professional coaching and mentoring programs. They literally wrote the books on nonprofit marketing. Check out *The Nonprofit Marketing Guide: High-Impact, Low-Cost Ways to Build Support for Your Good Cause, Content Marketing for Nonprofits: A Communications Map for Engaging Your Community, Becoming a Favorite Cause,* and *Raising More Money.* www.nonprofitmarketingguide.com

Nonprofit Tech for Good

With 100,000 monthly visitors and more than one million followers on social networks, Nonprofit Tech for Good is a leading mobile and social media blog for nonprofit professionals worldwide. They focus on providing easy-to-understand news and resources related to nonprofit technology, social media, online fundraising, and mobile communications. www.nptechforgood.com

NTEN is a community of nearly 70,000 nonprofit professionals that transforms technology into social change. NTEN connects its members

to each other through networking and events, provides professional development opportunities, educates their constituency on issues of technology use in nonprofits, and spearheads groundbreaking research, advocacy, and education on technology issues affecting the entire nonprofit technology community—from fundraising to technology leadership. www.nten.org

OneStar Foundation is a nonprofit corporation designated by the Governor to build a stronger nonprofit sector in Texas. OneStar is recognized statewide as a leading voice of the sector, a neutral convener, and a respected business partner to foundations, state agencies, and the business community. OneStar is home to Texas Connector, an online nonprofit mapping tool with the most robust nonprofit data set in the country overlaid with socioeconomic and demographic data for grant writing and community needs assessments. http://onestarfoundation.org

The Peace and Collaborative Development Network (PCDN) is one of the leading online networks connecting the global social change community. PCDN is a rapidly growing social enterprise that gathers over 35,000 professionals and organizations, offering a one-stop shop to inspire, connect, inform, and provide the tools and resources to scale social change. The network has extensive resources on all aspects of fundraising, including many grant, crowdfunding, and related opportunities. www.internationalpeaceandconflict.org

PeerSpring is a civic-tech education company dedicated to strengthening collaboration among students, teachers, and their communities. They work with educators, nonprofits, and youth leaders to connect real-world problems with skills-based education programs implemented inside secondary and higher education classrooms. Nonprofits are invited to submit "challenges" for secondary and higher-ed students to "solve." www.peerspring.com

PeerToPeer
Professional Forum

The Peer-to-Peer Professional Forum (formerly the Run Walk Ride Fundraising Council) was launched in May 2007 to support the professionals who manage peer-to-peer fundraising events, who collectively raise in excess of $1 billion a year for charities. Their conference and workshops, webinars, and online services provide access to practical information on producing more successful programs, valuable contacts, and recognition for outstanding work. www.peertopeerforum.com

 **Plenty**

Plenty is a peer-to-peer fundraising consultancy with unmatched experience helping organizations harness the power of networks, the possibility of community, and the potential of peer-to-peer, so they can raise more money, build larger movements, and create a lasting difference in the world. www.plentyconsulting.com

POINTS
OF LIGHT

Points of Light—the world's largest organization dedicated to volunteer service—mobilizes millions of people to take action and change the world. Through affiliates in 250 cities and partnerships with thousands of nonprofits and corporations, Points of Light engages four million volunteers in 30 million hours of service each year. They bring the power of people to bear where it's needed most. www.pointsoflight.org

 RSF
Social Finance

RSF Social Finance is a financial services organization dedicated to transforming the way the world works with money. RSF offers investing, lending, and giving services that generate positive social and environmental impact, while fostering community and collaboration among participants. Since 1984, RSF has made more than $275 million in loans and $130 million in grants to nonprofits (and for-profit social enterprises), working in the fields of Food and Agriculture, Education and the Arts, and Ecological Stewardship. www.rsfsocialfinance.org

Sea Change Strategies raises money by building relationships. They believe that the change organizations are seeking in the world will accelerate when they understand their donors, what they value, and how to build close ties with them. They do audience research and create research-backed fundraising strategies to give donors amazing experiences that keep them giving. www.seachangestrategies.com

Selfish Giving helps do-gooders, nonprofits, and businesses create win-win partnerships that raise money, build stakeholder loyalty, and change the world. The site's founder, Joe Waters, is co-host of CauseTalk Radio and the author of three books. His latest is *Fundraising with Businesses: 40 New (and Improved!) Strategies for Nonprofit*s. www.Selfishgiving.com

The Social Good Summit is a two-day conference examining the impact of technology and new media on social good initiatives around the world. Held annually during UN Week, the Social Good Summit unites a dynamic community of global leaders and grassroots activists to discuss solutions for the greatest challenges of our time. During the Summit, global citizens around the world unite to unlock the potential of technology to make the world a better place. www.mashable.com/sgs

S⦿CIAL MEDIA
─── For Nonprofits ───

Social Media for Nonprofits (SM4NP) powers social change globally by building the digital media capacity of nonprofits to use social media tools and platforms and better meet their missions. SM4NP is the only nonprofit with a vast global and digital footprint, including a presence in thirteen cities and three countries, dedicated solely to this work. In addition to training programs, they convene global leaders around the role of social media in social change movements to help elevate global movements like the ALS Ice Bucket Challenge, BlackLivesMatter, and more. www.sm4np.org

Socialbrite is a leading social media consultancy for nonprofits and a digital learning hub that brings together top experts in social causes and social media. They help nonprofits with all facets of social media: strategy, social PR, trainings, website design, community building, multimedia storytelling, and fundraising campaigns. In addition, they provide thousands of free articles, tutorials, and resources to the social good community. www.socialbrite.org

 StartSomeGood

StartSomeGood is a crowdfunding platform for social good project. They work with nonprofits, social enterprises, and community groups to help them develop and launch their campaigns. With a curated platform and emphasis on providing great advice and support, StartSomeGood has one of the highest success rates of any crowdfunding platform, with 53 percent of projects reaching their goals. www.startsomegood.com

 Stifter-helfen.net

Stifter-helfen.de—IT für Non-Profits—is the online portal for IT donations to nonprofits in Germany, Austria, and Switzerland. A regional TechSoup Global affiliate, they offer nonprofits discounted access to over 30 IT providers, including Adobe, Cisco, Microsoft, and Symantec. They also offer access to refurbished hardware and produce workshops and webinars to build nonprofits' IT knowledge and digital competence. They recently launched ConnectingHelp (www.connectinghelp.de), a new one-stop marketplace for donations of all kinds to nonprofits in Germany, including IT and other product donations, competitions, grant opportunities, requests for proposals, webinars, and pro bono activities of companies, foundations, and other organizations. www.Stifter-helfen.de

SUPPORT CENTER
| PARTNERSHIP IN
| PHILANTHROPY
| Change Consulting | Executive Search | Training

The Support Center/Partnership in Philanthropy has been dedicated to improving society by increasing the effectiveness of nonprofit leaders and their organizations since 1986. Their services—including change consulting, executive search, training, and grantmaker partnerships—strengthen nonprofit and philanthropic leaders and their organizations. They work with organizations of different sizes and stages of growth to develop practical knowledge, build productive relationships, and find the information and resources they need to further their mission. www.supportcenteronline.org

taproot
FOUNDATION

The Taproot Foundation connects nonprofits and social change organizations with passionate, skilled volunteers who share their expertise pro bono. Through their programs, business professionals deliver marketing, strategy, HR, and IT solutions that nonprofits need to achieve their missions. More and more nonprofits are thinking comprehensively about "resource-raising" to include pro bono service. Imagine what your organization could do for the communities you serve if you could secure 20 percent of your budget through pro bono service. www.taprootfoundation.org

techsoup

TechSoup is a global network of 63 partner NGOs that connects over 600,000 nonprofits in every country around the globe to the technology, support, and resources they need to enhance social impact. They are best known for running the world's largest technology philanthropy program in partnership with leading technology companies, offering nonprofits access to a wide array of discounted and donated hardware, software, and services. www.techsoup.org

Thrive™
The Alliance of Nonprofits
for San Mateo County

Thrive—San Mateo County's Nonprofit Alliance—is a robust, trusted network of nonprofit organizations, businesses, government agencies, elected officials, and civic leaders. Thrive helps build the capacity of nonprofits and strengthen San Mateo County's critical community organizations by providing over 230 members with invaluable connections, collaboration opportunities, and resources to help them fulfill their mission and fundraising goals. www.thrivealliance.org

UniversalGiving connects people with quality giving and volunteering opportunities worldwide. Unique to UniversalGiving, 100 percent of donations given through their online platform go directly to nonprofits. UniversalGiving Corporate consults Fortune 500 companies on scaling their Corporate Social Responsibility programs. www.universalgiving.org

VolunteerMatch believes everyone should have the chance to make a difference. As the Web's largest volunteer engagement network, they connect good people with great causes. To date, they've helped nonprofits attract more than $6.8 billion worth of volunteer services—and research shows that two out of three volunteers also donate money to the organizations to which they donate their time. www.volunteermatch.org

WVDO is a member-based organization in Oregon open to anyone who engages in professional fundraising activities, including volunteers, board members, executive directors, development directors and assistants, event planners, grant writers, consultants, foundations, and business professionals. They empower members to learn together and support one another as they develop resources for fundraising excellence. Through educational programming and job placement services, WVDO works tirelessly to improve nonprofits and the communities they serve. www.wvdo-or.org

YES! is a nonprofit that connects, inspires, and collaborates with changemakers to co-create thriving, just, and sustainable ways of life for all. They work at the meeting point of internal, interpersonal, and systemic

transformation. YES! supports leaders and visionaries to access and expand the resources inside of themselves, their communities, and the wider world at all levels. www.yesworld.org

YOUTH LEADERSHIP INSTITUTE

The Youth Leadership Institute (YLI) builds communities where young people and their adult allies come together to create positive community change. They bring over 20 years of social justice work to their California community-based programs—in San Francisco, Marin, San Mateo, and Fresno Counties—and their national training and consulting services. YLI is committed to engaging and developing young people of color, low-income youth, and other non-traditional leaders as agents of social change. www.yli.org

About the Authors

"The purpose of life is a life of purpose."

—Robert Byrne

Darian Rodriguez Heyman is an accomplished fundraiser, social entrepreneur, and author. His work "helping people help" started during his five-year tenure as executive director of Craigslist Foundation, where he launched their Nonprofit Boot Camp and educated and inspired more than 10,000 nonprofit leaders. He edited the best-selling book, *Nonprofit Management 101: A Complete and Practical Guide for Leaders and Professionals* (John Wiley & Sons), after which he co-founded the only conference series devoted to social media for social good, Social Media for Nonprofits.

Heyman also co-founded Sparrow: Mobile for All, which powers mobile campaigns for nonprofits and government agencies serving the poor, and served as a commissioner for the environment for the City and County of San Francisco, where he helped pass the largest solar rebate program in U.S. history. He is a frequent keynote speaker at nonprofit, fundraising, youth leadership, and environmental events around the globe and thrives on connecting social change leaders to the best practices, resources, and contacts needed to maximize impact. Heyman can be reached at darian@darianheyman.com and strives to personally and promptly respond to all inquiries and requests for support.

Laila Brenner is a writer and veteran fundraiser who has worked with a variety of national organizations including Habitat for Humanity, The Trust for Public Land, Craigslist Foundation, and KCETLink. In 2010 she received her master's degree in nonprofit administration from the University of San Francisco and founded LB Writing Services. Brenner has worked raising money for and promoting a variety of causes within the sector, including education and literacy, access to technology, affordable housing, environmental conservation, community building, performing arts, volunteerism, women's rights, media impact and reform, and more. She has also served as executive director for Atmos Theatre and co-founded The Women's Service Club and Nonprofits101.

Index

Page references followed by *fig* indicate an illustrated figure.

A

A/B email testing, 169–170
"ABC: Always Be Cropping" (Kawasaki), 189
Aberdeen Group, 121
Accenture Consulting, 130
Achieve, 144, 149
Advertisements. *See* Media sponsorships
Advocates (Triple A framework for the Ask), 91
AdWords, 122
AFP's 2014 *Fundraising Effectiveness Survey Report*, 88
Ali, Muhammad, 10
ALS Association, 182–184
Ambassadors (Triple A framework for the Ask), 91
American Cancer Society (ACS), 37, 40–41, 43
American Express, 129
American Marketing Association, 252
"Angels," 281–282
Annual appeal campaigns: critical skills and competencies for successful, 108–114; do's and don'ts for, 114–115; as great way to connection with donors and potential donors, 107–108
Annual unrestricted donations, 92–93
APANO (Asian Pacific American Network of Oregon) case study, 41–42
API (application programming interface), 58
Apple Watch, 201
Apps (mobile fundraising), 195
APRA (Association of Professional Researchers for Advancement), 48, 52–53, 54
Asker (Triple A framework for the Ask), 91
Association of Fundraising Professionals, 252
Aubry, Rick: on earned income strategies, 275–284; professional background of, 276, 284

B

"B to the Y," 292
Baby Boomers (born 1946-1964): critical skills and competencies for fundraising to, 145–148; do's and don'ts of fundraising to, 149; what fundraisers need to know about, 145

Ben & Jerry's Ice Cream, 281
Beneficiary testimonials, 167
Benefits (job), 18
Beth's Blog: How Nonprofits Can Use Social Media (Kanter), 186
Beyond Fund Raising (Grace), 88, 96
Big Duck, 108, 115
Bill Bradley Presidential Campaign, 130
Bioneers, 222
Bittel, Lester R., 13
Blackbaud, 59, 66, 70, 74, 113
Board chairs: creating a board development committee with focus on fundraising, 31; responsibility to make personal asks of each board member, 32; taking charge of getting other board members involved in fundraising, 31
Board development committee: created to focus on fundraising, 31; to drive recruitment and onboarding board members, 28
Board engagement: as critical for fundraising success, 25–26; critical skills and competencies for developing, 26–33; do's and don'ts of creating a, 33–34
Board engagement skills/competencies: 1: know what you're looking for by creating a matrix, 26–28; 2: set expectations for board members, 28–29; 3: provide board members with training and support, 30; 4: engage each board member individually, 30–31; 5: let your board lead, 31–32; 6: maximize board meetings, 32–33
Board matrix: how to introduce it to your board members, 27–28; Nonprofit Board Matrix Template for, 27; as powerful tool clarifying what you need in board meetings, 26
Board meetings: introducing your board matrix at a, 27–28; maximize your, 32–33; sharing fundraising success stories at, 32; start with ten minutes of silence during review of the docket agenda, 32–33
Board member expectations: annual capacity gift of every board member as, 29, 82; as basis for annual board reviews, 28–29; a minimum number of donor, finder, and sponsor prospect introductions annually as, 29

319